CAMBRIDGE

EMPOWER

SECOND EDITION

STUDENT'S BOOK WITH DIGITAL PACK

A2 ELEMENTARY

Adrian Doff, Craig Thaine
Herbert Puchta, Jeff Stranks, Peter Lewis-Jones

EMPOWER SECOND EDITION is a six-level general English course for adult and young adult learners, taking students from beginner to advanced level (CEFR A1 to C1). *Empower* combines course content from Cambridge University Press with validated assessment from the experts at Cambridge Assessment English.

Empower's unique mix of engaging classroom materials and reliable assessment enables learners to make consistent and measurable progress.

Content you love. Assessment you can trust.

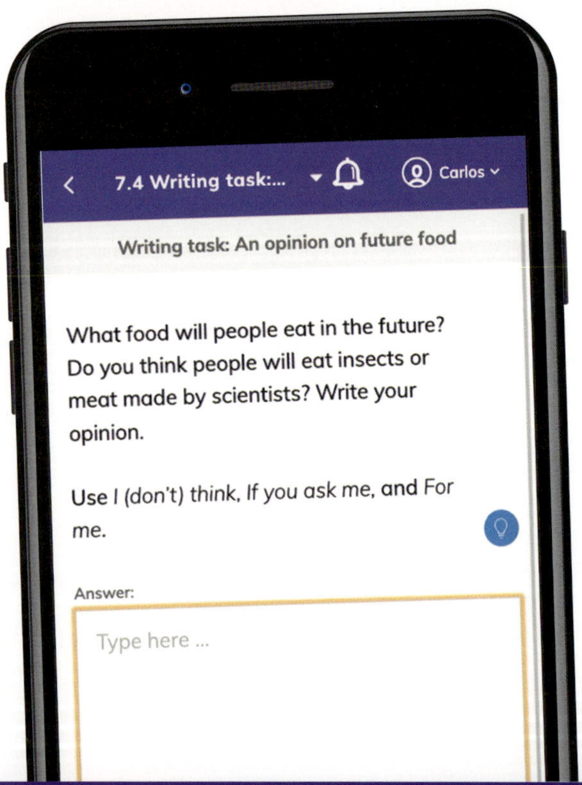

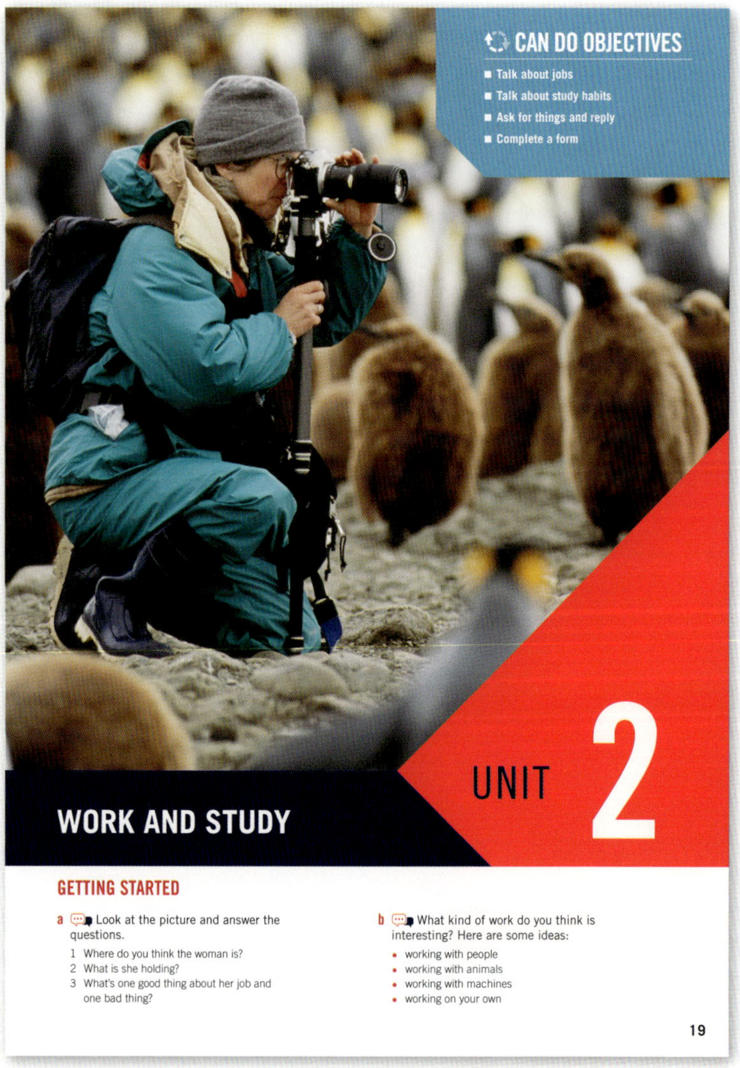

Better Learning with *Empower*

Better Learning is our simple approach where **insights** we've gained from research have helped shape **content** that drives **results**.

Learner engagement

1 Content that informs and motivates

Insights
Sustained motivation is key to successful language learning and skills development.

Content
Clear learning goals, thought-provoking images, texts and speaking activities, plus video content to arouse curiosity.

Results
Content that surprises, entertains and provokes an emotional response, helping teachers to deliver motivating and memorable lessons.

2A SHE LOVES HER JOB

Learn to talk about jobs
G Present simple: positive and negative
V Jobs

1 READING

a Look at the pictures. Answer the questions.
1 Where is this woman?
a in a park c by a river
b at home
2 Do you think ... ?
a she's a tourist b she works here
3 What do you know about alligators?

b Read the article and check your answers.

c Choose the correct answers.
1 Most people *like / don't like* alligators.
2 Gabby Scampone *likes / doesn't like* alligators.
3 Alligators *like / don't like* people swimming near them.
4 It *is / is not* dangerous to give alligators food.
5 Gabby has *one job / two jobs*.

d Read the article again. Find two reasons why Gabby's work is interesting.

e Talk about the questions.
1 Would you like Gabby's job? Why / Why not?
2 What other unusual jobs do you know?

GATOR GIRL

Everglades Holiday Park is an animal park in the USA. It's in Florida. It has birds, fish and … alligators! Many tourists visit the park every year. They come to look at the alligators. Most people think alligators are interesting, but they don't really like them, and they don't go too close to them!

Gabby Scampone is different. She lives in Florida, and she works at the park. She loves her job – and she also loves alligators. In her work, she teaches visitors about alligators. She tells visitors that alligators are not always dangerous animals. Usually, alligators don't attack people, but they don't like it when people swim in the water near them. Also, if people give food to alligators, sometimes the alligators get too close, and that can be dangerous.

Gabby doesn't always work at the park. She also has a second job: she catches wild alligators. If a wild alligator goes near a person's house, Gabby and some other people catch it. They take the alligators back to the park. Her parents and friends think she's crazy, but she really enjoys the job. Gabby thinks many people don't understand alligators very well, but that alligators are smart and amazing animals. And so far she still has all of her fingers!

Gabby Scampone with an alligator

20

UNIT 2

2 VOCABULARY Jobs

a Match words 1–9 with pictures a–i.
1 ☐ nurse 4 ☐ dentist 7 ☐ cleaner
2 ☐ shop assistant 5 ☐ pilot 8 ☐ photographer
3 ☐ police officer 6 ☐ engineer 9 ☐ taxi driver

b 02.01 Pronunciation Listen to the words and underline the stressed syllable.
police officer engineer photographer dentist

c Complete the sentences with jobs from 2a. Talk about your answers.
1 A(n) ________ has a dangerous job.
2 A(n) ________ has an easy job.
3 A(n) ________ has an exciting job.
4 The pay for a(n) ________ isn't very good.

d Now go to Vocabulary Focus 2A on p. 163 for more jobs vocabulary.

3 GRAMMAR Present simple: positive and negative

a 02.03 Look at the sentences from 1b and complete them with the verbs from the box. Listen and check.

catches come doesn't don't (x2) go attack think work works

	I / we / you / they	he / she / it
+	Tourists ____ to look at the alligators. Her parents ____ she's crazy.	She ____ at Everglades Holiday Park. She ____ wild alligators.
–	They ____ ____ too close to them. Alligators ____ ____ people.	Gabby ____ always ____ at the park.

b Underline more present simple verbs in the text in 1b. Make two lists: positive and negative forms.

c Now go to Grammar Focus 2A on p. 140.

d Underline the verbs in sentences 1–2.
1 She loves her job.
2 She catches wild alligators.

e 02.05 Pronunciation Which verb in 3d has an extra syllable when we add the letter -*s*? Listen and check.

f Underline the correct answers.
1 After the sounds /z/, /s/, /dʒ/ (spelled *j*), /ʃ/ (spelled *sh*) and /tʃ/ (spelled *ch*), we *add / don't add* an extra syllable.
2 We *add / don't add* an extra syllable after other sounds.

g 02.06 Listen to these verbs. Tick (✓) the verbs that have an extra syllable.
☐ works ☐ eats ☐ teaches
☐ finishes ☐ listens ☐ stops
☐ drives ☐ uses ☐ watches

h Communication 2A Student A: Go to p. 130. Student B: Go to p. 133.

4 SPEAKING

a Think about your job or the job of someone you know. Write four sentences about the job: two positive (+) and two negative (–). Use the verbs in the box.

work drive have like study
speak go start leave know

\+ I start work at 7:00 in the morning.
– I don't drive to work.

b Tell your partner your sentences. Can they guess the job?

c Tell other students about your partner's job. Can they guess it?

She starts work at …

21

2 Personalised and relevant

Insights
Language learners benefit from frequent opportunities to personalise their responses.

Content
Personalisation tasks in every unit make the target language more meaningful to the individual learner.

Results
Personal responses make learning more memorable and inclusive, with all students participating in spontaneous spoken interaction.

"There are so many adjectives to describe such a wonderful series, but in my opinion it's very reliable, practical and modern."

Zenaide Brianez, Director of Studies, Instituto da Língua Inglesa, Brazil

Measurable progress

1 Assessment you can trust

Insights
Tests developed and validated by Cambridge Assessment English, the world leaders in language assessment, to ensure they are accurate and meaningful.

Content
End-of-unit tests, mid- and end-of-course competency tests, and personalised CEFR test report forms provide reliable information on progress with language skills.

Results
Teachers can see learners' progress at a glance, and learners can see measurable progress, which leads to greater motivation.

Results of an impact study showing % improvement of Reading levels, based on global *Empower* students' scores over one year.

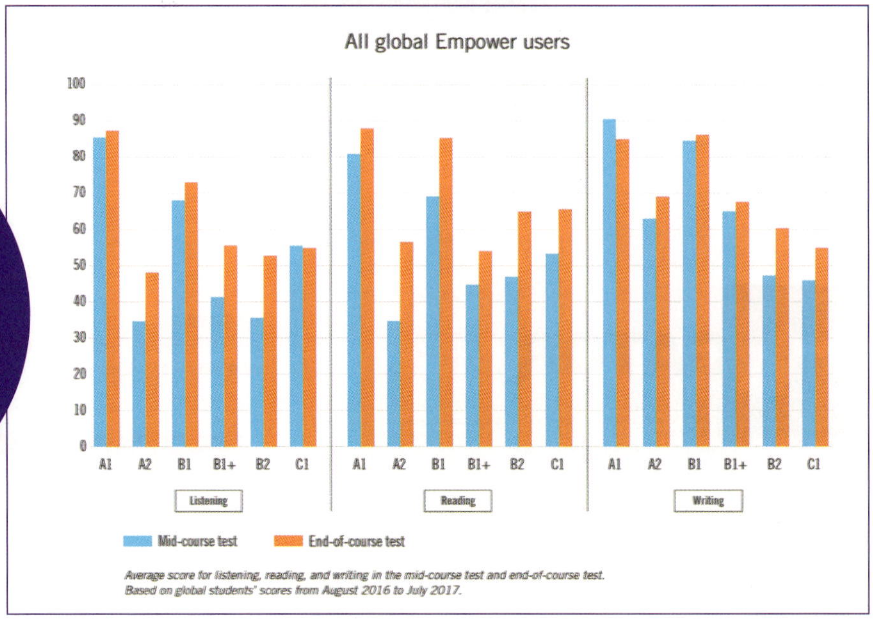

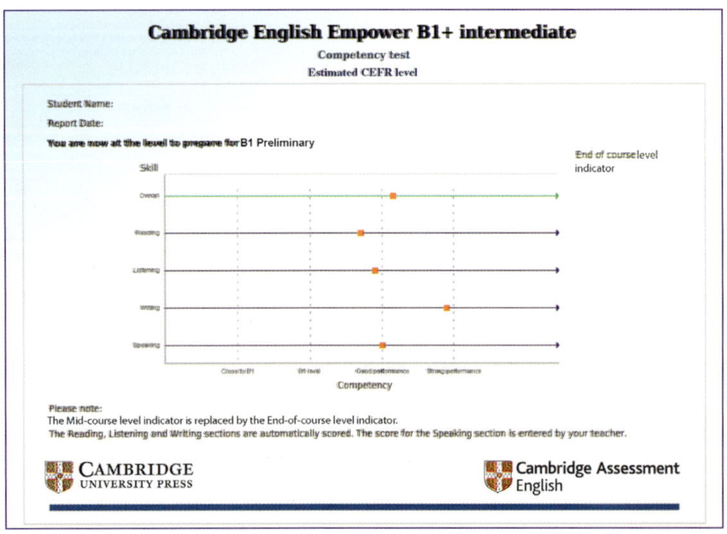

"We started using the tests provided with Empower and our students started showing better results from this point until now."

Kristina Ivanova, Director of Foreign Language Training Centre, ITMO University, Saint Petersburg, Russia

2 Evidence of impact

Insights
Schools and colleges need to show that they are evaluating the effectiveness of their language programmes.

Content
Empower (British English) impact studies have been carried out in various countries, including Russia, Brazil, Turkey and the UK, to provide evidence of positive impact and progress.

Results
Colleges and universities have demonstrated a significant improvement in language level between the mid- and end-of-course tests, as well as a high level of teacher satisfaction with *Empower*.

Manageable learning

1 Mobile friendly

Insights
Learners expect online content to be mobile friendly but also flexible and easy to use on any digital device.

Content
Empower provides easy access to Cambridge One: Digital Workbook content that works on any device and includes practice activities with audio.

Results
Cambridge One: Digital Workbook content is easy to access anywhere and produces meaningful and actionable data so teachers can track their students' progress and adapt their lesson accordingly.

I had been studying English for ten years before university, and I didn't succeed. But now with Empower *I know my level of English has changed.*

Nikita, *Empower* Student, ITMO University, Saint Petersburg, Russia

2 Corpus-informed

Insights
Corpora can provide valuable information about the language items learners are able to learn successfully at each CEFR level.

Content
Two powerful resources – Cambridge Corpus and English Profile – informed the development of the *Empower* course syllabus and the writing of the materials.

Results
Learners are presented with the target language they are able to incorporate and use at the right point in their learning journey. They are not overwhelmed with unrealistic learning expectations.

Rich in practice

1 Language in use

Insights
It is essential that learners are offered frequent and manageable opportunities to practise the language they have been focusing on.

Content
Throughout the *Empower* Student's Book, learners are offered a wide variety of practice activities, plenty of controlled practice and frequent opportunities for communicative spoken practice.

Results
Meaningful practice makes new language more memorable and leads to more efficient progress in language acquisition.

2B DO YOU WORRY ABOUT EXAMS?

Learn to talk about study habits
G Present simple: questions and short answers
V Studying; Time

1 READING

a Ask and answer the questions.
1 Are you good at exams?
2 Do you worry about exams and tests?
3 Do you study a lot for an exam or test?

b Read comments 1–3 in the online chat and match them with pictures a–c.

c Read the comments again and answer the questions with a partner.
1 Which study habits are ... ?
• useful • funny
2 Put the study habits in the order you want to try them from 1 (really want to try) to 3 (don't want to try).

2 VOCABULARY Studying

a Look at the underlined words in questions 1–7. Match them with pictures d–j below.
1 Do you have a break in the middle of your English lesson?
2 Do you have a timetable for your study routine?
3 Do you take notes when you read something in English?
4 Do you get good marks in English tests?
5 How many weeks is a term at your school?
6 Do you have an exam at the end of the year?
7 Do you and your friends enjoy your studies?

b Match the words in the box with 1–4. You can use some of the words more than once.

get good pass bad take fail

1 an exam 3 notes
2 marks 4 a test

c Ask and answer the questions in 2a.

CHAT Home Forums Articles Archives

Exam stress!
Hi guys! I have a big exam on Friday. It's really hard to study. I read my study notes for an hour and then I watch really bad TV programmes! What about you? Do you worry about exams? What are your study habits?
MIMI23

1 Yeah, I hate tests. They're really difficult and I can't always remember everything. I need to study every day and take a lot of notes. It's not easy, but it helps to listen to R&B music – really loud! It helps me think.
SOUL BOY2 REPLY

2 I agree – exams and tests are really, really hard. In my study breaks I play with my pet cat. Some people say that animals stop stress and relax people. I think it's true, well, for me it is! Everybody needs a cat to help them study!
CAT LOVERS REPLY

3 I think it helps to have a good study routine. I make a study timetable and that helps me to pass my exams. I always plan a lot of breaks and have a cup of tea and something small to eat. I don't want to get tired when I study! But the breaks are only short – about five or ten minutes. Then I go back to studying hard for one or two hours. Good marks come from a lot of hard work!
BOOKWORM8 REPLY

Tania and Jack

3 LISTENING

a Jack talks to Tania about her study habits. Listen and tick (✓) the things they talk about.
1 places to study 3 exams
2 hours of study 4 free time

b Listen again. Complete the information about Tania's studies.
• Part-time or full-time student? • When?
• Hours a week? • Where?

4 VOCABULARY Time

a Match the times that Tania talks about with the clocks.
1 Usually at **half past eight** ...
2 ... last night at **a quarter past eleven**.

b Complete the sentences with the words in the box.

to past o'clock half

1 four ___ 3 (a) quarter ___ four
2 ___ past four 4 (a) quarter ___ five

c Now go to Vocabulary Focus 2B on p. 164 for more practice with time vocabulary.

UNIT 2

5 GRAMMAR Present simple: questions

a Look at the questions. Which is correct? Listen and check.
1 You study full-time or part-time?
2 Do you study full-time or part-time?
3 Study you full-time or part-time?

b Complete the questions with one word.
___ you study engineering?
___ they like tests?

c Jack asks Tania about her daughter, Ellie. Listen and complete the information about Ellie's studies.
• Hours a week?
• When?
• Where?

d Read the question Jack asks Tania.
Does she study more before an exam?
Look at the questions in 5b. How are they different? Why?

e Now go to Grammar Focus 2B on p. 140.

f Put the questions in the correct order. Listen and check.
1 a week / do you study / hours / how many ?
2 study grammar / or vocabulary / do you ?
3 you / when / study / do ?
4 study / do / where / you ?

g Pronunciation Notice the pronunciation of *do you* in each question. Can you hear both words clearly?

6 SPEAKING

a Look at the questions in 5f. Write another question about studying.

b Ask and answer your question in 6a.

c Do you have any new ideas about studying now?

Natalia studies very early in the morning because she isn't very tired. I think it's a good idea, but I prefer to sleep!

2 Beyond the classroom

There are plenty of opportunities for personalisation.

Elena Pro, Teacher, EOI de San Fernando de Henares, Spain

Insights
Progress with language learning often requires work outside of the classroom, and different teaching models require different approaches.

Content
Empower is available with a print workbook, online practice and documentary-style videos that expose learners to real-world English, plus additional resources with extra ideas and fun activities.

Results
This choice of additional resources helps teachers to find the most effective ways to motivate their students both inside and outside the classroom.

Unit overview

Unit Opener

Getting started page – Clear learning objectives to give an immediate sense of purpose.

Lessons A and B

Grammar and Vocabulary – Input and practice of core grammar and vocabulary, plus a mix of skills.

Digital Workbook (online, mobile): Grammar and Vocabulary

Lesson C

Everyday English – Functional language in common, everyday situations.

Digital Workbook (online, mobile): Listening and Speaking

Unit Progress Test

Lesson D

Integrated Skills – Practice of all four skills, with a special emphasis on writing.

Digital Workbook (online, mobile): Reading and Writing

Review

Extra practice of grammar, vocabulary and pronunciation. Also a 'Review your progress' section for students to reflect on the unit.

Mid- / End-of-course test

Additional practice

Further practice is available for outside of the class with these components.

Digital Workbook (online, mobile)

***Workbook* (print)**

Components

Resources – Available on cambridgeone.org

- Audio
- Video
- Unit Progress Tests (print)
- Unit Progress Tests (online)
- Mid- and end-of-course assessment (print)
- Mid- and end-of-course assessment (online)
- Digital Workbook (online)
- Photocopiable Grammar, Vocabulary and Pronunciation worksheets

CONTENTS

WELCOME!

G Possessive adjectives; Question words; *a/an*; Regular plural forms
V Numbers; The alphabet; Colours; Classroom objects and instructions

a

b

c

1 FIRST CONVERSATIONS

a 00.02–00.06 Listen to five short conversations. Match them with pictures a–e.

b 00.02–00.06 Listen again. Who says these sentences? Match them with pictures a–e.

1 [b] Nice to meet you.
2 [ ] How are you?
3 [ ] What's your name and address?
4 [ ] How do you spell that?
5 [ ] Can we pay, please?
6 [ ] Is that your flat?

2 SAYING HELLO

a Read Conversation 1. Put the sentences in the correct order.

[ ] Hello. Nice to meet you. I'm Pierre.
[ ] Hello, Pierre. Nice to meet you.
[ ] Hello. I'm Tony, and this is my wife, Joanna.

00.02 Listen and check your answer.

b In pairs, say hello and say your name.

c In groups of four, say hello. Say your name and introduce your partner.

d 00.03 Read Conversation 2 and complete the sentences. Listen and check your answers.

fine thanks how

A Hi, Nick. [1]__________ are you?
B I'm [2]__________, thanks. And you?
A I'm OK, [3]__________.

e Meet other students. Have a conversation with two or three people in the class.

d

3 NUMBERS

a 00.04 Listen to Conversation 3. Complete the bill.

ITEM	NO.	PRICE
COFFEE	(2)	€ ______
ICE CREAM	(2)	€ ______
Total		€ ______

THANK YOU

How much do they pay? € ______

b 00.07 Listen and circle the numbers you hear. Then say all the numbers.

13 15 16 17 12
30 50 60 70 20

c Choose the correct answer.

25 = twenty and five / twenty-five
61 = sixty-one / one and sixty
110 = a hundred ten / a hundred and ten

d Read the numbers aloud. Then say the next three numbers.

1, 2, 3, 4, …
10, 20, 30, …
15, 25, 35, …
31, 33, 35, …
50, 100, 150, …

4 THE ALPHABET

a 00.08 Listen to the letters of the alphabet and say them.

A B C D E F G

H I J K L M N

O P Q R S T U

V W X Y Z

b **Pronunciation** Which letters have … ?

1 the same long sound as s**ee** /iː/
2 the same long sound as d**ay** /eɪ/
3 the same short sound as **e**gg /e/

c Test a partner. Student A, point to a letter. Student B, say the letter.

d Say these colours and spell the words.

e Write two words you know in English. Say the word and ask your partner to spell it.

f 00.05 Listen to Conversation 4 and complete the name and address.

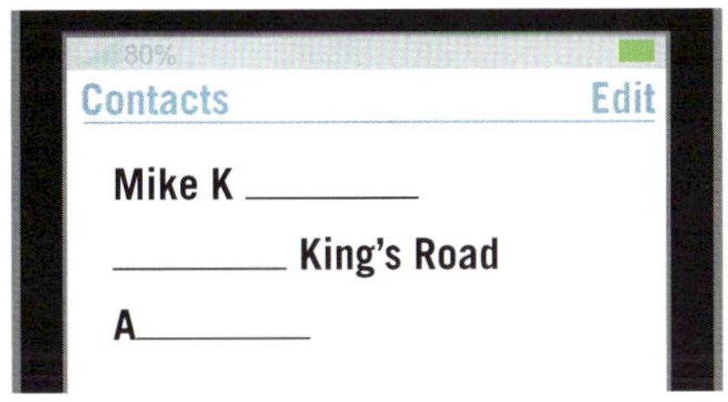

g Work in pairs. Student A, tell Student B:

- your first and last name
- your address

Student B, ask Student A to spell their name and address. Write the information down. Then swap roles.

How do you spell your … ?

5 POSSESSIVE ADJECTIVES

a 00.06 Read and listen to Conversation 5. Underline the correct answer.

A This is a nice photo. This is *my* / *your* wife and *his* / *her* brother.
B Oh, yes. Is that *our* / *your* flat?
A Yes, that's *our* / *their* flat in London.
B Mmm, it's very nice.

b Complete the table.

our their her his

I live here.	This is __my__ flat.
Do you live here?	Is this __your__ flat?
He lives here.	This is ____ flat.
She lives here.	This is ____ flat.
We live here.	This is ____ flat.
They live here.	This is ____ flat.

c Complete the sentences with a word from the table in 5b.

1 This is my brother. ____ name is George.
2 Jenny and Phil are old friends, and that's ____ car.
3 That's a good photo of you. And is that ____ daughter?
4 In this photo, we're on holiday with ____ friends Sue and Bill.
5 I know that girl in the photo. What's ____ name?

6 CLASSROOM OBJECTS

a Match objects 1–10 with a–j in the picture.

1 a notebook
2 a dictionary
3 a projector
4 a question
5 a pen
6 a cupboard
7 a desk
8 a whiteboard
9 an answer
10 a coursebook

b 00.09 **Pronunciation** Notice the stressed syllable in the words in 6a. Listen, then practise saying the words.

c When do we usually use *an*? Choose the correct answer.

a before *a, e, i, o, u*
b before other letters

d Write *a* or *an* next to each word.

1  ____ book
2  ____ apple
3  ____ camera
4  ____ glass
5  ____ egg
6  ____ baby
7  ____ box
8  ____ ice cream

e Choose one of the words from 6a or 6d. Other students ask questions to guess the word.

Is it big? No. Is it white? No.

f Look at how words change in the plural. Complete the rules.

Singular → Plural	Rule
a pen → pens	Most words add ____ in the plural.
a baby → babies	Change a final *-y* to ____ and add ____.
a glass → glasses	If a word ends in *-s*, *-x*, *-sh* or *-ch*, we add ____.

7 CLASSROOM INSTRUCTIONS

a 00.10 Listen and follow the instructions you hear. Then listen again. Which verbs do you hear each time?

open close look at read turn to write ask work

b 00.11 Underline the correct words. Listen and check.

1 *What's / Who's* this? An apple or an orange?
2 *When's / Where's* Tokyo?
3 *How / What* do you say this word?
4 *Who's / When's* the president?
5 *When's / What's* your English lesson?

c Match questions 1–4 with answers a–d.

1 What's 'amigo' in English?
2 How do you spell 'night'?
3 What's a 'ferry'?
4 How do you say this word?

a It's a boat for cars and people.
b 'Pee-pl'.
c Friend.
d N-I-G-H-T.

d Write a question like questions 1–4 in 7c. Then ask other students your question.

CAN DO OBJECTIVES

- Talk about where you're from
- Talk about people you know
- Ask for and give information
- Write an online profile

UNIT 1 PEOPLE

GETTING STARTED

a Look at the picture and answer the questions.

1 What different countries are the people from?

2 Why are they together?

- for a sports game
- for a party
- for a music concert

3 How do they feel? Here are some ideas:

a bored
b excited
c good
d happy
e sad
f tired

b When do you meet people from other countries? Here are some more ideas:

- on holiday
- on a language course
- never
- at work
- at parties

1A I'M FROM FRANCE

Learn to talk about where you're from

G *be*: positive and negative

V Countries and nationalities

1 LISTENING AND READING

a Look at pictures a–f and answer the questions.

1 What sport do all the people like?

2 Match countries 1–6 with pictures a–f.

1 ☐	Brazil	4 ☐	Japan
2 ☐	Spain	5 ☐	Russia
3 ☐	Germany	6 ☐	France

b 01.01 Listen and check. Practise saying the countries.

c 01.02 Thomas and Lena are at the World Cup. Listen and tick (✓) the three things they talk about.

1 ☐	football	4 ☐	a city
2 ☐	countries	5 ☐	TV
3 ☐	food		

d 01.02 Listen again. Complete the conversation.

THOMAS Hi there! My name's Thomas. What's your [1]_________?
LENA I'm Lena.
THOMAS Hi, Lena! Where are you [2]_________? Russia?
LENA Yeah, you're right! I'm Russian. I'm from St Petersburg.
THOMAS Oh, yes! It's a really beautiful city.
LENA Yes, I think so too. So, [3]_________ are you from, Thomas?
THOMAS Me? I'm from [4]_________. I'm French.
LENA Oh, the French team's really good!
THOMAS Of course! We're [5]_________!

e Are sentences 1–4 true (*T*) or false (*F*)? Correct the false sentences.

1 Thomas and Lena are friends.
2 Lena is from Russia.
3 Thomas likes St Petersburg.
4 Lena says the football team from France is very bad.

f Underline the two nationalities in the conversation in 1d.

2 VOCABULARY
Countries and nationalities

a Thomas says:

I'm from **France**. I'm **French**.

01.03 Find other pairs of countries and nationalities in the box below. Listen and check.

Ru|ssia Bra|zil|i|an Spa|nish Ja|pan Ru|ssian
Ger|many Ja|pan|ese Ger|man Bra|zil Spain

b 01.03 **Pronunciation** Notice how many syllables each word has. Underline the stressed syllable in each word in the box in 2a.

c 01.03 Listen again and repeat.

d Make sentences about the people below with the words in 2a.

1 Lena: She's Russian. She's from ________.
2 The people in pictures a–f: They're ________. They're from ________.

e Look at the conversation in 1d again. Complete the question. Then ask your partner.

________ are you from?

I'm from ________.
I'm ________.

f Now go to Vocabulary Focus 1A on p. 162 for more countries and nationalities.

c

f

3 GRAMMAR
be: positive and negative

a 01.06 Listen to the next part of the conversation between Thomas and Lena. What do they talk about?

a their football teams
b the town where Thomas is from

b 01.06 Underline the correct answers. Listen again and check.

1 Thomas *is* / *isn't* from Paris.
2 Lena's friends *are* / *aren't* Russian.
3 Her friends *are* / *aren't* at the match.
4 *It's* / *It isn't* 8:00.

c Look at the pairs of sentences and complete the rule.

1 It's a town near Paris. It isn't very big.
2 They're all in the hotel. They aren't here.
3 I'm from France. I'm not from Paris.

To make *am*, *is* and *are* negative, we add ________.
We often use contractions for the verb:
it **is** not = it is**n't** they **are** not = they are**n't**
I **am** not = I**'m** not

The match isn't on yet.
Her friends aren't at the match.

d Complete the table with the correct forms of the verb *be*.

Positive (+)	Negative (–)
I'm from St Petersburg.	I ____ French.
He ____ a really good player.	She ____ from Moscow.
They say they ____ tired.	They ____ at the match.

e Now go to Grammar Focus 1A on p. 138.

f Thomas and Lena talk more in the café. Add the verb *be* to make correct sentences.

Thomas says: 1 My brother at university in Madrid.
2 My mother and father not here.

Lena says: 3 Russia not very hot in April.
4 My friends really interesting and fun.

g Write two positive and two negative sentences about you with the verb *be*. Make two of them false.

h Read your sentences to a partner and say if your partner's sentences are true or false.

4 SPEAKING

a **Communication 1A** Student A: Go to p. 130. Student B: Go to p. 133.

b Work in small groups. Tell other students:

- your name
- your home town
- your country and nationality

1B SHE'S A LOVELY PERSON

Learn to talk about people you know

G *be*: questions and short answers

V Adjectives

1 READING

a Look at pictures a–d. Where do you think the people are?

b Read the texts and match them with pictures a–d. Are your ideas in 1a correct?

c Who do you think says sentences 1–4?

1 'I have four classes every day.'
2 'It's fun to travel with friends.'
3 'My family members live in different places.'
4 'She speaks two languages – Spanish and Portuguese.'

d Who would you like to meet: Suzi, James, Alex or Saddah? Why?

Now Photo!

Suzi

This is me in Rio de Janeiro with my friend Claudia. She lives in Brazil, but she's from Spain. She's a lovely person – very warm and kind.

view Suzi's photos   leave Suzi a message

James

In this photo I'm chatting with my cousin, Eric. He lives in Sydney. He's Australian, but I'm from England – Eric's mother and my father are brother and sister. Eric is a really pleasant guy and he's a brilliant doctor. He's well known in his part of Sydney.

view James's photos   leave James a message

Alex

In this photo I'm on holiday with my friend Tom. He's a fantastic friend and he's very cool. He's a great person to be on holiday with.

view Alex's photos   leave Alex a message

Saddah

This is my colleague Maram. We're teachers and we work together in a school. She's quiet, but she's really friendly. She's also very popular with her students.

view Saddah's photos   leave Saddah a message

2 VOCABULARY Adjectives

a Look at the sentence. The underlined words are adjectives. Are they about Rio de Janeiro or Claudia?

She's a lovely person – very warm and kind.

b Underline nine more adjectives in the texts. Then put them in the correct blanks.

1 very good: ____________, ____________, ____________, ____________
2 nice: *lovely, warm, kind* ____________, ____________
3 famous: ____________
4 he/she doesn't talk much: ____________
5 people like him/her: ____________

c Pronunciation Three words in the texts have the /k/ sound:

kind cool quiet

Underline the /k/ sound in these words. Which two words do not have /k/?

cold car cheap kitchen like
coffee quick back key know
come make school cat

d Talk about people you know. Use adjectives from 2b.

My friend Emma's very friendly and very popular.

My best friend Joe's a cool guy.

My aunt Sophia's fantastic – she's a very warm and friendly woman.

e Now go to Vocabulary Focus 1B on p. 163 for more adjectives.

3 LISTENING

a 01.12 Listen to the conversations. Complete the nationalities (1–3) on the profiles below.

b 01.12 Listen again. Complete the profiles with adjectives 4–6.

Name Roman
Nationality 1____________
Personality 4____________

Names Diego and Mia
Nationality 2____________
Personality 5____________

Name Laura
Nationality 3____________
Personality 6____________

4 GRAMMAR *be*: questions and short answers

a 01.13 Complete the answers with the words in the box. Listen and check.

aren't isn't is are

1 Is she Italian? No, she ____________. She's from Spain.
2 Is he from Poland? Yes, he ____________.
3 Are they married? Yes, they ____________.
4 Are they Spanish? No, they ____________. They're from Mexico.

b Complete the table with the correct forms of the verb *be*.

Questions (?)	Short answers	
Are you Australian?	Yes, I am.	No, I'm not.
______ you Brazilian?	Yes, we are.	No, we aren't.
______ he/she Turkish?	Yes, he/she ______.	No, he/she ______.
______ they Italian?	Yes, they ______.	No, they ______.

c Now go to Grammar Focus 1B on p. 138.

d 01.15 Complete the conversations. Use contractions *'s, 're* and *isn't* if possible. Listen and check.

A My friend Tony 1*'s* English. He 2______ very kind.
B 3______ he from London?
A Yes, he 4______.

A My friends, Joe and Mel, 5______ American. They 6______ very warm and friendly.
B 7______ they married?
A No, they 8______ . They 9______ just good friends.

5 SPEAKING

a Write down words about friends, family and famous people you know from other countries.

Camilla – British, cool, popular *Gabriel – Mexican, quiet, kind*

b Talk about the people you know. Look at the conversations in 4d to help you.

1C EVERYDAY ENGLISH

What's your surname?

Learn to ask for and give information

S Checking understanding

P Consonant clusters

1 LISTENING

a Look at the pictures of Dan and Leo. Use personality adjectives from p. 12 to describe them.

b 01.16 Watch or listen to Part 1. Choose the correct answer.

1 Dan wants to: a finish something b do some exercise.
2 Leo wants to: a do an exercise class b go for a run.
3 Martina is: a in the office b at the gym.

c 01.17 Leo talks to the gym receptionist. Watch or listen to Part 2. What does Leo want to do? Choose the correct answer.

a join the gym b book a fitness class
c pay for a fitness class.

d 01.17 Watch or listen to Part 2 again. Are the sentences true (*T*) or false (*F*)? Correct the false sentences.

1 The class starts at 7:20.
2 Ten people can go to the fitness class.
3 The class is in Studio 2.

2 USEFUL LANGUAGE
Asking for and giving information

a Who says sentences 1–7 at a gym: the receptionist (*R*) or a visitor (*V*)?

1 What time's the next class? a Seymour.
2 And what's your address? b You're welcome.
3 How can I help? c S–E–Y–M–O–U–R.
4 Thanks for your help. d It's at twenty past seven.
5 Can you spell that, please? e It's in Studio 1.
6 And where's the class? f I'd like to do a fitness class.
7 What's your surname? g 18 New Street.

b 01.18 Match 1–7 with a–g. Listen and check.

c Underline the correct answers.

1 It's **in** *ten past four* / *Room 6*.
2 It's **at** *eight o'clock* / *Studio 4*.

d 01.19 A is a receptionist and B wants information. Complete the conversation. Look at 2a and 2b to help you. Listen and check.

A Hello. How can I [1]__________ you?
B I'd [2]__________ to do a computer course.
A No problem.
B When's the first lesson?
A It's tomorrow at eight o'clock.
B And [3]__________ the lesson?
A It's here in Room 5.
B Great. Can I book a place?
A Certainly. [4]__________ your surname?
B Moore.
A Can you [5]__________ that, please?
B M–O–O–R–E.
A Thank you. Enjoy the class.

e In pairs, practise the conversation in 2d. Use your own surname. Take turns being A and B.

3 LISTENING

a 01.20 Watch or listen to Part 3. Leo talks to Martina at the gym. Answer the questions.

1 Who is Martina?
2 What does she say about Dan?
   a He's very busy. b He's a bit lazy.

b What is a good time to go to the gym?

- before work / school
- after work / school
- at lunchtime
- never

4 CONVERSATION SKILLS
Checking understanding

a Complete the mini-conversations with the words in the box.

so that's	sorry

SONIA It's at twenty past seven.
LEO [1]_____?
SONIA 7:20.

SONIA It's in Studio 1.
LEO [2]_____ 7:20 in Studio 1?

b Which expression in 4a means:

1 I'm not sure and I want to check.
2 I don't understand. Can you say that again?

c 01.21 **Pronunciation** Listen to what Leo says in 4a. Does the intonation go up ↗ or down ↘ on 1 and 2?

d Work in pairs. Use the dialogue map to practise checking understanding. Take turns being A and B.

A	B
Tell each other your surname and spell it →	
	Answer with sorry?
← Repeat the information.	

5 PRONUNCIATION
Consonant clusters

a 01.22 Listen to the time. Notice how the consonant clusters in **bold** are pronounced.

ei**ght** o'**cl**o**ck**
/t/ /kl/ /k/

b 01.23 Listen to the words below. How many consonant sounds do the letters in **bold** have?

three si**x** ei**ght**y

c 01.24 Practise saying these times. Listen and repeat.

1 seven o'clock (7:00)
2 six ten (6:10)
3 eight twenty (8:20)
4 three forty (3:40)
5 six thirty (6:30)
6 twelve twenty (12:20)

6 SPEAKING

a **Communication 1C** Student A: Go to p. 131. Student B: Go to p. 133.

UNIT PROGRESS TEST

→ CHECK YOUR PROGRESS

You can now do the Unit Progress Test.

1D SKILLS FOR WRITING

I'm Carla and I'm from Italy

Learn to write an online profile

W Capital letters and punctuation

1 SPEAKING AND LISTENING

a Ask and answer the questions.

1 Do you use social media?
2 Do you have an online profile?
3 Which of the following information is on it?

- your name
- your age
- your nationality
- where you live
- your job
- things you like

b Look at Kate and Carla's profiles and complete the table with yes (✓), no (✗) or don't know (*DK*).

She's …	20 years old	from London	Italian	a teacher	a student
Kate	DK				
Carla	✓				

KATE MARKS

Teacher, International College

Age: -

Lives in London, UK

About Kate

Friends: 132 VIEW

Photos VIEW

CARLA DI MAMBRO

Student, University of Milan

Age: 20

Lives in Milan

From Varese, Italy

About Carla

Friends: 189 VIEW

Photos VIEW

c 01.25 The people in the picture are on an English course. Listen and answer the questions.

1 Is this the first or the last day of the course?
2 What city are they in?

d 01.25 Listen again. Complete the table.

Name	Country	One other thing we know
Kate and Mike	UK	They're __________.
Carla	Italy	She's a __________.
Masato		English is __________ for his work.
Carmen		She's a __________ of IT.
Orhan		His __________ is in London.
Marisa		Her __________ is in London.

e Work in groups of five or six. It's your first day at International College.

Student A: You're the teacher.
The others: You're one of the students in the picture.

Say who you are and add one more thing.

I'm Masato.
My home town is Kyoto.

2 READING

a Read Kate and Carla's profiles for the new course. Underline any new information.

I'm Kate Marks. I'm from Wigan. It's a small town near Manchester in England. I live in London and I'm a teacher at International College. I'm married and I have two small children: a boy and a girl.

I like languages, music and films.

< Back

I'm Carla Di Mambro. I'm Italian. I'm from Varese, but I study marketing at the University of Milan. It's my first time in London and I'm very happy to be here. Are other people new to London?

I like running, swimming and yoga.

< Back

3 WRITING SKILLS
Capital letters and punctuation

a Look at the profiles in 2a. Tick (✓) the words that have capital letters.

1 ☐ first names of people
2 ☐ last names of people
3 ☐ names of companies, schools, universities
4 ☐ names of countries and nationalities
5 ☐ names of sports
6 ☐ names of towns or cities
7 ☐ all nouns
8 ☐ all words at the start of a sentence
9 ☐ the word *I*

b *I'm* = *I am*. What are the full forms of these contractions?

1 it's
2 she's
3 you're
4 isn't
5 aren't

c Correct the words. Add an apostrophe (') to each word.

1 Im
2 arent
3 isnt
4 hes
5 were
6 theyre

d Look at the commas (,) and full stops (.) in the online profiles. Which do we use … ?

a at the end of a sentence
b after words in a list

e Correct the sentences. Add capital letters and punctuation (. , ' ?).

i live in paris its amazing → *I live in Paris. It's amazing.*
1 im from shanghai its a big city in china
2 i like basketball old cars and jazz
3 im a french teacher in australia
4 this isnt my first time in london
5 are all the teachers from britain

4 WRITING

a Write a profile about yourself. Use the profiles in 2a to help you. Give this information:

- your name
- your nationality
- your home town
- your job
- what you like

b Swap profiles with another student and check the capital letters and punctuation.

Update Your Profile

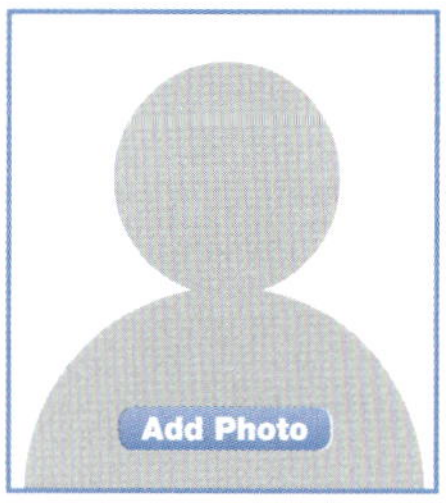

Add Photo

Upload File Take a Photo

I'm ______________________________

I like ______________________________

Save

UNIT 1
Review and extension

1 VOCABULARY

a Complete the sentences with the correct nationality word.

1 Vera's from Rio de Janeiro. She's ______________.
2 Pedro's from Madrid. He's ______________.
3 Kurt and Erika are from Berlin. They're ______________.
4 Ellen's from Melbourne. She's ______________.
5 Claude and Sabine are from Paris. They're ______________.
6 Takashi's from Tokyo. He's ______________.

b Complete the text about Vera with the correct adjective.

Vera's family members are all [1]f______c. Her mother's [2]w______m and [3]k______d, and her father is very [4]n______e. He's a [5]b______t doctor. Her sister Pia is [6]q______t, but she's very [7]f______y.

2 GRAMMAR

a Complete the text with the correct form of the verb *be*. Use contractions where possible.

Hi. I [1]______ Paolo and I [2]______ from Sydney, Australia. I [3]______ a university student. I [4]______ really lucky because I live near my sister Barbara. She [5]______ an English teacher, and she [6]______ very popular with her students. She [7]______ very kind and friendly. We [8]______ Australian, but our parents [9]______ from Italy. They [10]______ doctors.

b Write questions for the answers. Use the word in *italics* to start your question.

1 *Are ...?* No, I'm not. I'm Brazilian.
2 *Is ...?* Yes, she's very kind.
3 *Are ...?* No, they aren't. They're from Germany.
4 *What's ...?* My name's Abdulaziz.
5 *Where ...?* I'm from Venezuela.

c Write questions and short answers.

1 you Turkish? Yes
2 she your sister? No
3 they friendly? Yes
4 you both from the USA? No
5 he well known? No

d Complete the conversation with one word in each blank. A contraction (*I'm, you're, he's*) is one word.

A Hello. What's [1]__________ name?
B I'm Juan.
A [2]__________ you from Mexico?
B Yes, [3]__________ from Jalisco.
A And that woman over there. Is [4]__________ your sister?
B No, she [5]__________. She's a student at my school.
A OK. And [6]__________ she from?
B She's Italian. [7]__________ from Venice.

e Practise the conversation in 2d with a partner and use your own personal information.

3 WORDPOWER *from*

a Match sentences 1–4 with pictures a–d.

1 Is the flight **from** Hong Kong here?
2 I'm not American. I'm **from** Canada.
3 The shops are open **from** 9:00 am to 6:00 pm.
4 My house is about five kilometres **from** the city centre.

a

b
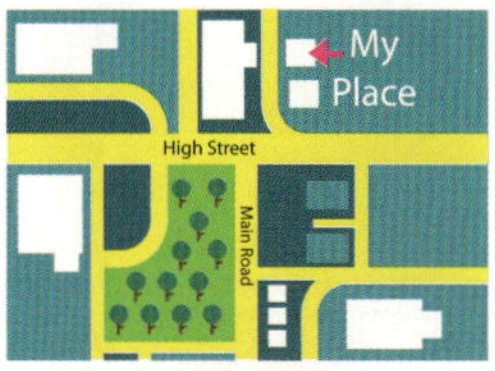

c

d

b Match examples 1–4 in 3a with rules a–d.

We use ***from*** to talk about:
a times
b a starting place
c our country or city
d how far away something is

c Match sentences 1–4 with rules a–d in 3b.

1 Our lunch break is from 12:30 to 1:30.
2 Our hotel's about five kilometres from the airport.
3 The train from Paris is now at platform two.
4 I'm from Argentina.

d Add *from* in the correct place in these sentences.

1 This postcard is New Zealand.
2 Breakfast is seven o'clock to ten o'clock every morning.
3 The bank's only 200 metres here.

e Put the phrases in the correct order to make sentences.

1 from / Denmark / I'm
2 open from / the supermarket's / 7:30 am to 9:30 pm
3 my place is / from school / two kilometres

f Are the sentences in 3e true for you? Change them to make them true.

I'm not from Denmark. I'm from Australia.

REVIEW YOUR PROGRESS

How well did you do in this unit? Write 3, 2 or 1 for each objective.

3 = very well 2 = well 1 = not so well

I CAN ...	
talk about where I'm from	☐
talk about people I know	☐
ask for and give information	☐
write an online profile.	☐

CAN DO OBJECTIVES

- Talk about jobs
- Talk about study habits
- Ask for things and reply
- Complete a form

UNIT 2

WORK AND STUDY

GETTING STARTED

a Look at the picture and answer the questions.

1 Where do you think the woman is?
2 What is she holding?
3 What's one good thing about her job and one bad thing?

b What kind of work do you think is interesting? Here are some ideas:

- working with people
- working with animals
- working with machines
- working on your own

2A SHE LOVES HER JOB

Learn to talk about jobs

G Present simple: positive and negative

V Jobs

1 READING

a Look at the pictures. Answer the questions.

1. Where is this woman?
   a in a park
   b at home
   c by a river
2. Do you think ... ?
   a she's a tourist
   b she works here
3. What do you know about alligators?

b Read the article and check your answers.

c Choose the correct answers.

1. Most people *like* / *don't like* alligators.
2. Gabby Scampone *likes* / *doesn't like* alligators.
3. Alligators *like* / *don't like* people swimming near them.
4. It *is* / *is not* dangerous to give alligators food.
5. Gabby has *one job* / *two jobs*.

d Read the article again. Find two reasons why Gabby's work is interesting.

e Talk about the questions.

1. Would you like Gabby's job? Why / Why not?
2. What other unusual jobs do you know?

Gabby Scampone with an alligator

GATOR GIRL

Everglades Holiday Park is an animal park in the USA. It's in Florida. It has birds, fish and ... alligators! Many tourists visit the park every year. They come to look at the alligators. Most people think alligators are interesting, but they don't really like them, and they don't go too close to them!

Gabby Scampone is different. She lives in Florida, and she works at the park. She loves her job – and she also loves alligators. In her work, she teaches visitors about alligators. She tells visitors that alligators are not always dangerous animals. Usually, alligators don't attack people, but they don't like it when people swim in the water near them. Also, if people give food to alligators, sometimes the alligators get too close, and that can be dangerous.

Gabby doesn't always work at the park. She also has a second job: she catches wild alligators. If a wild alligator goes near a person's house, Gabby and some other people catch it. They take the alligators back to the park. Her parents and friends think she's crazy, but she really enjoys the job. Gabby thinks many people don't understand alligators very well, but that alligators are smart and amazing animals. And so far she still has all of her fingers!

2 VOCABULARY Jobs

a Match words 1–9 with pictures a–i.

1 ☐ nurse	4 ☐ dentist	7 ☐ cleaner
2 ☐ shop assistant	5 ☐ pilot	8 ☐ photographer
3 ☐ police officer	6 ☐ engineer	9 ☐ taxi driver

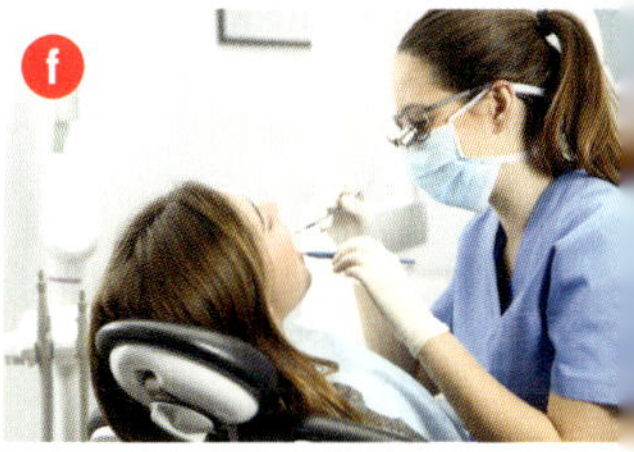

b 02.01 **Pronunciation** Listen to the words and underline the stressed syllable.

police officer   engineer   photographer   dentist

c Complete the sentences with jobs from 2a. Talk about your answers.

1 A(n) ________ has a dangerous job.
2 A(n) ________ has an easy job.
3 A(n) ________ has an exciting job.
4 The pay for a(n) ________ isn't very good.

d Now go to Vocabulary Focus 2A on p. 163 for more jobs vocabulary.

3 GRAMMAR
Present simple: positive and negative

a 02.03 Look at the sentences from 1b and complete them with the verbs from the box. Listen and check.

catches come doesn't don't (x2) go attack think work works

	I / we / you / they	*he / she / it*
+	Tourists ____ to look at the alligators. Her parents ____ she's crazy.	She ____ at Everglades Holiday Park. She ____ wild alligators.
–	They ____ ____ too close to them. Alligators ____ ____ people.	Gabby ____ always ____ at the park.

b Underline more present simple verbs in the text in 1b. Make two lists: positive and negative forms.

c Now go to Grammar Focus 2A on p. 140.

d Underline the verbs in sentences 1–2.

1 She loves her job.
2 She catches wild alligators.

e 02.05 **Pronunciation** Which verb in 3d has an extra syllable when we add the letter *-s*? Listen and check.

f Underline the correct answers.

1 After the sounds /z/, /s/, /dʒ/ (spelled *j*), /ʃ/ (spelled *sh*) and /tʃ/ (spelled *ch*), we *add / don't add* an extra syllable.
2 We *add / don't add* an extra syllable after other sounds.

g 02.06 Listen to these verbs. Tick (✓) the verbs that have an extra syllable.

☐ works	☐ eats	☐ teaches
☐ finishes	☐ listens	☐ stops
☐ drives	☐ uses	☐ watches

h **Communication 2A** Student A: Go to p. 130. Student B: Go to p. 133.

4 SPEAKING

a Think about your job or the job of someone you know. Write four sentences about the job: two positive (+) and two negative (–). Use the verbs in the box.

work drive have like study
speak go start leave know

+ I start work at 7:00 in the morning.
– I don't drive to work.

b Tell your partner your sentences. Can they guess the job?

c Tell other students about your partner's job. Can they guess it?

She starts work at …

2B DO YOU WORRY ABOUT EXAMS?

Learn to talk about study habits

- **G** Present simple: questions and short answers
- **V** Studying; Time

1 READING

a Ask and answer the questions.

1 Are you good at exams?
2 Do you worry about exams and tests?
3 Do you study a lot for an exam or test?

b Read comments 1–3 in the online chat and match them with pictures a–c.

c Read the comments again and answer the questions with a partner.

1 Which study habits are ... ?
   - useful
   - funny
2 Put the study habits in the order you want to try them from 1 (really want to try) to 3 (don't want to try).

2 VOCABULARY Studying

a Look at the underlined words in questions 1–7. Match them with pictures d–j below.

1 Do you have a break in the middle of your English lesson?
2 Do you have a timetable for your study routine?
3 Do you take notes when you read something in English?
4 Do you get good marks in English tests?
5 How many weeks is a term at your school?
6 Do you have an exam at the end of the year?
7 Do you and your friends enjoy your studies?

b Match the words in the box with 1–4. You can use some of the words more than once.

get good pass bad take fail

1 an exam
2 marks
3 notes
4 a test

c Ask and answer the questions in 2a.

d

CHAT Home Forums Articles Archives

a

b

c

Exam stress!

Hi guys! I have a big exam on Friday. It's really hard to study. I read my study notes for an hour and then I watch really bad TV programmes! What about you? Do you worry about exams? What are your study habits? **MIMI23**

1 Yeah, I hate tests. They're really difficult and I can't always remember everything. I need to study every day and take a lot of notes. It's not easy, but it helps to listen to R&B music – really loud! It helps me think.
SOUL BOY2 REPLY

2 I agree – exams and tests are really, really hard. In my study breaks I play with my pet cat. Some people say that animals stop stress and relax people. I think it's true, well, for me it is! Everybody needs a cat to help them study!
CAT LOVER5 REPLY

3 I think it helps to have a good study routine. I make a study timetable and that helps me to pass my exams. I always plan a lot of breaks and have a cup of tea and something small to eat. I don't want to get tired when I study! But the breaks are only short – about five or ten minutes. Then I go back to studying hard for one or two hours. Good marks come from a lot of hard work!
BOOKWORM8 REPLY

e

f

g
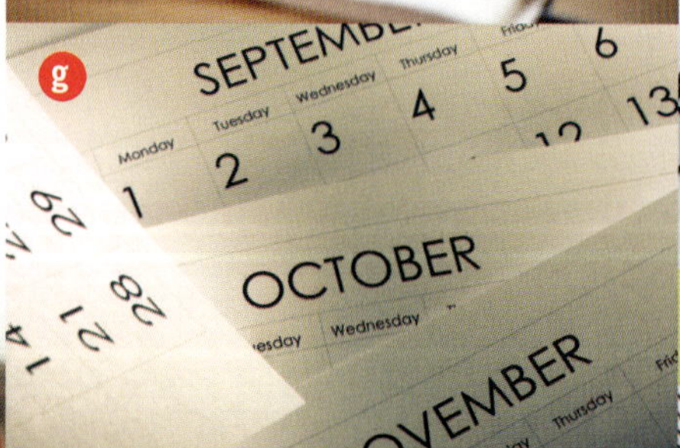
h

i

j

Tania and Jack

3 LISTENING

a 02.07 Jack talks to Tania about her study habits. Listen and tick (✓) the things they talk about.

1 ☐ places to study
2 ☐ hours of study
3 ☐ exams
4 ☐ free time

b 02.07 Listen again. Complete the information about Tania's studies.

- Part-time or full-time student?
- Hours a week?
- When?
- Where?

4 VOCABULARY Time

a Match the times that Tania talks about with the clocks.

1 Usually at **half past eight**
2 … last night at **a quarter past eleven**.

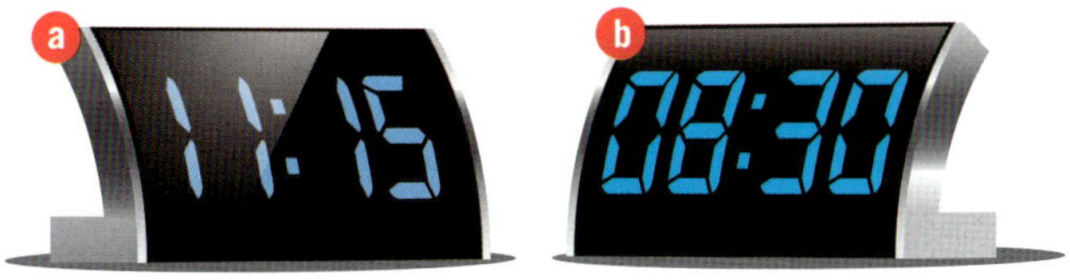

b Complete the sentences with the words in the box.

to past o'clock half

1 four ____ 
2 ____ past four 
3 (a) quarter ____ four 
4 (a) quarter ____ five 

c >>> Now go to Vocabulary Focus 2B on p. 164 for more practice with time vocabulary.

5 GRAMMAR Present simple: questions

a 02.09 Look at the questions. Which is correct? Listen and check.

1 You study full-time or part-time?
2 Do you study full-time or part-time?
3 Study you full-time or part-time?

b Complete the questions with one word.

____ … you study engineering?
… they like tests?

c 02.10 Jack asks Tania about her daughter, Ellie. Listen and complete the information about Ellie's studies.

- Hours a week?
- When?
- Where?

d Read the question Jack asks Tania.

Does she study more before an exam?

Look at the questions in 5b. How are they different? Why?

e >>> Now go to Grammar Focus 2B on p. 140.

f 02.12 Put the questions in the correct order. Listen and check.

1 a week / do you study / hours / how many ?
2 study grammar / or vocabulary / do you ?
3 you / when / study / do ?
4 study / do / where / you ?

g 02.12 **Pronunciation** Notice the pronunciation of *do you* in each question. Can you hear both words clearly?

6 SPEAKING

a Look at the questions in 5f. Write another question about studying.

b Ask and answer your question in 6a.

c Do you have any new ideas about studying now?

Natalia studies very early in the morning because she isn't very tired. I think it's a good idea, but I prefer to sleep!

2C EVERYDAY ENGLISH
I'd like a latte

Learn to ask for things and reply

- S Reacting to news
- P Sound and spelling: *ou*

1 LISTENING

a Look at picture a. Dan and Leo are in a cafeteria. Do you think they're:

1 at the airport 2 at work 3 in a shopping centre?

b 02.13 Watch or listen to Part 1 and check your answer in 1a.

c Work in pairs. Choose the correct answers.

1 Dan orders a *small* / *large* tea, a *small* / *large* latte and *one croissant* / *two croissants*.
2 It costs *£3.60* / *£4.60*.
3 Dan asks Leo to pass the *milk* / *sugar*.

d 02.13 Watch or listen to Part 1 again and check your answers in 1c.

e 02.14 Watch or listen to Part 2. Annie wants to do an online course. What's her problem? Choose one answer.

She can't decide … .

a which course to do b how much to pay c when to start

f 02.14 Watch or listen to Part 2 again. Are the sentences true (*T*) or false (*F*)? Correct the false sentences.

1 Annie asks Dan for help.
2 Dan's free tonight.
3 Annie isn't free on Friday.
4 Annie's happy about dinner.

g Where do you usually meet friends and family?

- in your home
- in their home
- in a café
- in a different place

2 USEFUL LANGUAGE
Asking for things and replying

a Look at these ways to ask for things. Who says them: Dan (*D*) or Annie (*A*)?

1 Can I have a tea and a latte, please?
2 Could I come to your place tonight?
3 Could we chat about it now?
4 I'd like some help.

b 02.13–02.14 Watch or listen to Parts 1 and 2 again and check. Match a–d with 1–4 in 2a.

a Certainly. Small or large?
b Sorry, I have another meeting in five minutes.
c Sure, no problem.
d Sorry, we're not at home tonight.

c In pairs, take turns asking for things and replying. Use the phrases from 2a and 2b.

d 02.15 Listen to three short conversations. Where are they? Match them with pictures a–c.

e 02.15 Complete the sentences from the conversations in 2d. Listen again and check your answers.

1 ________ some water, please?
2 ________ a chicken sandwich, please.
3 ________ you this afternoon?

f Look at the situations. What can A and B say? Use expressions from 2a and 2b.

	A	B
1	You're in B's home. Ask for some water.	Say yes.
2	You're in a café. Ask for a small espresso.	You're the waiter. Say yes.
3	You have a problem at work. Ask for some help.	Say no. (You're busy.)
4	You want to meet B on Saturday.	Say no. (You aren't free then.)

g Work in pairs. Use the dialogue maps to ask for things and reply. Take turns being A and B.

3 CONVERSATION SKILLS
Reacting to news

a 02.16 Complete the mini-conversations with words in the box. Listen and check your answers.

problem	pity

LEO Sorry, I have another meeting in five minutes.
DAN OK, no [1]________. We can do it later.

DAN Sorry, we're not at home tonight.
ANNIE Oh, that's a [2]________.

b Read the mini-conversations in 3a again. Which phrase means ... ?

1 'It's not important.'
2 'I'm not happy about it.'

c Match a–d with 1 or 2 in 3b.

a Never mind.
b I'm sorry about that.
c It doesn't matter.
d What a shame.

4 PRONUNCIATION
Sound and spelling: *ou*

a 02.17 Listen to the sound of the letters *ou* in **bold**.

1 col**ou**r
2 an online c**ou**rse
3 h**ou**se

Do the letters in 1–3 have different sounds?

b 02.18 Do these words sound like *1*, *2* or *3* in 4a? Listen and check. Listen again and repeat.

out __3__ four _____ neighbour _____
about _____ sound _____

5 SPEAKING

a Communication 2C Student A: Go to p. 130. Student B: Go to p. 133.

UNIT PROGRESS TEST

CHECK YOUR PROGRESS

You can now do the Unit Progress Test.

2D SKILLS FOR WRITING

I need English for my job

Learn to complete a form

W Spelling

1 SPEAKING AND LISTENING

a Why do you want to study English?

- to get a good job
- to meet new friends
- for travel and tourism
- to study something in English
- a different reason

b 02.19 Listen to three International College students talk about where they're from and their reasons for studying English. Underline the correct answers.

I'm from *Acapulco / Mexico City* and I need English for my *job / studies*.

Daniela

Said

I'm from *Riyadh / Jeddah* and I need English for my *job / studies*.

I'm from *Krakow / Warsaw* and I need English for my *job / studies*.

Justyna

c 02.19 Listen again and complete the table with the words in the box.

grammar   the lessons   the teacher
reading and writing   listening   the timetable

	Likes at the college	Needs to improve
Daniela		
Said		
Justyna		

d Talk about the questions with other students.

1 What do you need to improve in English?
2 Why is this important for you?

e 02.20 Listen to Kate talk about a competition at International College. What can you win?

f 02.20 Listen again. Answer the questions.

1 Can students who don't go to International College enter the competition?
2 Is it OK to use a computer for the entry form?
3 Where can students get entry forms?

2 READING

a Look at the information about Daniela. Complete Part 1 of the form. Can you remember her nationality?

From: EIC Student Care
To: danielar@supermail.com

Dear Daniela

We're looking forward to welcoming you to International College on 6th July.

You will be in class P1 and your teacher will be Kate Marks. We hope …

INTERNATIONAL COLLEGE COMPETITION ENTRY FORM

Part 1

First name: ____________

Last name: Romero

Gender: ☐ female ☐ male

Nationality: ____________

Mobile (UK): 074822 294576

Email address: ____________

Your class: ____________

Course start date: ____________

Part 2

Why is English important for you?

I work as a(n) [1] ________ in Mexico City. I love my job except for the [2] ________! Every day they speak to me and ask me for information. I can't understand them and it is difficult for me to answer. English is important for me because it helps me do my [3] ________ well.

What do you want to improve in your English?

I think my speaking in English is OK for my level. But [4] ________ and understanding is still very difficult for me. I really want to stay an extra month at your school and improve my listening.

b Read Part 2 of Daniela's form. Complete it.

c 02.21 Listen to Daniela again and check your answers.

3 WRITING SKILLS Spelling

a Read Daniela's first draft of her entry form. Cover p. 26. Look at the example spelling problem. Find eight more spelling problems.

b Tick (✓) when it's important to have correct spelling.

1 ☐ a first draft of a text
2 ☐ a final draft of a text
3 ☐ a text other people read
4 ☐ a text only you read

c Find and correct a spelling mistake in each sentence.

1 I really love swimming in the see.
2 Can you please right your name on the form?
3 I don't no the answer to this question.
4 Can you speak up? I can't here you.
5 Where can I bye bread?

d In what way are the incorrect and correct words in 3c the same?

4 WRITING

a Complete the form with your information.

b Use your ideas in 1d to write answers to the questions in Part 2.

c Swap forms with another student. Are your ideas in Part 2 the same?

INTERNATIONAL COLLEGE COMPETITION ENTRY FORM

Part 2

Why is English important for you?

I work as a ~~trafic~~ traffic police offiser in Mexico City. I love my job except for the toorists! Every day they speak to me and ask me for informashion. I can't understand them and it is dificult for me to anser. English is important for me becos it helps me do my job well.

What do you want to improve in your English?

I think my speaking in English is OK for my level. I also find reading and writing quite easy. But listning and understanding is still very hard for me. I really want to stay an extra month at your scool and improve my listening.

INTERNATIONAL COLLEGE COMPETITION ENTRY FORM

Part 1

First name: ______

Last name: ______

Gender: ☐ female ☐ male

Nationality: ______

Mobile (UK): ______

Email address: ______

Your class now: ______

Course start date: ______

Part 2

Why is English important for you?

______

What do you want to improve in your English?

______

UNIT 2
Review and extension

1 GRAMMAR

a Complete the text with the correct form of the verb in brackets.

I'm a university student, but I [1]_________ (work) in a clothes shop every weekend. On Saturday I [2]_________ (start) work at 9:00 am, but on Sunday I [3]_________ (not start) until 11:00 am. My sister's a nurse, so she [4]_________ (not have) a normal timetable. She sometimes [5]_________ (work) all night, but she [6]_________ (not like) it. My parents are both teachers, so they [7]_________ (work) from Monday to Friday.

b Write possible questions for the answers.

1 **A** What _________? **B** I'm a receptionist.
2 **A** Do _________? **B** No, I don't. I work in a hospital.
3 **A** Do _________? **B** Yes, I do. It's great.
4 **A** When _________? **B** I start at 9 o'clock in the morning.
5 **A** Does _________? **B** Yes, he does. My husband is a teacher.
6 **A** Where _________? **B** He works in a local school.
7 **A** Does _________? **B** Yes, he does. He loves it.

c Practise the conversation in 1b with a partner. Then answer about your own life.

2 VOCABULARY

a Put the letters in brackets in the correct order to complete the job.

1 n _________ e (s r u)
2 d _________ t (t e i s n)
3 p _________ t (l o i)
4 e _________ r (n n i e g e)
5 c _________ r (e e n a l)
6 p _________ r (o o h e h p r a t g)

b Write the times in words.

10:15 – *(a) quarter past ten or ten fifteen*

1 11:30 3 6:00 5 2:40
2 12:45 4 8:15 6 5:20

c Match 1–5 with a–e to complete the sentences.

1 Read the text and take
2 I'm not worried because I usually get good
3 I hope we have
4 He is worried because he often fails
5 I need to study for the end-of-

a a break soon because I'm tired.
b important exams.
c notes on a piece of paper.
d term test next week.
e marks in tests.

3 WORDPOWER work

a Match sentences 1–3 with pictures a–c.

1 I **work in** a hospital.
2 I **work for** Larkin Computers.
3 I **work as** a receptionist.

b Look at the phrases in **bold** in 3a. Match them with 1–3.

1 the job I do
2 the place of work
3 the company

c Is *work* a verb or a noun in sentences 1–5?

1 I start **work** at 8:00 am each day.
2 She leaves **work** at about 6:00 pm.
3 I can't talk to you now – I'm at **work**.
4 I'm an actor, but I'm out of **work** at the moment.
5 They go to **work** very early in the morning.

d Which *work* phrase in 3c do we use when … ?

a we don't have a job
b we are at the place we work

e Put the word in brackets in the correct place in the sentence.

1 He works a nurse at night. (as)
2 We all work at 6:00 pm. (start)
3 She'd like a job because now she's of work. (out)
4 She's a photographer and works *The Times*. (for)
5 When I'm work, I have no free time. (at)
6 We both work a large office in the city centre. (in)

f Write four sentences about people you know. Use *work* in different ways.

My brother works in a shoe shop in the city centre.

REVIEW YOUR PROGRESS

How well did you do in this unit? Write 3, 2 or 1 for each objective.
3 = very well 2 = well 1 = not so well

I CAN ...	
talk about jobs	☐
talk about study habits	☐
ask for things and reply	☐
complete a form.	☐

CAN DO OBJECTIVES

- Talk about routines
- Talk about technology in your life
- Make arrangements
- Write an informal invitation

UNIT 3

DAILY LIFE

GETTING STARTED

a Look at the picture and answer the questions.

1 What country do you think this is? Why?
2 What time is it: morning or evening? Why?
3 Where do these people go when they get off the train?
4 What are their jobs?

b In pairs, ask and answer the questions.

1 What things do you do every day?
- take a bus or train
- buy a cup of coffee
- check social media
- go for a walk

2 What do you do on a train or bus?
- read
- talk to other passengers
- listen to music
- use your phone

3A SHE OFTEN GOES TO AN ENGLISH LESSON

Learn to talk about routines

G Position of adverbs of frequency

V Time expressions; Common verbs

A Regular Office Job – Or Not?

Nora is 24 and she works in the marketing department of a large media company in Oslo. She works hard, but her company wants her to take breaks during the day, so she goes to lessons and sometimes plays with animals.

Nora gets up every weekday at 6:15 am. She eats breakfast and then she leaves for work at 7:00 am. She usually arrives at work at about 8:15 am – the journey takes more than an hour and the trains are always crowded.

From 8:30 am until 9:00 am, Nora reads her emails and talks to her colleagues. Then everyone in her department gets together for a short meeting. The manager tells everyone any important information, and workers can ask questions. Nora thinks it's a nice way to start the day – with everyone together.

At about 10:15 or 10:30, Nora usually takes a break. She often goes to an English lesson, but she sometimes goes to a knitting lesson. The company pays for these lessons. At 12:30, she has lunch with her colleagues. Most people at the company bring lunch – called a 'matpakke'. It is usually a sandwich with fish or cheese.

In the afternoon, Nora always takes another break at about 3:00 pm. She goes to the pet floor of her office building. The company has cats, dogs and rabbits that workers can play with on their breaks. Nora feeds the rabbits, and she often takes one of the dogs for a walk. The pet floor is Nora's favourite part of the office.

Nora never leaves the office before 5:30 pm. She often has dinner with her colleagues at the company restaurant. The meal doesn't cost a lot of money. She goes home at 7:30 pm.

1 READING

a Look at the pictures of an office in Oslo and answer the questions. What do you think?

1 What kind of company is it?
2 What job do the people do?
3 Is their work life easy or hard?

b Read the article about Nora and answer the questions.

1 Is her work life easy or hard?
2 What is unusual about her work life?

c Read the article again. Are the sentences True (*T*) or false (*F*)? Correct the false sentences.

1 Nora has her breakfast on the train to work.
2 Her journey to work takes a long time.
3 Early in the morning, Nora goes to a meeting with her colleagues.
4 During her morning break, she goes to a knitting lesson and then an English lesson.
5 Nora likes the pet floor in her office building.
6 Nora always goes home at 5:30 pm.

d What are the good things about Nora's work life?

2 GRAMMAR Position of adverbs of frequency

a Look at this sentence from the article. The adverb of frequency is underlined.

She usually arrives at work at about 8.15 am.

Underline more adverbs of frequency in the article.

b Put the adverbs of frequency in the correct place on the time line.

~~sometimes~~ usually never often always

0% — sometimes — 100%

c Now go to Grammar Focus 3A on p. 142.

d Talk about the questions.

1 What do you always do in the morning?
2 What do you usually do in the afternoon?
3 What do you sometimes do in the evening?

I always get up at 6 o'clock.

I often play tennis in the afternoon.

3 LISTENING

a Ask and answer the questions.

1 Do you spend a lot of time with your family? Why / Why not?
2 What do you like doing with your family?

b 03.02 Listen to Martin and Katherine. Answer the questions.

1 Do they talk about their jobs or free time?
2 What does Martin want the family to do?

c 03.02 Listen again. Complete the timetable with the correct activity from the box.

Spanish lesson   band practice   work late   volleyball training

d Talk about the questions.

1 Is your family routine like the Lawsons' or is it different?
2 In your country, do families spend a lot of time together? What do they do?

The Lawson Family's Week

	Martin	Katherine	Liz	Pete
Monday				
Tuesday				
Wednesday				
Thursday				
Friday				

4 VOCABULARY Time expressions

a 03.03 Complete the sentences. Listen and check.

twice   a   every   once

1 I go to my Spanish lesson __________ a week.
2 She goes to volleyball training __________ a week, on Monday and Thursday.
3 He has band practice three times __________ week.
4 I work late __________ Tuesday.

b Underline the correct answer to complete the rule.

We put time expressions *before the verb* / *at the end of a sentence.*

c 03.04 **Pronunciation** Listen to the question and answer. Notice the stressed words.

MARTIN How often does she go?
KATHERINE Twice a week, on Monday and Thursday.

d Which words do we usually stress? Choose the correct answer.

a Important words like time expressions and verbs.
b Less important words.

e 03.05 Put the words in each sentence in the correct order to make a conversation. Listen and check.

A you and your family do / how often do / things together?
B a week / about once.
A you do / what do?
B we usually / to a restaurant / go for a picnic or.
A do that at / do you / the weekend?
B but we sometimes / yes, every Sunday / go to the cinema.
A do anything else / do you?
B away for a weekend / a year we go / well, about twice.
A with your family / a nice time / it sounds like you have.

f Now go to Vocabulary Focus 3A on p. 165 for common verbs.

5 SPEAKING

a Think of a group of people you know well. Think of things you do together every day, week or year. Make notes.

My parents – have a cup of tea every morning
Rob and Andy – usually go on holiday every June
My classmates – study English three times a week

b Talk about what you do with the people you know well and how often. Look at the conversation in 4e to help you.

3B IMAGINE YOU HAVEN'T GOT THE INTERNET

Learn to talk about technology in your life

G *have got*
V Technology

1 READING

a How do you use the Internet? Tick (✓) the things you sometimes do. Tick (✓✓) the things you do every day.

☐☐ find information	☐☐ post pictures
☐☐ talk to friends	☐☐ play games
☐☐ send emails	☐☐ buy things
☐☐ watch films or TV	☐☐ download music

b Talk about your answers with other students.

c Read the first part of the blog post.

1 Is it about … ?
   a using the Internet more
   b using the Internet less
2 What is unusual about the Walker family this month?

d Read the interview and answer the questions.

1 Which of the activities (a–f) does Alfie do more without the Internet?
   a reading
   b going out
   c shopping
   d doing things with his father
   e chatting with friends
   f watching TV
2 What activities are now more difficult for Alfie and his parents?

e Talk about the questions.

1 Would you like to live without the Internet? Why / Why not?
2 What do you think is good and bad about the Internet?

2 VOCABULARY Technology

a Match the words in the box with pictures 1–10.

computer smartphone tablet smartwatch speaker
keyboard printer headphones camera laptop

1 
2 
3 
4 
5 
6 
7 
8 
9 
10 

b 03.08 **Pronunciation** Listen and repeat the words in 2a. Underline the stressed syllable in each word.

c What are the people talking about? There is sometimes more than one answer.

1 I talk to my friends on it.
2 I use it to write emails.
3 I use these when I listen to music.
4 I often print out maps, so it's very useful.
5 I use it on the train.

TechBlog

HOME REVIEWS **FORUMS** DOWNLOADS LOGIN SEARCH

This month on TechBlog

These days, we all use the Internet – for everything. It's on our computers, our smartphones … it's everywhere. But imagine you haven't got the Internet. So you can't send emails, you can't post photos and you can't go online to get information.

How long could you live like that? A day? A week maybe, if you're on holiday? A month?

Here at TechBlog we asked the Walker family in Birmingham, England, to live without the Internet for a whole month. Read our interview with Alfie Walker, 17, about what it's like to go offline.

THE INTERVIEW

Alfie, is your life different without the Internet?

Yes, it's really different! We usually get our TV through the Internet, so now I don't watch TV. And I usually go online to find information. But now we haven't got the Internet, so I go to the library and do my homework there.

What about your parents?

It's not easy for them either! My mum usually does her shopping online, but now she goes to the supermarket every weekend. My dad likes to read the news online, but now he hasn't got the Internet, so he usually buys a newspaper. The good thing is, he doesn't do any work at home now, so he's got more free time and he plays chess with me.

What about friends?

That is a big problem. If I'm not on social media, I have no idea what my friends are doing. But I think life is good without the Internet. I can't chat online now, so now I go out and see my friends and we do things together. But one month without the Internet is enough. I can't wait to get back online again!

3 LISTENING

a 03.09 Listen to Don, Bella and Chris's answers. Match the people with the questions.

1 Have you got a computer?
2 Have you got a smartphone?
3 Have you got a digital camera?

b 03.10 Listen to the conversations and complete the table.

	Gadgets	Do they often use them?
Don	1	
Bella	1 2	
Chris	1 2	

c 03.10 Listen again and check.

4 GRAMMAR *have got*

a Look at the sentences. Which are from the Reading text (R) and which are from the Listening (L)?

1 I've got my daughter's phone.
2 He's got more free time.
3 She's got a new phone.
4 Imagine you haven't got the Internet.
5 Now he hasn't got the Internet.
6 Have you got a digital camera?

INTERNET FACT FILE

- The average teenager spends about nine hours a day online.
- Every minute, more than 500 hours of video are uploaded to YouTube.

b Underline the forms of *have got* in 1–6 in 4a.
Does *I've got* mean ... ?

a I am b I have c I get

c Complete the table.

	I / We / You / They	He / She
+	I _____ got her old phone.	She _____ got a new phone.
–	I _____ got a PC, but I've got a laptop.	He _____ got his phone with him. It's at home.
?	_____ you got a computer at home? Yes, I have. / No, I haven't.	_____ she got a new camera? Yes, she has. / No, she hasn't.

d 03.11 **Pronunciation** Listen to the sentence. The main stress is on *camera*, the last important word.

I've got a digital camera.

e 03.12 Listen to sentences 1–3. Underline the main stress.

1 They've got a computer.
2 He's got a smartphone.
3 She's got a new laptop.

f 03.12 Listen again. Does the intonation go up ↗ or down ↘ on the main stress?

g Now go to Grammar Focus 3B on p. 142.

h Write sentences that are true for you. Use *have got* or *haven't got* and the words and phrases in the box.

a laptop a camera a car a smartwatch a tablet
a lot of online friends friends in another country

I've got a smartphone.

i Write three *have got* questions with words and phrases in 4h.

Have you got a smartphone?

5 SPEAKING

a Put the words in the correct order to make questions.

1 use it / how often / you / do ?
2 you / do / like it ?
3 it / is / what kind ?
4 is / it / how old ?
5 where / they / do / live ?
6 like one / would / you ?

b Work with a partner. Ask and answer your questions in 4i. Then ask some of the questions from 5a to find out more.

Have you got a laptop?
Yes, I have.
What kind is it?
It's a ...

c Work in new pairs. Tell a new partner what you know about other students.

Onur's got a tablet. It's one year old and he uses it every day.

3C EVERYDAY ENGLISH
How about next Wednesday?

Learn to make arrangements

- S Thinking about what you want to say
- P Main stress

1 LISTENING

a Ask and answer the questions.

1 How often do you watch TV?
2 Are there programmes you watch every week?
3 Do you have a favourite TV programme? Who do you watch it with?

b 03.14 Watch or listen to Part 1. Do Martina, Annie and Dan all like the same TV programme?

c 03.14 Watch or listen to Part 1 again. Are the sentences true (*T*) or false (*F*)? Correct the false sentences.

1 The programme Annie wants to watch is *Best Cook*.
2 Martina and Dan don't see this programme very often.
3 Annie loves everything to do with eating.

d 03.15 Watch or listen to Part 2. What do they plan to do?

e 03.15 Answer the questions. Watch or listen to Part 2 again and check your answers.

1 Which day does Martina work late?
2 Which day do they decide to go out?
3 Who does Dan want to ask to dinner?
4 How does Annie feel about Dan's idea?

2 USEFUL LANGUAGE
Making arrangements

a Match beginnings 1–6 with endings a–f.

1 Why	a be great.
2 How	b free next Friday?
3 Are you	c don't we try it?
4 That'd	d love to.
5 That's a	e about next Wednesday?
6 I'd	f good idea.

b Which questions in 2a do we use to make suggestions? Which sentences do we use to say *yes* to suggestions?

c Martina says *no* to an idea. Underline the phrase that means *no*.

MARTINA I'm sorry, I can't. I need to work late next Wednesday.

d 03.16 Put the conversation in the correct order. Listen and check.

B ☐ I'm sorry, I can't. I'm away this weekend.
A [1] Why don't we go to the cinema?
B ☐ Yes, Monday's fine.
A ☐ How about this Saturday?
A ☐ Are you free on Monday?
B ☐ The cinema? That's a good idea.

e Practise the conversation in 2d. Then have similar conversations using your own ideas.

Why don't we go for a picnic?

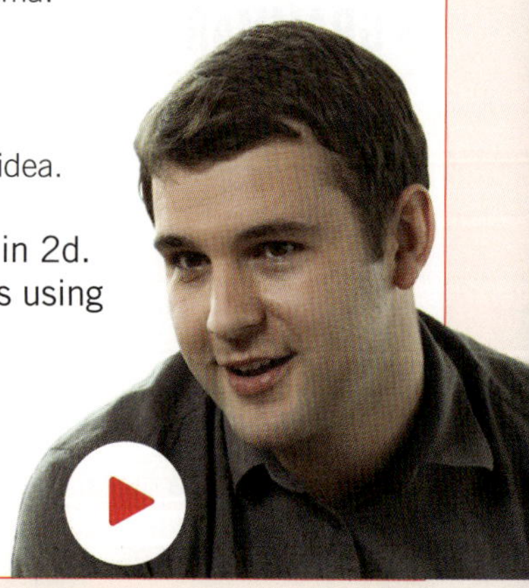

3 PRONUNCIATION Main stress

a 03.17 Listen to the sentences. Notice the main stress in each sentence.

1 That'd be great. 2 That's a good idea. 3 I'd love to.

b Choose the correct answer.

The words in 3a that have the main stress are … .
a short and loud b long c long and loud

c 03.18 Listen to the sentences. Underline the main stress.

1 We'd love to.
2 That'd be good.
3 That's a lovely idea.
4 That'd be fantastic.

d Practise the sentences in 3c.

4 CONVERSATION SKILLS
Thinking about what you want to say

a Look at the underlined phrases in the conversation. Choose the correct answer below.

ANNIE How about next Wednesday?
MARTINA Mm, maybe. Let me see. I'm sorry, I can't. I need to work late next Wednesday.
ANNIE Are you free next Friday?
MARTINA Mm, possibly. Friday's fine. Dan?
DAN Friday? Sure, I'd love to.

Martina uses the underlined phrases because they … .
a have an important meaning in the conversation
b give her time to think

b 03.19 **Pronunciation** Listen and notice how *Mm* is pronounced. Do you have short words or sounds like this in your language?

c In pairs, ask and answer the questions. Think about your answer before you reply.
1 Are you free this weekend?
2 Do you want to have a coffee after the lesson?
3 Would you like to go to the cinema tomorrow?
4 Why don't we do our homework together?

5 SPEAKING

a **Communication 3C** Student A: Look at the information below. Student B: Go to p. 132.

Conversation 1. Read your first card. Think about what you want to say. Then start the conversation with Student B.

1 You want to have a picnic on Saturday morning with Student B. Decide the following and invite Student B.
- where to have the picnic
- what time
- what you'd like to do/eat

b **Conversation 2.** Now look at your second card. Listen to Student B and reply.

2 You aren't free next Friday after work/school because you have an exercise class at the gym. You'd like to go out on Saturday night.

c Tell other students about arrangements in each role play.

UNIT PROGRESS TEST
CHECK YOUR PROGRESS
You can now do the Unit Progress Test.

3D SKILLS FOR WRITING
Can you join us?

Learn to write an informal invitation

W Inviting and replying

1 SPEAKING AND LISTENING

a Ask and answer the questions.

1 Have you got family or friends in other countries or in other places in your country?
2 Where are they?
3 What do they do?
4 How often do you see them?

b 03.20 Emrah from Turkey talks about his family. Listen and number the countries where he's got family in the order you hear them.

☐ England	☐ Italy
☐ France	☐ Sweden
☐ Germany	☐ Turkey

c 03.20 Listen again. Correct the mistakes in the text below.

Emrah comes from a large family and [1]they all live in Izmir in Turkey. [2]He hasn't got any brothers or sisters. His family keep in contact by Skype, and every [3]ten years they all meet in [4]London. They stay [5]in a large hotel and they have a big [6]meal. This [7]is only for people in the family – they [8]don't invite friends.

1 *They live in many different countries.*

2 READING

a Read Emrah's emails to his brother and sister. Why does he email them?

b Complete the information about the family party.

- Place
- Date
- How many days?
- Where to stay?

Family party

From: EBoztepe12@supermail.com
To: M_Boztepe@supermail.com

Hi Mustafa,

[1]How are you? Hope the family's well.

[2]In September it's our family party again and we all plan to meet in Izmir as usual. [3]We're there from Friday 14th to Sunday 16th September. [4]Would you like to come? I hope so, as I'd love to see you. [5]Mert (you know, my friend from school) says he's got a bedroom free so you can stay at his house. [6]Please let me know if you would like to join us. I hope you can come!

Love,
Emrah

Family party

From: EBoztepe12@supermail.com
To: Ayda99@email.com

Hi Ayda,

[1]How are things? Hope you like your new job.

[2]In September it's our family party again and we all plan to meet in Izmir as usual. [3]We're there from Friday 14th to Sunday 16th September. [4]Can you join us? I hope you can, as it would be great to see you. [5]Melis (you know, my friend from school) says she's got a bedroom free so you can stay at her house. [6]Please let me know if you can come. Hope you can make it!

Love,
Emrah

Izmir

3 WRITING SKILLS Inviting and replying

a Read Emrah's email to Ayda again. In which of sentences 1–6 does he … ?

a [4] invite Ayda
b [ ] ask how she is
c [ ] ask her to reply
d [ ] give the reason for his message
e [ ] talk about where to stay
f [ ] give details of dates

b Compare sentences 1–6 in Emrah's emails to Mustafa and Ayda on p. 36. Underline phrases that are different.

c Tick (✓) the correct questions to invite people.

1 [ ] Can you come?
2 [ ] Can you join?
3 [ ] Can you join us?
4 [ ] Can you to join us?
5 [ ] Would you like come?
6 [ ] Would you like to come?
7 [ ] Would you like to join us?

d Put the words in the correct order. Add question marks (?) and full stops (.).

1 things / are / how
2 you / see / to / be / it / would / great
3 hope / it / can / you / make
4 to / I'd / you / love / see
5 are / you / how
6 I / can / come / you / hope

e Which sentences and questions in 3d mean the same?

f Read the emails from Mustafa and Ayda. Can they come?

Re: Family party

From: M_Boztepe@supermail.com
To: EBoztepe12@supermail.com

Hi Emrah,

It's good to hear from you and many thanks for the invitation. Yes, I'd love to come. I'm really looking forward to it. Please tell Mert I'd love to stay with him if he's got a free room. See you soon.

Love,
Mustafa

Re: Family party

From: Ayda99@email.com
To: EBoztepe12@supermail.com

Hi Emrah,

Great to hear from you and thanks for the invitation. I'd love to come but I'm afraid I can't. I've got a business trip to Los Angeles that weekend, and I can't change it.

Hope you all have a great time, and hope to see you soon.

Keep in touch!

Love,
Ayda

g Underline phrases in the emails from Mustafa and Ayda that mean … .

1 I want to come
2 I can't come
3 Have a good time

4 WRITING AND SPEAKING

a Plan a party or other event. Write notes.

- Where?
- When?
- Why?
- Who?

b Talk about your plan with other students.

My party is at the Grand Hotel.

It's at 7 pm on Saturday.

It's for my brother's birthday.

c Write an invitation to your event to another student in your class. Use the emails on p. 36 to help you.

d Swap invitations with another student and check the information. Does it include the information in 4a?

e Write a reply to the invitation. Use the emails in 3f to help you. Give your reply back to the student who invited you.

UNIT 3
Review and extension

1 GRAMMAR

a Put the frequency adverbs in the correct place in the sentences.

1 He gets up at about 10 or 11. (often)
2 He goes to bed before 2:00 am. (never)
3 He studies all night. (sometimes)
4 He has black coffee and toast for breakfast. (usually)
5 He is away for a week or more. (often)
6 His windows are closed, even in summer. (always)

b Complete the text with the correct forms of *have got* or *haven't got*.

My brother and I are very different. He and his wife [1]______ good jobs and they [2]______ a large house near London. Their house [3]______ a big garden with a swimming pool. They both work ten hours a day, so they [4]______ any free time and they never go on holiday.

I'm a school teacher, so I [5]______ much money, but I [6]______ a lot of free time in the holidays. Every summer I travel to a different country and I [7]______ friends all over the world.

c Make the notes into questions with *have got* or *has got*.

1 you – a car? *Have you got a car? No, I haven't.*
2 your neighbours – children?
3 your flat or house – a garden?
4 you – TV in your bedroom?
5 someone in your family – a smartwatch?
6 you – a lot of free time?

d Ask and answer the questions in 1c.

2 VOCABULARY

a Change the words in *italics* into a time expression.

1 She calls ~~on Tuesday and Sunday~~. *twice a week*
2 There are English courses *in March, May and October.*
3 We go on holiday *in June and in January.*
4 There's a boat *on Monday, Wednesday and Saturday.*
5 I check my emails *before I start work and in the evening.*
6 Her mother phones on *Monday, Tuesday, Wednesday and Thursday.*

b Write the names of the objects.

3 WORDPOWER Prepositions of time

a Match sentences 1–5 with pictures a–e.

1 He relaxes outside in the summer.
2 He works all the time – in the morning, in the evening, sometimes even at night.
3 He gets up at 6 am, but he finishes work at 1 pm.
4 He works on weekday mornings, but on Sunday he gets up late.
5 In January he works at a ski resort.

a

b

c

d

e

b Answer the questions.

1 Do we use *at*, *in* or *on* with a–f?
   a times
   b days
   c months
   d parts of days (morning, afternoon)
   e seasons (summer, winter)
   f the words *the weekend* and *night*

2 How many examples of a–e can you find in 3a?

c Add *at*, *in* or *on* in the correct place in these sentences. Some sentences may need more than one word.

1 I always get up 6:30 the morning weekdays.
2 It's usually cold here the winter, and it often snows January.
3 Are you free the weekend? I've got tickets for a concert Saturday. It starts 7:30 pm.

d When do you usually do these things? Write sentences.

1 get up
2 go to bed
3 have lunch
4 go on holiday
5 go shopping
6 drink coffee or tea
7 clean your flat or house
8 cook meals

e Ask and answer questions about when you usually do the things in 3d.

REVIEW YOUR PROGRESS

How well did you do in this unit? Write 3, 2 or 1 for each objective.
3 = very well 2 = well 1 = not so well

I CAN ...	
talk about routines	☐
talk about technology in my life	☐
make arrangements	☐
write an informal invitation.	☐

CAN DO OBJECTIVES

- Talk about the food you want
- Talk about the food you eat every day
- Arrive at and order a meal in a restaurant
- Write a blog post about something you know how to do

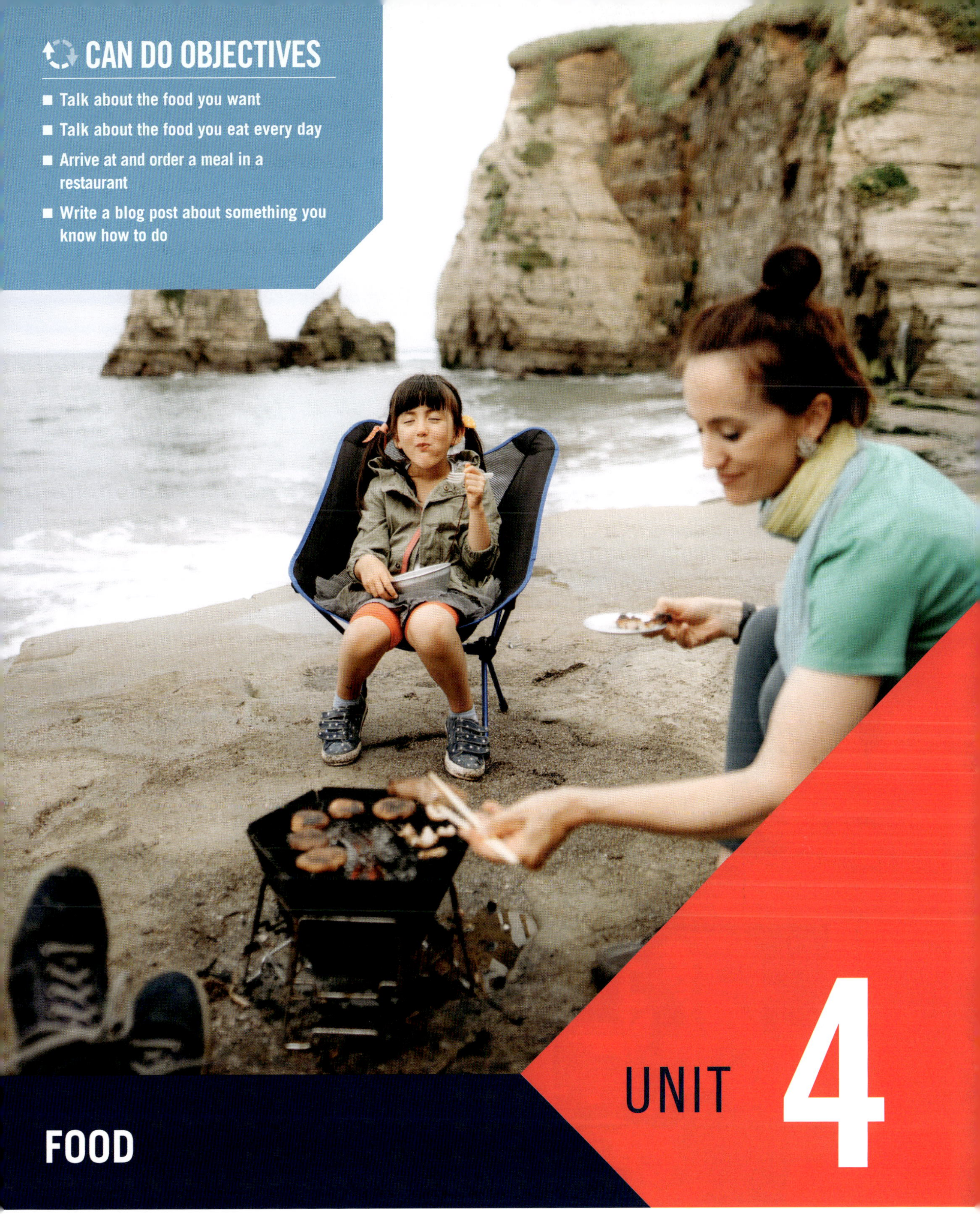

UNIT 4

FOOD

GETTING STARTED

a Look at the picture and answer the questions.

1 Do you think these people are friends or family?
2 What meal is this – breakfast, lunch or dinner?
3 Is it the beginning, middle or end of the meal?

b In pairs, ask and answer the questions.

1 How often do you eat together as a family?
2 What do you usually have for … ?
- breakfast
- lunch
- dinner

3 What things do you talk about when you eat together?

4A TRY SOME INTERESTING FOOD

Learn to talk about the food you want

G Countable and uncountable nouns; *a / an, some, any*

V Food

1 READING

a Look at the pictures of places to buy food. Which one would you like to visit? Why?

b Read the article and match 1–3 with pictures a–c.

c Read the sentences. Where is each person?

SAM I love these pickled vegetables – they're great!
MAISIE I really only need a snack, but look at all the food I can buy!
SARAH Now I know a new way to cook these potatoes.

d Talk about the questions.

1 Are there any markets in your town? What do they sell?
2 Where do you prefer shopping for food: at a market or a supermarket? Why?

2 GRAMMAR Countable and uncountable nouns

a Look at the four nouns from the article. Which two have plural endings?

fruit vegetables tomatoes cheese

b Complete the rule.

We can't count some nouns (they are uncountable nouns). We *always* / *never* add *-s* or *-es*.

c Look at the table. Add food nouns from the article.

Countable nouns (You can say *1, 2, 3 vegetables.*)	Uncountable nouns (You can't say ~~*1, 2, 3 fruits.*~~)
vegetables, tomatoes	fruit, cheese

WORLD MARKETS

Markets can be the best places to see the daily life of a city and to eat some fantastic local food. Today, read about different markets around the world.

COOK AS YOU SHOP

1 **If you want to buy food and learn how to cook it** at the same time, go to the Union Square Greenmarket in New York. It's open four days a week and it has about 250,000 customers. Farmers from all over New York State sell food there. You can find different kinds of fruit and vegetables, such as potatoes, carrots, mushrooms and tomatoes. The farmers show the best ways to cook the food and you can even try the dishes they make for free!

A TASTE OF SÃO PAULO

2 **The Municipal Market of São Paulo, Brazil** is so large that people call it Mercadão (or big market). You can find almost any kind of food here, including fruit and vegetables, pasta, fresh meat, excellent cheese, spices, bread, chocolate and more. Both tourists and locals like to shop and eat in this beautiful and historic building. You can try some of São Paulo's most famous food items here, such as the local sandwiches or pastries. There's something for everyone in the Mercadão!

KYOTO'S KITCHEN

3 **One of the best places to try Japanese food** is in Kyoto, Japan. There you can find Nishiki Market. It's famous for its traditional Japanese food. It is over 700 years old and its nickname is 'Kyoto's kitchen'. Most of the foods at Nishiki Market are local foods, so they come from Kyoto. The best chefs in Kyoto buy their ingredients here because the food is amazing! At Nishiki Market, you can try local foods such as tofu, pickled vegetables, grilled fish and sweets.

3 VOCABULARY Food

a Match the food words with pictures 1–10.

beans lemons chicken
mushrooms onions lamb
pears steak carrots grapes

b Underline the different word in 1–3. Why is it different?

1 lemon pear carrot grape
2 bean lamb onion mushroom
3 steak chicken grape lamb

c 04.01 **Pronunciation** Answer the questions. Then listen and check.

1 What is the same about the spelling of these words?
• steak • bean • pear
2 Which word above has the same sound as these words?
green /iː/ hair /eə/ make /eɪ/

d 04.02 What sound do the letters in **bold** have in the words in the box? Add the words to the sound groups below. Listen and check.

eat wh**ere** th**ese** **eigh**t r**ai**n gr**ee**n w**ea**r d**ay** f**air**

Sound 1 /eɪ/	Sound 2 /iː/	Sound 3 /eə/
steak	bean	pear

e Talk about the food you like and don't like.

f Now go to Vocabulary Focus 4A on p. 166 for more food vocabulary.

4 LISTENING

a Ask and answer the questions.

1 Do you like cooking?
2 How often do you (or does someone in your family) buy food to cook?

b 04.06 Listen to Tom and Milly's conversation and answer the questions.

1 Does Milly want to cook?
2 Who doesn't want to go to the supermarket at the weekend – Tom or Milly?
3 Where do they decide to buy food – at the supermarket or farmers' market?
4 Who says they can pay – Tom or Milly?

c 04.06 Listen again. Tick (✓) the food on the shopping list that Tom and Milly need.

Meat:
☐ chicken ☐ steak ☐ fish

Vegetables:
☐ carrots ☐ an onion ☐ potatoes
☐ tomatoes ☐ mushrooms

5 GRAMMAR *a / an, some, any*

a 04.07 Complete the sentences with the words in the box. Listen and check.

some a/an any (x2)

1 We've got ________ potatoes.
2 Have we got ________ mushrooms?
3 And I need ________ onion and a chicken.
4 I haven't got ________ money.

b Complete the chart with *a*, *an*, *some* and *any*.

	Countable	Uncountable
+	___a___ potato ______ potatoes	______ fruit
– / ?	______ onion ______ onions	______ cheese

c Now go to Grammar Focus 4A on p. 144.

d 04.09 Complete the conversation with *a/an*, *some* or *any*. Listen and check.

SARAH Hello, I'd like [1]________ lemon and [2]________ onion, please.
STALLHOLDER Just one?
SARAH Yes, and I'd like [3]________ potatoes, too.
STALLHOLDER Is this bag OK?
SARAH Yes, fine. Have you got [4]________ small tomatoes?
STALLHOLDER I'm sorry, but I haven't got [5]________ small tomatoes.
SARAH OK, the big ones there are fine. Also I'd like [6]________ cheese.
STALLHOLDER I'm sorry, I don't sell cheese. Try that guy over there.

6 SPEAKING

a **Communication 4A** Student A: Go to p. 130. Student B: Go to p. 133.

4B HOW MUCH CHOCOLATE?

Learn to talk about the food you eat every day

G Quantifiers: *much, many, a lot (of)*

V Cooking

1 READING

a Answer the questions with other students.

1. Do you have any famous TV programmes about cooking in your country?
2. Do you like the food they make on those programmes? Why / Why not?
3. Do you know the chef in the picture?
4. Read the information about Albert Adrià. Would you like to try his food? Why / Why not?

b Read Josh's email to his father. Answer the questions.

1. Who lives in Barcelona – Josh or his dad?
2. Which restaurant does Josh want to go to?
3. Why does Josh want to go to this restaurant?

c Read his dad's reply. Does he want to go to *Tickets*?

d Read his dad's email again. What does he think about these things? Underline the correct answers.

1. Albert Adrià's food: *boring / different*
2. His wife's food: *normal / strange*
3. The restaurant: *expensive for him / expensive for Josh*

e Talk about the questions.

1. Do you like going to restaurants with your family? Or do you prefer to eat at home? Why / Why not?
2. Do you like trying new food? Why / Why not?

Introducing... Albert Adrià

Who is Albert Adrià?

A famous chef and film director, Albert Adrià has written several cookbooks and owns a group of restaurants in Barcelona called *elBarri* – including the very popular *Tickets* restaurant.

What's he famous for?

Albert makes creative dishes, such as spicy tuna with cherries and an orange salad with olive juice. You can try making his mussels with tomato sauce – the recipe is in his cookbook *Tapas – Tickets Cuisine*!

visit

From: Josh1994@supermail.com
To: MrBLJohnson@supermail.com

Hi Dad,

When you come to Barcelona next week, I want to take you out to dinner. Would you like to go to Albert Adrià's restaurant *Tickets*? It looks fun and I can pay! Do you remember my friend Pete? Well, he goes to *Tickets* every time his parents are in town. He always has the lettuce tacos and he says they're amazing! And his mum says the smoked eel is great, too. I really want to take you there!

Josh

Re: visit

From: MrBLJohnson@supermail.com
To: Josh1994@supermail.com

Hi Josh,

Thanks for the invitation to *Tickets*. I know about that guy Albert Adrià from TV. His food is interesting and it's certainly pretty unusual. But really I'm happy to go to a normal restaurant and have something simple like fried chicken with boiled potatoes or roasted vegetables, like your mum makes at home. Or I'm also fine with a tin of soup at your flat. It's a nice idea to go to the restaurant, but it will be expensive for you. You don't need to do anything special for me.

Dad

2 VOCABULARY Cooking

a Read the cooking instructions 1–5 and match them with the pictures a–e.

1 **Fry** the onions in a little oil.
2 Put water and rice in a pan and **boil** for 12 minutes.
3 **Grill** the chicken for 10 minutes until it's brown.
4 Put some oil on the lamb and **roast** it in the oven.
5 **Bake** the bread in a hot oven for 30 minutes.

b 04.10 Complete the table. Use verbs from 2a and adjectives from Josh's dad's email. Listen and check.

Verb	Adjective
boil	
	fried
	grilled
	baked
roast	

c Complete the examples with adjectives in 2b.

- add *-ed* — *boiled* ________
- add *-d* ________
- changes *-y* to *-ied* ________
- ends with the sound /t/ ________

d Talk about the questions.

1 Which kinds of cooking do you think are healthy? Which do you think are unhealthy?
2 Choose two kinds of food. What is your favourite way to cook that food?

e Now go to Vocabulary Focus 4B on p. 166 for containers vocabulary.

3 LISTENING

a 04.12 Listen to Olivia and Harry talk about recipes. Tick (✓) which two recipes they choose.

☐ Ultimate mashed potato ☐ Three times cooked chips
☐ Cheese-on-toast ice cream ☐ Coffee and chocolate sauce

b 04.12 Listen again. Underline the correct food words in the instructions for Olivia and Harry.

1 Olivia needs *potatoes* / *chips* and *cream* / *butter*.
2 She needs to *boil* / *roast* the ingredients.
3 Harry needs *honey* / *sugar*, *coffee beans* / *black coffee* and *milk chocolate* / *dark chocolate*.
4 He needs to *grill* / *boil* the ingredients.

c Which recipe would you like to make?

4 GRAMMAR Quantifiers: *much, many, a lot (of)*

a 04.13 Complete the sentences with the correct words in the box. Listen and check.

much a lot many a little

1 That's ________ of butter.
2 How ________ chocolate? Only ________.
3 How ________ grams of butter?

b Look at the phrases in italics in 1–3. Can you use them with countable (*C*) or uncountable (*U*) nouns or both (*B*)?

1 **A** *How much* butter does Olivia need?
B *A lot* / *Quite a lot* / *A little* / *Not much*.
2 **A** *How many* beans does Harry need?
B *A lot* / *Quite a lot* / *A few* / *Not many*.
3 I need *a lot of* / *quite a lot of* potatoes and chocolate.

c Now go to Grammar Focus 4B on p. 144.

d 04.16 Complete the conversation. Then put the conversation in order. Listen and check.

B ☐ A [1] ________ – about five or six pieces.
A ☐ Really? That's [2] ________ a lot.
B ☐ About four or five.
A ☐ And what about drinks? How [3] ________ cups of coffee do you have a day?
A 1 How [4] ________ fruit do you eat a day?

e Do you think that Speaker B in 4d is healthy or unhealthy? Why?

5 SPEAKING

a Write questions to ask your partner about the food they eat.

Do you eat much fish?
What fruit do you like?
How many pieces of bread do you eat a day?
How much rice do you eat a week?

b Ask your questions and write down your partner's answers.

c Go to Communication 4B on p. 131 and read about food that is healthy to eat every day. Look at your partner's answers and decide if your partner eats in a healthy way.

4C EVERYDAY ENGLISH
Do we need a reservation?

Learn to arrive at and order a meal in a restaurant

S Changing what you say

P Word groups

1 LISTENING

a Ask and answer the questions.

1 How often do you go to a restaurant?
2 What kind of restaurant do you like?
3 Do people eat out a lot in your country?

b Work in pairs. Look at picture a. Why do you think the restaurant is empty? Choose an answer.

1 The restaurant isn't open.
2 People think the waiter isn't very nice.
3 It's very early.

c 04.17 Watch or listen to Part 1 and check your answers in 1b.

d 04.17 Watch or listen to Part 1 again. Are the sentences true (*T*) or false (*F*)? Correct the false sentences.

1 They have a reservation for four people.
2 They want a table by the door.
3 Annie finds it difficult to choose a table.

2 USEFUL LANGUAGE
Arriving at a restaurant

a Read the sentences. Who is the waiter – A or B?

A No problem.
B Can we have a table by the window?
A Good evening. Do you have a reservation?
A Yes, of course. This way, please.
B No, we don't. We'd like a table for four.

b 04.18 Put the sentences in 2a in the correct order. Listen and check your answers.

c Practise the conversation with a partner.

d Change what B says in 2a. Use the sentences below.

1 We'd like a table outside.
2 Yes, we have a reservation for two people. The name's Morton. But we're twenty minutes late.

3 LISTENING

a Read the restaurant menu. Read what the friends say about food in picture b. What do you think they choose for their main course?

Martina ________ Dan ________
Annie ________ Leo ________

b 04.19 Watch or listen to Part 2.

1 Which of your answers in 3a are correct? Change the wrong answers.
2 Who can't decide what they want to have?

c Do you sometimes find it difficult to choose at a restaurant? Why / Why not?

Starters

Smoked chicken salad
Mixed bean salad
Fried fish in lemon sauce
Fresh mushroom soup

Main course

Spaghetti with tomato sauce
Egg and vegetable pie
Lamb with roast potatoes
Thai chicken curry

4 USEFUL LANGUAGE Ordering a meal in a restaurant

a Complete the conversations from Part 2 with the words in the box.

have then with I'll like

WAITER	What would you like for your starter?
MARTINA	I'd [1]________ the mushroom soup, please.
WAITER	And for your main course?
MARTINA	[2]________ have the lamb with roast potatoes.
WAITER	And for your starter, sir?
DAN	I'll [3]________ chicken salad.
WAITER	Chicken salad.
DAN	[4]________ lamb with roast potatoes.
WAITER	Would you like rice [5]________ that?
LEO	Yes, please.

b Tick (✓) the two phrases we use when we want to order food in a restaurant.

1 ☐ I have
2 ☐ I'd like
3 ☐ I'd want
4 ☐ I'll have

c 04.20 Put the words in the correct order to make sentences. Listen and check.

1 salad / my / bean / I'd / starter / for / like
2 course / I'll / my / spaghetti / for / have / main
3 I'd / rice / chicken / like / with / curry

5 PRONUNCIATION Word groups

a 04.21 Listen to the sentences. In each sentence there are two or more word groups. Write ‖ where you hear the start of a new word group.

1 For my starter ‖ I'd like raw fish.
2 And I'll have vegetable pie for my main course.
3 I'd like chicken salad for my starter.

b 04.21 Listen again. Notice the main stress in each word group.

c 04.22 Write ‖ where you hear the start of a new word group. Listen and check.

For my starter ‖ I'll have mushroom soup. And then I'd like chicken curry for my main course. And I'll have some rice with my curry.

d In pairs, practise saying the order in 5c.

6 CONVERSATION SKILLS Changing what you say

a Look at the two sentences from the conversation. Underline the phrases Annie uses when she wants to change what she wants to say.

1 **ANNIE** What about the one on the right?
DAN If you prefer …
ANNIE Maybe not. The one on the left is fine …

2 **ANNIE** OK, for a starter I'll have the fish. No, wait. I'll have chicken salad.

b 04.23 Complete the sentences. Listen and check.

1 I'll have mushroom soup. Maybe _____. I'd like the chicken salad.
2 I'd like spaghetti, I think. No, _____. I'll have the vegetable pie.

7 SPEAKING

a Work in groups of three or four. Use the menu on p. 44. Write one more starter and one more main course.

b You are at a restaurant. Take turns to be the waiter and the customer. Order a meal from the menu. Use phrases from 4a to help you. Practise changing what you say when you order.

UNIT PROGRESS TEST

CHECK YOUR PROGRESS

You can now do the Unit Progress Test.

4D SKILLS FOR WRITING
Next, decide on your menu

Learn to write a blog post about something you know how to do

W Making the order clear

1 SPEAKING AND LISTENING

a Ask and answer the questions.

1 Which of the dishes in pictures a–d would you like to eat?
2 Can you make any dishes like these?
3 Who does most of the cooking in your house: you or another person? Why?

a

b

c

d

b 04.24 Four people talk about cooking. Listen and underline the correct answers.

Name	Talks about		
Jake	*himself* / *his wife*	*a good* / *bad* cook	picture *a* / *b* / *c* / *d*
Rosie	*herself* / *her husband*	*a good* / *bad* cook	picture *a* / *b* / *c* / *d*
Johanna	*herself* / *her father*	*a good* / *bad* cook	picture *a* / *b* / *c* / *d*
Toby	*himself* / *his mother*	*a good* / *bad* cook	picture *a* / *b* / *c* / *d*

c 04.24 Listen again. Answer the questions.

1 Who always wants to eat more?
2 Who can only make one thing?
3 Who doesn't understand how you can make a really good dish from only a few things?
4 Who enjoys their own food?

d Think of someone you know who is a good cook. Make notes.

- Who?
- Why?
- What dishes?

e Ask and answer about the good cook you know.

Who do you know who is a good cook?

My father – he's a great cook.

Why is your father a good cook?

He can cook many different things.

What does he make?

He makes fantastic chicken salad.

2 READING

a Read the blog description. Who is it for?

a people who know how to cook very well
b people who want to learn how to cook

JAKE COOKS!

I'm not a good cook, but I want to improve. I just want to learn how to cook simple dishes and eat well. I don't want to cook difficult things and I don't want to be a famous chef. In this blog, I want to tell you about the help I get from my family and friends, and the things I try out. So if you want to be a better cook, but not a chef, then maybe I can help you!

b Read the blog post below. What does Jake talk about?

a the food he eats
b planning a dinner

c Read the blog post again. Are the sentences true (*T*) or false (*F*)? Correct the false sentences.

1 Jake hopes the blog can help other people plan dinner for friends.
2 It's not a good idea to invite a lot of people for dinner.
3 It's always fun to try a new dish because friends can tell you if it's good or not.
4 Choose the night of the dinner and then tell your friends.
5 It helps to do all the cooking before your friends come.

d Do you prefer making meals for other people or going to someone's home for a meal? Why?

3 WRITING SKILLS Making the order clear

a In Jake's blog post, the words *first* and *next* help make the order clear. Underline two more phrases in the blog post that also make the order clear.

b Answer the questions.

1 Which two phrases can we change with *then*?
2 What punctuation do we use after these phrases?

c Read the recipe for a bean salad. Only sentences *1* and *5* are in the correct order. Put the other sentences in the correct order.

[1] Cook the beans in hot water with a little salt.
[ ] Add salt and pepper and mix everything together.
[ ] Put lemon and oil on the warm beans – not too much.
[ ] Leave the beans until they are warm.
[5] Place the bean salad in a nice bowl and serve to your guests.

d Add the words in the box to the sentences in 3c.

first	after that	next	then	finally

First, cook the beans in hot water …

4 WRITING

a Plan a blog post about something you know how to do.

- What are good ideas to improve?
- What's a good order to do things?

b Write your blog post. Use *My food – shared!* to help you.

c Swap blog posts with another student and check to see if the order is clear.

JAKE COOKS!

My food – shared!

Added at 12:47 today

Do you like the idea of cooking dinner for friends? Here are my ideas for planning a dinner for friends – I hope you find them useful …

First, think about how many people you want to invite. Don't invite too many – I think four people is a good number.

Next, call or text to invite your friends and agree on a night that's good for everyone.

After that, decide on your menu. Only choose food that you know how to prepare. Don't choose new and difficult dishes – it's just too hard. Your friends know that you are not a chef and your house is not a restaurant!

Finally, on the day of the dinner, you need a lot of time to prepare everything – the food and the table. (The weekend is good because you have all day to prepare.) If everything is ready before your guests arrive, you can enjoy the dinner much more.

Cooking for friends can be easy and fun. I hope it is for you!

UNIT 4
Review and extension

1 GRAMMAR

a Correct the words (1–10) that are wrong.

There's a very good market near my home. I always go there to buy [1]*food*. Some stalls sell [2]*vegetable* and [3]*fruits*. I usually buy [4]*potato* and [5]*onions* there because they're very cheap. At my favourite stall, a woman sells [6]*butters*, [7]*cream* and [8]*egg* from her own farm. There is also a building where they sell [9]*fishes* and [10]*meat*.

b Underline the correct answers.

1 Have we got *an / any* onions?
2 How *much / many* coffee do you drink?
3 How *much / many* bananas would you like?
4 Can you buy *a / some* spaghetti?
5 Is there *any / many* milk in the fridge?
6 How *a lot of / much* money have you got?

c Choose the correct answers.

1 I haven't got ____ money, but I can buy a cup of coffee.
a some b many c much
2 There aren't ____ bananas. Let's buy some more.
a much b many c some
3 The party's going to be great – ____ people want to come.
a much b a lot of c any
4 He's got ____ good books about food and cooking.
a some b much c any

2 VOCABULARY

a Match the words in the box with 1–5. Then add one more word to each group.

pear chicken grape cheese grilled
lamb potato boiled carrot yoghurt

1 kinds of meat
2 vegetables
3 kinds of fruit
4 things that come from milk
5 ways of cooking food

b Look at 1–9. Which are normal (✓) and which are unusual (or impossible) (✗)?

1 grilled chicken ☑
2 roasted butter ☒
3 boiled egg ☐
4 grilled rice ☐
5 fried fish ☐
6 fried grapes ☐
7 roasted chicken ☐
8 fried mushrooms ☐
9 boiled potatoes ☐

3 WORDPOWER *like*

a Read the three conversations. Which one matches the picture?

1 **A** What kind of fruit **do you like**?
B I like most kinds of fruit, but not bananas.
2 **A** What vegetables **would you like**?
B I'd like potatoes and carrots, please.
3 **A** We want to have a party. **Would you like** to join us?
B Yes, thanks. I'd love to.

b Look at the questions in 3a. Which question … ?

1 is about what B wants now
2 invites B to go somewhere
3 is about what B likes in general (not just now)

c Match a–c with 1–3 in 3b.

a I don't like *The Voice*. I think it's a terrible programme.
b Would you like to come to my birthday party?
c I'd like two lemons, please.

d Match the words in **bold** in 1–4 with meanings a–d.

1 **What's it like** to live without the Internet?
2 They haven't got a computer. I couldn't live **like that**.
3 I eat a lot of fruit, **like** apples, pears, melons and bananas.
4 She's 20 and she studies Russian, just **like** me.

a the same as
b how is it
c for example
d in that way

e Write a question or a sentence with *like* for each situation.

1 Invite a friend to the cinema on Friday.
2 You're in a shop. Ask for some apples.
3 You're a waiter or waitress in a café. A customer says 'A coffee, please'.
4 Someone is a guest in your home. You want to know what to cook for him/her.
5 At a party, someone says he/she lives in New York. Ask him/her about the city.

f Ask and answer the questions in 3e with a partner.

REVIEW YOUR PROGRESS

How well did you do in this unit? Write 3, 2 or 1 for each objective.
3 = very well 2 = well 1 = not so well

I CAN ...	
talk about the food I want	☐
talk about the food I eat every day	☐
arrive at and order a meal in a restaurant	☐
write a blog post about something I know how to do.	☐

CAN DO OBJECTIVES

- Talk about towns
- Describe rooms and furniture in your home
- Ask for and give directions
- Write a description of your neighbourhood

UNIT 5

PLACES

GETTING STARTED

a Talk about the picture. Which ideas do you think are true?

1 A family lives here.
2 People go here for a quiet weekend.
3 Wild animals live inside.
4 You can stay here on holiday.
5 People use it when it rains a lot and the river is high.

b In pairs, ask and answer the questions.

1 Why is this a good place for a home?
2 Why is it a bad place?
3 What is a 'good home'? Here are some ideas:

- It's in a quiet place.
- It's expensive.
- It's in the city centre.
- It's got lots of rooms.
- It's got a garden.
- It's modern.

5A THERE AREN'T ANY PARKS OR SQUARES

Learn to talk about towns

G *there is / there are*

V Places in a city

1 READING

a Look at the pictures of Whittier, Alaska. How do you think the town is unusual?

b Read the article and check your answer.

UNUSUAL TOWNS

Whittier, Alaska

Do you want to go to the supermarket? In most towns you walk down a street, or maybe you go by bus. Do you need to go to work? In most places, you probably take a bus or go by car. But in Whittier, you never go outside when you do these things. That's because almost the whole town is in one huge building with fourteen floors. In this one building, there are shops, there's a church, there's a police station and there's even a hospital. There are also many flats for the people who live there, and there are offices where people work, all under one roof. Only 220 people live in Whittier, so there isn't a college or university in the town, but there's one school for all the children. And of course everything is inside, so there aren't any parks or squares, and there aren't any street cafés like in other towns.

So why is it like that? Well, Whittier is on the coast of Alaska, and the weather is terrible most of the year. In summer it often rains, and there's a lot of snow in winter (about seven metres), and also very strong winds. So people in Whittier are happy to stay inside most of the time.

It isn't easy to get to and from Whittier because there isn't a normal road. The only way to get there on land is through a long tunnel. It's 3 km long, and it's very narrow, so cars can only go through it once every hour. And the tunnel closes at 10:30 pm. After that, you have to stay the night in Whittier and leave in the morning.

Do people like living there? Yes, they do! As one man from Whittier says: 'It's safe here, it's quiet, and people are friendly. And there are beautiful mountains and forests all around. I love it here!'

c Can you do these things in Whittier?

1 go to work by bus
2 sit outside in a café
3 go shopping
4 go for a walk in July
5 go for a walk in January
6 drive into Whittier at 3:00 in the morning

d Talk about the questions.

1 Would you like to visit Whittier? Why / Why not?
2 Would you like to live there? Why / Why not?

2 VOCABULARY Places in a city

a Underline 12 words in the article for places in a town or city. Which are … ?

1 buildings or in buildings
2 outside

b Now go to Vocabulary Focus 5A on p. 164.

c Work with other students. Write words for more places in a city. Think of:

- places to go in the evening
- things to see
- places to relax in the daytime

d Talk about three places you like in your town or city.

3 GRAMMAR *there is / there are*

a Complete the sentences from the article with *there's*, *there are*, *there isn't* or *there aren't*.

1 ___________ any parks or squares.
2 ___________ a church.
3 ___________ much to do around Whittier.
4 ___________ offices where people work.

b Complete the table with forms of *there is* or *there are*.

+	–
There _'s_ a police station.	There ___ a normal road.
There ___ a few shops.	There ___ any street cafés.

c Match questions 1–4 about Whittier with answers a–d.

1 Is there a road to Whittier?
2 Is there a university?
3 Are there any parks in the town?
4 Are there mountains near the town?

a Yes, there are. They're very beautiful.
b Yes, there is. It goes through a tunnel.
c No, there isn't, but there's a school.
d No, there aren't. The town is inside a building.

d Complete the table with forms of *there is* or *there are*.

Yes/No questions	Short answers	
___ ___ a good hotel in the town?	Yes, there ___.	No, there ___.
___ ___ any good restaurants?	Yes, ___ ___.	No, ___ ___.

e Go to Grammar Focus 5A on p. 146.

f 05.04 **Pronunciation** Listen to the sentences.

1 When do the speakers use *there's*?
a in questions
b in short answers
c in sentences

2 Does the word *there* have:
a a long vowel sound
b a short vowel sound?

g **Communication 5A** Student A: Go to p. 131. Student B: Go to p. 132.

4 SPEAKING

a 05.05 Tom asks his friend, Sofia, about visiting Vienna, her home town. Complete the conversation with the correct form of *there is* or *there are*. Listen and check your answers.

TOM Is Vienna a good place to visit?
SOFIA Oh, it's a fantastic city to visit. [1]___________ lots of interesting old buildings and [2]___________ some beautiful palaces.
TOM [3]___________ any good restaurants?
SOFIA Yes, [4]___________, and the street food is good, too.
TOM What about coffee shops? [5]___________ any good coffee shops?
SOFIA Oh yes, [6]___________ lots of good coffee shops. The coffee's very good in Vienna.
TOM And what about family activities? [7]___________ a beach in Vienna?
SOFIA No, [8]___________ a beach, but [9]___________ lots of parks and the famous big wheel!

b Work in groups of four: Pair A and Pair B.

shops and markets things to see
buses and trains restaurants and cafés
parks famous buildings bridges

Pair A: You are visitors to a town or city. Write questions to ask about the things in the box.

Is there a …? Are there any …?
Can I …? Where can I …?

Pair B: Think about a town or city that you know well. Make notes about the things in the box.

The city is great to visit because … and …
There's a famous … It's called …
There are a lot of …

c Use the conversation in 4a and your notes in 4b to have a conversation.

Pair A: Ask about the town.
Pair B: Answer the questions about the town.

5B WHOSE WARDROBE IS THAT?

Learn to describe rooms and furniture in your home

G Possessive pronouns and possessive *'s*

V Furniture

1 VOCABULARY Furniture

a Ask and answer the questions.

1 Do you live in a house or a flat?
2 How old is your home?
3 Where can you buy furniture in your country?

My flat is very old.

I always buy furniture online.

b Read the advertisement for a furniture shop. Who is the shop for?

a people who like expensive furniture
b people who don't want to spend too much money on furniture

c Match the words in the box with pictures 1–12.

mirror washing machine bookcase curtains sink bedside table armchair wardrobe lamp chest of drawers cooker sofa

d 05.06 **Pronunciation** Listen to the pronunciation of the letters in **bold**. Are the sounds long or short?

1 **a**m	3 w**ar**drobe	5 c**u**t
2 c**ur**tains	4 **ar**mchair	6 b**a**d

e Answer the questions.

1 What letter is in the spelling of all the long sounds in 1d?
2 Can you hear this letter in the examples?
3 Match *far*, *her* and *door* with three words with the same long sound in 1d.

f Look at the room you are in now. Write a list of the furniture in it.

g Compare your list with a partner.

What have you got?

I've got …

2 LISTENING

a Ask and answer the questions.

1 Which is your favourite room in your home?
2 Do you have a favourite piece of furniture?

b 05.07 Jim's sister, Ruth, comes to visit him in his new flat. Listen to their conversation. Which rooms does Jim show Ruth?

a the kitchen
b the living room
c the bathroom
d the bedroom

c 05.07 Listen again and write down the furniture they talk about in each room.

Room 1 ____________________
Room 2 ____________________

d What does Ruth think about the furniture in Jim's flat?

3 GRAMMAR
Possessive pronouns and possessive *'s*

a 05.08 Complete the conversation with words from the box. Listen and check your answers.

your Mum and Dad David's mine
yours of David Mum and Dad's

RUTH I love that armchair.
JIM Yes, it's quite … interesting.
RUTH Is it [1]____________?
JIM No, it's [2]____________. He's my flatmate.
RUTH I love it. That mirror over there. Is that [3]____________?
JIM Well, yes, but really it's [4]____________ now.

b Tick (✓) the correct sentences.

1 ☐ It's the flat of Jim.
2 ☐ It's Jims flat.
3 ☐ It's Jim's flat.
4 ☐ It's my parent's flat.
5 ☐ It's the flat of my parents.
6 ☐ It's my parents' flat.

Jim and Ruth

Jim's flatmate, David

c Look at the sentences and answer the questions.

Whose mirror is that? a *It's my mirror.*
b *It's mine.*

1 Do we need to repeat *mirror* in the answer?
2 Which answer is better?

d Complete the sentences with the words in the box.

yours hers mine his theirs

1 It's my bed. → It's ____________.
2 It's your lamp. → It's ____________.
3 It's her sofa. → It's ____________.
4 It's their mirror. → It's ____________.
5 It's his chair. → It's ____________.

e Now go to Grammar Focus 5B on p. 146.

f 05.12 Read about Jean-Paul's flat. Complete the text with the words in the box. Listen and check your answers.

sister's parents' mine (x3)
mother's hers yours

I live in a flat with seven rooms. It's not [1]____________ – it's my [2]____________. In my bedroom, there's a really big bookcase that I love. It's my [3]____________, but she doesn't live at home now, so I don't think it's [4]____________ any more – it's [5]____________ now. My father's got a study with a beautiful old desk. It's really my [6]____________, but Dad always says to Mum, 'It's not [7]____________ now, it's [8]____________.'

4 SPEAKING

a Write four sentences about your home, the furniture in it, and whose furniture it is. Look at Jean-Paul's words in 3f to help you.

b Read your sentences to a partner. Listen to your partner's sentences and try to remember the information.

c Tell your partner what you remember about their home. Who can remember the most?

In the living room there's a very large sofa.

No, there are two large sofas.

The lamp in your bedroom is your brother's.

Yes, that's right.

5C EVERYDAY ENGLISH
Is there a bank near here?

Learn how to ask for and give directions

- **S** Checking what other people say
- **P** Sentence stress

1 LISTENING

a Answer the questions about pictures a and b.

1 Where do you think Dan and Leo want to go? Say why.
 a shopping c the gym
 b a meeting d lunch
2 There's a problem. What do you think it is?

b 05.13 Watch or listen to Part 1 and check your answers in 1a.

c 05.13 Watch or listen to Part 1 again. Choose the correct answer.

1 The street name on Leo's phone is … .
 a Bedford Street b Park Road
2 Leo says South Street is … .
 a off Park Road b off North Street
3 Dan doesn't want to be … .
 a too early b late

2 CONVERSATION SKILLS
Checking what other people say

a 05.14 Look at the sentences from Part 1 and answer the questions.

DAN Are you **sure** it's here?
LEO I think so.

DAN Are you **certain**?
LEO Yes.

1 Are the questions still correct if we swap the two words in **bold**?
2 Why does Dan ask the questions? Choose the correct answer.
 a He agrees with Leo.
 b He wants to check something with Leo.

3 LISTENING

a When you're lost, what do you usually do? Choose one idea.

1 Look again for the correct street on your phone.
2 Continue along the street and look for the correct street.
3 Ask someone for help to find the correct street.

b 05.15 Watch or listen to Part 2. Do Dan and Leo have the same idea as you in 3a?

c 05.15 Watch or listen to Part 2 again. Are the sentences true (*T*) or false (*F*)? Correct the false sentences.

1 Dan and Leo want to find a bank that is on the corner of Park Road and South Street.
2 The man on the street says there's a bank 150 metres away.

d Work in pairs. Look at picture c. Dan and Leo find a bank, but there's another problem. What do you think it is?

e 05.16 Watch or listen to Part 3. Answer the questions.

1 Do they find the right bank?
2 Does the woman they talk to know where South Street is?

f 05.16 Watch or listen to Part 3 again. Follow the woman's directions. Write *South Street* in the correct place on the map.

4 USEFUL LANGUAGE
Asking for and giving directions

a Complete the questions with the words in the box.

tell where there how

1 Is ____________ a bank near here?
2 Can you ____________ us how to get to South Street?
3 ____________ do I get to Park Road?
4 ____________ can I find a supermarket?

b Look at the phrases for giving directions. Change the words in **bold** for the words in the box.

a supermarket on left

1 Go straight **along the road**.
2 The bank is on your **right**.
3 Go straight on until you come to **Park Road**.

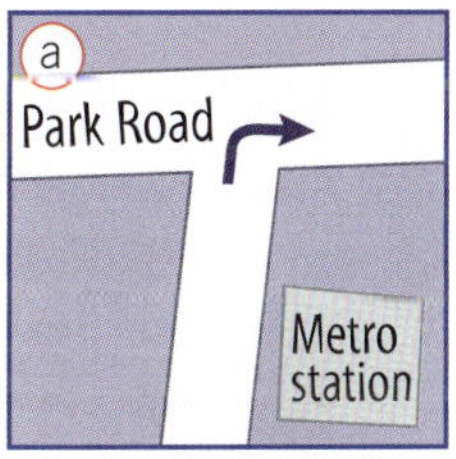

c Match the directions with maps a–b.

1 Turn right **at** the metro station.
2 Turn right **into** Park Road.

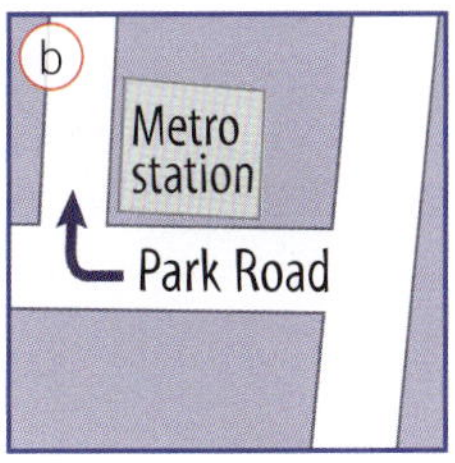

d 05.17 Complete the conversation with the words in the box. Listen and check.

go (x3) turn (x2) get can come

A Excuse me, [1]____________ you tell me how to [2]____________ to the park?
B Yes, [3]____________ straight on and [4]____________ right at the corner.
A Is that right into King Street?
B Yes, and [5]____________ along King Street until you [6]____________ to Park Road, then [7]____________ left.
A Left into Park Road?
B Yes, and [8]____________ straight on for about 50 metres. The park is on your right.
A Thank you very much.

e In pairs, practise the conversation in 4d. Take turns being A and B.

5 PRONUNCIATION
Sentence stress

a 05.18 Read and listen to B's directions in 4d. Notice the stressed words.

Go straight on and turn right at the corner. Go along King Street until you come to Park Road, then turn left. Go straight on for about fifty metres. The park is on your right.

b Choose the correct answer.

When we give directions, we stress … .
1 only the verbs and nouns
2 the words for direction and place
3 the little words that join ideas

c In pairs, take turns asking for and giving directions like the conversation in 4d. Use phrases from 4, the map in 3f and give directions to different places.

6 SPEAKING

a Communication 5C Student A: Go to p. 131. Student B: Go to p. 132.

UNIT PROGRESS TEST

CHECK YOUR PROGRESS

You can now do the Unit Progress Test.

5D SKILLS FOR WRITING

It isn't very exciting, but it's a nice place to live

Learn to write a description of your neighbourhood

W Linking ideas with *and*, *but* and *so*

1 SPEAKING AND LISTENING

a What makes a good neighbourhood? Tick (✓) four ideas.

☐ a lot of shops	☐ a lot of cafés and restaurants
☐ a football stadium	☐ a cinema
☐ no shops or cafés	☐ a sports centre
☐ a supermarket	☐ a museum

b Talk about your ideas in 1a.

c 05.19 Antonella, Keith and Jia talk about what they think makes a good neighbourhood. Listen and answer the questions.

1 Who likes a neighbourhood that is … ?
   a new   b busy   c quiet
2 Who do you agree with?

d 05.19 Listen again. Write the places in the box next to the people who talk about them.

houses   restaurants   shopping mall   clubs
shops   cafés   museum   cinema   park

1 Antonella ________________
2 Keith ________________
3 Jia ________________

Who likes their neighbourhood? Who doesn't?

e Ask and answer questions about your neighbourhood.

Are there any shops in your neighbourhood?

Yes, there are lots.

There's a really good café near my house.

2 READING

a Read the blog description and answer the questions.

1 What can you read about on this website?
2 What does the website want you to do?

b Read *In my neighbourhood*. Do Anita and Blanca live in the same kind of neighbourhood?

c Underline the correct answers.

1 *Anita* / *Blanca* lives close to the city centre.
2 *Anita* / *Blanca* likes a neighbourhood that isn't noisy.
3 *Anita* / *Blanca* can often go shopping.
4 It's easy for *Anita* / *Blanca* to eat in a restaurant.
5 There's a place where *Anita* / *Blanca* can get some exercise near her home.

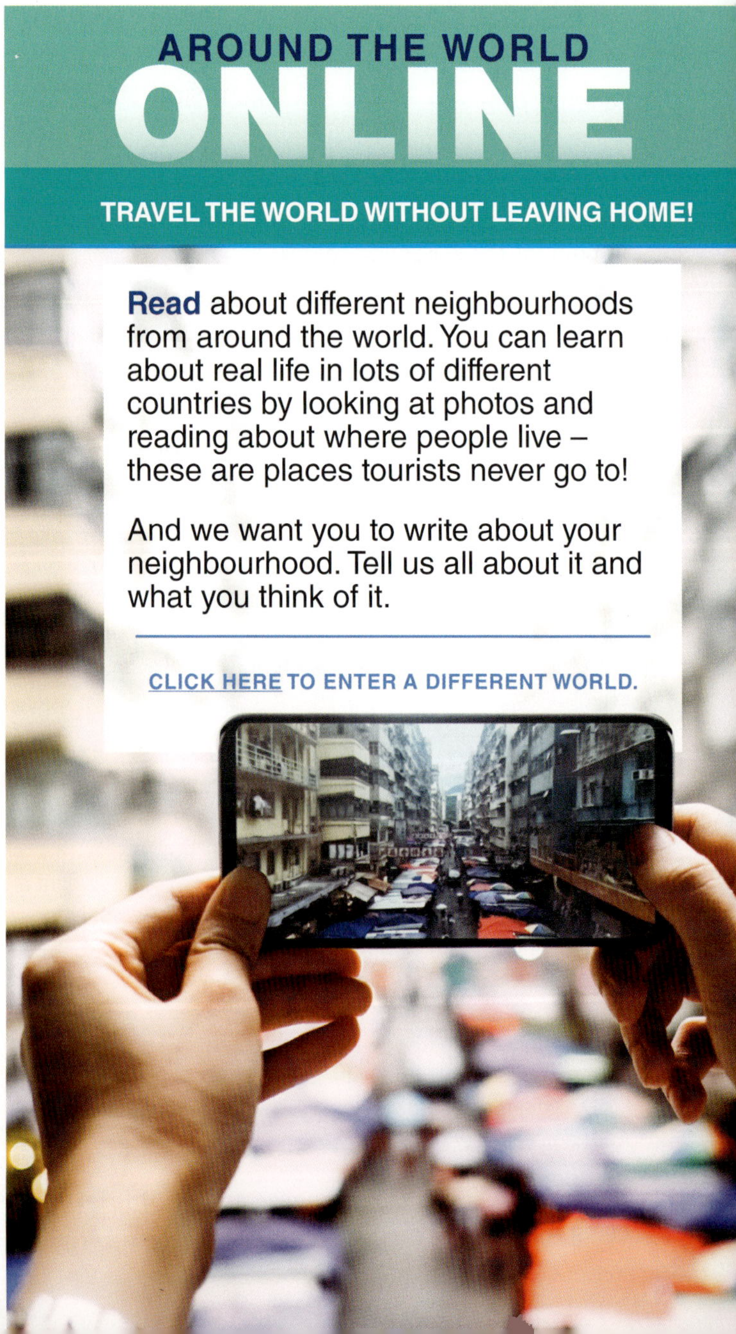

AROUND THE WORLD
ONLINE
TRAVEL THE WORLD WITHOUT LEAVING HOME!

Read about different neighbourhoods from around the world. You can learn about real life in lots of different countries by looking at photos and reading about where people live – these are places tourists never go to!

And we want you to write about your neighbourhood. Tell us all about it and what you think of it.

CLICK HERE TO ENTER A DIFFERENT WORLD.

3 WRITING SKILLS
Linking ideas with *and*, *but* and *so*

a Underline one word in each sentence below that links two ideas.

1 There are a lot of good restaurants in my neighbourhood and my flat's opposite a really good Thai restaurant, *Siam Café*.
2 My neighbourhood isn't very exciting, but it's a nice place to live.
3 There aren't any restaurants or bars in the area, so it's nice and quiet.

IN MY NEIGHBOURHOOD

My neighbourhood's about two kilometres from the centre of town. It's easy for me to get into the city centre, but everything I need is in my neighbourhood, so I don't go into the centre very often. It's near the City Museum and there are some beautiful old buildings here, so it's an interesting part of the city. There are lots of good restaurants in my neighbourhood and my flat's opposite a really good Thai restaurant, *Siam Café*. I love their food and it's cheap, so I eat there often.

Anita

My neighbourhood's about eight kilometres from the city centre, but there's a metro train station near my house, so it's easy to get there. There aren't any restaurants or bars in the area, so it's nice and quiet. About a kilometre away, there's a big shopping centre with a lot of shops. Opposite it, there's a park and a sports centre. I go there three times a week to use the gym. My neighbourhood isn't very exciting, but it's a nice place to live.

Blanca

b Look at the sentences in 3a and complete the rules with the words in the box.

so	and	but

1 We use ____________ when we want to add an extra idea.
2 We use ____________ when we want to add a different idea.
3 We use ____________ when we want to add an idea that is the result of the first idea.

c Read the blog post again. Underline sentences that contain linking words.

d Put the linking words in the correct place in the sentences.

1 My neighbourhood's in the centre of town there are a lot of different shops near my house. (and)
2 I live near the university there are a lot of interesting shops in my neighbourhood. (so)
3 My neighbourhood's quite busy during the day it's nice and quiet at night. (but)
4 My house is near a park there's a small river with a bridge in the park. (and)
5 My neighbourhood is very friendly it's a nice place to live sometimes it's noisy in the evening. (so, but)
6 There's a popular café in my neighbourhood I don't like coffee I never go there. (but, so)

4 WRITING

a Plan a description of your neighbourhood. Write notes.

- where
- near
- what
- adjectives

b Write about your neighbourhood. Use the blog post about Anita's and Blanca's neighbourhoods and your notes in 4a to help you. Use *and*, *but* and *so*.

c Swap descriptions with another student and check the linking words.

d Read about other students' neighbourhoods. Which one is most different from yours?

UNIT 5
Review and extension

1 GRAMMAR

a Complete the conversation with the correct form of *there is* or *there are*.

MARCEL Can you tell me about your free room?
LANDLADY [1]_______ a bed, two armchairs and a big window.
MARCEL [2]_______ a desk?
LANDLADY No, [3]_______, but [4]_______ a small table.
MARCEL And [5]_______ a shower?
LANDLADY No, but [6]_______ a bathroom on the same floor.
MARCEL I see. And [7]_______ other students in the house?
LANDLADY Yes. [8]_______ four other students.

b Change the words in *italics* to make them shorter. Use *mine*, *yours*, *his*, etc.

A Is this bag [1]*your bag*? yours
B No, it isn't [2]*my bag*.

A Look, I think this is Theresa's phone.
B I know it isn't [3]*our phone*, so maybe it's [4]*her phone*. Let's ask her.

A Whose car is that?
B It's [5]*my brother's car*. And the motorbike's [6]*his motorbike*, too.

A I think that's my book.
B No, this book's [7]*my book*. I don't know where [8]*your book* is.

2 VOCABULARY

a Underline the correct words.

1 They live in a big *flat* / *river* near the city centre.
2 It costs a lot to stay in this *bridge* / *hotel*.
3 There are a lot of good *restaurants* / *parks* in the main *river* / *square*.
4 Let's go to the *flat* / *park*. We can play football.
5 There's only one *square* / *bridge* over the river.
6 The train gets in to the *park* / *station* at 6:30.

b Complete the sentences with things you find in a room.

1 Look in the m_______. Your face is dirty.
2 I just want to wash my hands in the s_______.
3 You can put your clean clothes in the c_______ of d_______.
4 I'm tired. I'll lie on the s_______ for a bit.
5 Put your dirty clothes in the w_______ m_______.
6 Don't touch the c_______. It's hot!
7 I always keep a book on my b_______ t_______.

3 WORDPOWER Prepositions of place

a Match cafés 1–6 with a–f on the map below.

1 **Alpha Café** A busy student café on Newton Street, next to the Rex Cinema. Cheap, but usually full.

2 **Café Uno** On the corner of Newton Street and Green Street. Good coffee and great cakes, but expensive.

3 **Café Express.** A small café just in front of the train station.

4 **La Roma.** A small café on Green Street, between the market and the library. They have good pasta dishes.

5 **Shane's.** At the end of Newton Street, opposite the station. Popular with mothers and young children.

6 **Café Casablanca.** A Moroccan café with a nice garden. It's in a small street behind the Rex Cinema.

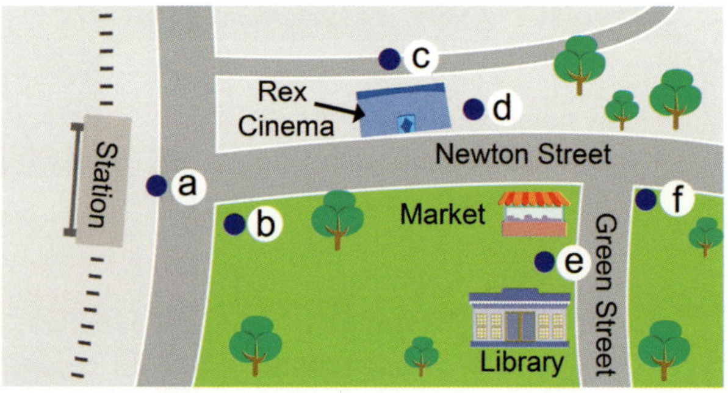

b Look at the underlined examples in 3a. Words like **on** and **next to** are prepositions of place that tell us where something is. Underline more prepositions of place in 3a.

c Add one more word to make the sentences correct.

1 The cinema is on King Street, next the supermarket.
2 There's a cash machine the end of Green Street.
3 I'll meet you in front the bank on Newton Street.
4 There's a new bookshop the corner of New Street.

d Work in pairs. Choose four numbers on the map below. Take turns describing and guessing where they are. Use prepositions of place.

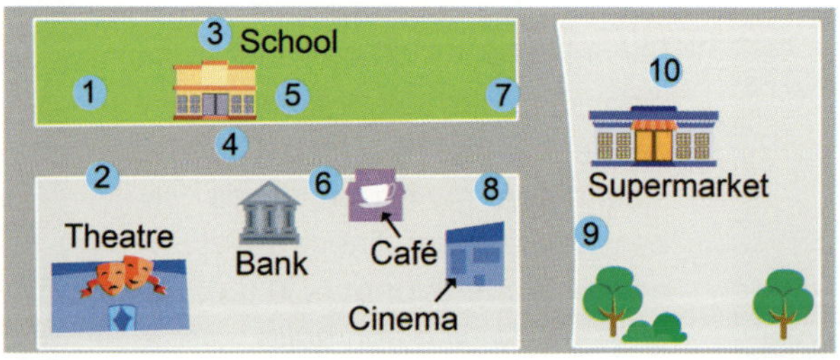

REVIEW YOUR PROGRESS

How well did you do in this unit? Write 3, 2 or 1 for each objective.
3 = very well 2 = well 1 = not so well

I CAN ...	
talk about towns	☐
describe rooms and furniture in my home	☐
ask for and give directions	☐
write a description of my neighbourhood.	☐

CAN DO OBJECTIVES

- Talk about your family and your family history
- Talk about past activities and hobbies
- Leave a voicemail message and ask for someone on the phone
- Write a life story

UNIT 6

FAMILY

GETTING STARTED

a Look at the picture and answer the questions.

1 Who do you think the people in this family are? Use family words you know, like 'mother' and 'sister'.
2 Do you think they all live together in one house?
3 Choose someone in the photo. Write two questions to ask them.

b Talk about a family you know well – not your own family.

1 How many people are there in the family? Who are they?
2 Who do you know the best in the family? Why?

6A THEY WERE MARRIED IN 1968

Learn to talk about your family and your family history

G Past simple: *be*

V Family; Years and dates

1 VOCABULARY Family

a Talk about your parents, brothers or sisters. Think about:

- their names
- what they do
- adjectives about them

b 06.01 Listen to Part 1. Greg talks about his family. Tick (✓) the people he talks about.

☐ aunt	☐ sister	☐ grandmother
☐ grandparents	☐ granddaughter	☐ cousin
☐ uncle	☐ brother	☐ grandfather
☐ grandchildren	☐ grandson	☐ parents

c Choose words in 1b to complete Greg's family tree.

d 06.01 Listen again and check your answers in 1c. Whose parents were born in Italy?

e 06.02 **Pronunciation** Listen to the letters in **bold**. Tick (✓) the words that have the same sound as *but* /ʌ/.

c**o**usin **u**ncle **au**nt grandm**o**ther grands**o**n

f Look at the family tree again. Who can say these sentences?

1 'Alice is my aunt.' Greg, Ella, Rick
2 'Simone's our uncle.' ____________
3 'Ella's our granddaughter.' ____________
4 'Rick, Ella and Greg are our cousins.' ____________
5 'We've got three grandchildren.' ____________

g Draw your own family tree. Show it to your partner and talk about how many people there are.

2 LISTENING

a 06.03 Put the life events in the correct order on the timeline. Listen again and check your answers.

1 got married
2 grandfather was born
3 grandmother retired from her job
4 photographer took the picture
5 grandmother was born

☐ 1943 ☐ 1945 ☐ 1968 ☐ 1969 ☐ 2010

Nathan and Sally

3 GRAMMAR Past simple: *be*

a Underline the correct words.

1 Greg's grandparents *are* / *aren't* still alive.
2 His grandmother *is* / *isn't* a doctor now.
3 His grandmother *was* / *wasn't* a doctor.
4 His grandparents *were* / *weren't* at the same school.
5 They *were* / *weren't* friends at school.

b Choose the correct answers to complete the rules.

1 We use *was* / *were* to talk about ...	a now	b the past
2 To make a negative sentence, we add ...	a *'nt*	b *n't*

c Complete the chart with *was*, *were*, *wasn't* or *weren't*.

+	–
I _was_ ill. She ____ a doctor.	I _wasn't_ ill. He ____ a teacher. He was a doctor.
We _were_ at school together. They ____ friends at university.	No, we ____ in the same class. In 1967, they ____ married.

d 06.04 Listen again and complete the conversation. Which words are repeated in the question and answer?

A What about your grandfather? [1]________ he a doctor, too?
B Yes, he [2]________.
A [3]________ they in the same class?
B No, they [4]________.
A When [5]________ she born?
B She [6]________ born in 1945, I think.

e Now go to Grammar Focus 6A on p. 148.

f 06.06 **Pronunciation** Listen to the sentences. If *was* or *were* are stressed, underline them.

1 She was a doctor.
2 They were at school together.
3 When was she born?
4 Was she a doctor? Yes, she was.

g Complete the rules with *are* or *aren't*.

[1]In positive sentences and questions, *was* and *were* ________ stressed.
[2]In short answers, *was* and *were* ________ stressed.

h Complete the questions with the correct past forms of the verb *be*.

1 Where ________ you born?
2 Who ________ your first teacher?
3 What ________ your first school called?
4 ________ yesterday a good day for you?

i Ask and answer the questions in 3h.

4 VOCABULARY Years and dates

a 06.07 In Part 2, Greg talks about years and dates. Listen and answer the questions.

1 How do we say 1945?
   a one thousand nine hundred and forty-five
   b nineteen forty-five
   c both a and b are correct
2 How do we say 2010?
   a two thousand and ten
   b twenty ten
   c both a and b are correct
3 What do we add to *16* when we say *16 July*?

b 06.08 Listen and tick (✓) the years you hear. Then practise saying them.

☐ 2002 ☐ 1930 ☐ 1918 ☐ 2011
☐ 2012 ☐ 1913 ☐ 1989 ☐ 2001

c Go to Vocabulary Focus 6A on p. 165.

5 SPEAKING

a Make notes about the people in your family tree in 1g.

- When were they born?
- Where do they live?
- How old are they?
- What do they do?

b Ask and answer questions about your family trees.

6B I PLAYED ANYTHING AND EVERYTHING

Learn to talk about past activities and hobbies

G Past simple: positive

V Past simple: irregular verbs

1 READING

a Ask and answer the questions.

1 Who's the man in the pictures?
2 What do you know about his company?
3 What do you know about his family life?

b The article is called *His Family Secret*. What do you think the secret is? Talk about the ideas and choose one.

1 His grandfather got married four times.
2 He had a secret sister.
3 His father was a famous actor.
4 He never met his brother.

c Read the article and check your answer in 1b.

d Put the events from Steve Jobs' life in the correct order.

a ☐ Steve started a new hobby: electronics.
b ☐ His sister Mona was born.
c ☐ Steve became friends with Steve Wozniak.
d ☐ Steve's birth parents couldn't keep him.
e ☐ Steve met his sister.
f ☐ Clara and Paul Jobs became Steve's parents.
g ☐ The two Steves became very rich.
h ☐ Apple Computers began.

HIS FAMILY SECRET

His name is famous around the world and every day millions of people use the products he made – our phones, computers, laptops, tablets and smartwatches. We all think we know his story from magazines, newspapers and the Internet, but how much do we really know about him?

Steve Jobs was born in San Francisco in 1955. His birth parents were university students. They decided not to keep their son and Steve was adopted by Clara and Paul Jobs.

The Jobs family lived in Mountain View, California. This area is now known as Silicon Valley, where there are a lot of big technology companies. Steve's hobby as a child was electronics. He made simple computers with his father at the family home. He met Steve Wozniak when he was at school. They both loved electronics and became good friends. In 1976, they started Apple Computers in Steve's parents' garage. They worked hard, and four years later the company was worth $1.2 billion.

Two years after that, Steve found out about his sister for the first time. After he was adopted, his birth parents had another child, Mona, who became a famous writer. This amazing brother and sister were close friends until he died in 2011. People will continue to remember Steve when they see or use an Apple product.

2 GRAMMAR Past simple: positive

a Underline the past simple form of verbs 1–5 in the text.

1 work
2 start
3 live
4 decide
5 love

b Complete the rule.

To form the past simple of regular verbs add _____ or _____.

c 06.11 **Pronunciation** Listen to the infinitive and the past simple form of the verbs in 1a. Which two verbs have an extra syllable in the past?

d Complete the rule with two sounds.

-ed endings have an extra syllable /ɪd/ only after _____ and _____.

e 06.12 Practise saying these past simple forms. Which have an extra syllable? Listen and check your answers.

- looked
- waited
- arrived
- finished
- hated
- wanted
- remembered
- needed

f Underline the past simple form of verbs 1–4 in *His Family Secret*. Are these verbs regular or irregular?

1 have 2 find 3 make 4 become

g Now go to Grammar Focus 6B on p. 148.

3 LISTENING

a Steve Jobs' hobby when he was a child was electronics. Tick (✓) the hobbies you had when you were a child.

- ☐ reading
- ☐ taking photos
- ☐ drawing pictures
- ☐ playing the guitar

Can you think of other hobbies?

b 06.14 Listen to Hannah and Charlie. What were their childhood hobbies?

c 06.14 Listen again and complete the notes about Hannah and Charlie.

	Hannah	Charlie
hobby details	basketball	cakes
parents' problem		
now		

4 VOCABULARY Past simple: irregular verbs

a Hannah and Charlie use the past simple irregular verbs in the box in their conversation. Match them with 1–9.

went spent got made told came bought cost ate

1 buy
2 eat
3 tell
4 go
5 cost
6 spend
7 make
8 get
9 come

b Now go to Vocabulary Focus 6B on p. 165.

c Use the verbs *go*, *eat*, *buy*, *make* and *get* to talk about things you did:

- last night
- yesterday
- last week
- last year

5 SPEAKING

a 06.18 Read about Becky's hobby. Complete the text with the past simple form of the verbs in the box. Listen and check your answers.

play buy like listen have start

When I was young, my hobby was playing the piano. I only [1]__________ jazz, not modern or classical music. My parents [2]__________ me a piano when I was eight years old, and I [3]__________ lessons then. They [4]__________ a lot of jazz CDs and I always [5]__________ to them. They were happy for me to play jazz. I [6]__________ jazz piano all the time. I still play the piano now and jazz is my favourite music.

b Think of a hobby you had when you were a child. Make notes. Read Becky's example in 5a to help you. Think about:

- what you did
- how your parents helped you

c Talk with a partner about your childhood hobby. Start the conversation with this question.

What was your hobby when you were a child?

6C EVERYDAY ENGLISH
Can you call me back?

Learn to leave a voicemail message and ask for someone on the phone

S Asking someone to wait

P Sound and spelling: *a*

1 LISTENING

a If you phone a friend and there's no answer, what do you usually do? Say why.

- leave a message
- send them a text
- call again later

b 06.19 Watch or listen to Part 1. Which two people leave messages?

c 06.19 Watch or listen to Part 1 again. Are the sentences true (*T*) or false (*F*)? Correct the false sentences.

1 Annie tells Dan to only call her on her mobile.
2 Dan tells Annie where he is.

2 USEFUL LANGUAGE
Leaving a voicemail message

a Which sentences do Dan (*D*) or Annie (*A*) say? Which are on their voicemail (*V*)?

1 Please leave a message after the tone.
2 Can you call me back?
3 Could you call me back?
4 You can call me on my work number or my mobile.
5 I'm not here right now.
6 Hi, Dan – it's Annie.

b 06.19 Watch or listen to Part 1 again and check your answers in 2a.

c 06.20 Complete the voicemail message and the caller's message with the words in the box. Listen and check.

this	message	it's	call	here	back

Voicemail
Hello, [1]_____ is Alex. Sorry, I'm not [2]_____ just now. Please leave a [3]_____ and I'll call you later.

Caller
Hi, [4]_____ Pam. Could you call me [5]_____? You can [6]_____ me at work.

d Work in pairs. Use the dialogue map to leave a message. Take turns being A and B.

A	B
Phone B →	Give your voicemail message
Leave a message ←	

3 LISTENING

a 06.21 Put events a–e in the order they happened. Watch or listen to Part 2 and check your answers.

a ☐ Annie chats to Leo.
b [1] Dan goes to make coffee.
c ☐ Leo answers the phone.
d ☐ Dan brings some coffee.
e ☐ Dan talks to Annie.

b Answer the questions.

1 What do Leo and Annie talk about?
   a how they are   b the weather   c work
2 How does Leo feel?

4 USEFUL LANGUAGE
Asking for someone on the phone

a 06.21 Look at Annie's questions and Leo's answers. Underline the correct words. Then watch or listen to Part 2 again and check your answers.

ANNIE Is Dan [1]*here / there*?
LEO He's not [2]*here / there* just now.
ANNIE Can he call me [3]*again / back*?
LEO He'll be [4]*back / there* soon.

b Work in pairs. Use the dialogue map to ask for someone. Take turns being A and B.

A: Phone Student B. You want to speak to another student.
B: Answer and say that he/she isn't here.
A: Ask him/her to call you back.

5 CONVERSATION SKILLS
Asking someone to wait

a Complete the conversation with the words in the box.

just wait minute (x2)

LEO Can you [1]_____ a [2]_____? He'll be back soon.
ANNIE Sure.

LEO It's Annie.
DAN Oh, good. [3]_____ a [4]_____.

b What does *a minute* mean in the conversation?

a exactly one minute   b a short time

c Practise the conversation in 4b again. Use expressions in 5a.

6 PRONUNCIATION
Sound and spelling: *a*

a 06.22 Listen to the sound of the letter *a* in the words below.

Sound 1 /æ/	Sound 2 /ɔː/	Sound 3 /ɪ/	Sound 4 /eɪ/
th**a**nks	c**all**	mess**a**ge	l**a**ter

b 06.23 What sound do the letters in **bold** have in the words in the box? Add them to the sound groups in 6a. Listen and check. Listen and repeat.

t**al**k vill**a**ge w**ai**t t**all** b**a**ck lugg**a**ge
voicem**ai**l s**a**me sm**all** t**a**ble bl**a**ck

c Work in pairs. Cover the table in 6a. Student A: Say a word from 6b. Student B: Say a word that has the same sound. Then swap roles.

7 SPEAKING

a 06.24 Listen and complete the phone conversation.

SUE Hello, Sue Parker.
NICK Hi, Sue. [1]__________ Nick. Is Melanie there, please?
SUE No, sorry. She's not [2]__________ just now. She's at her Spanish class. Do you want to leave a [3]__________?
NICK No, it's OK. Can she call me [4]__________?
SUE OK, I'll tell her.
NICK Thanks. She can [5]__________ me on my mobile.
SUE OK. … Just a [6]__________. I need to find a pen to write the number.
NICK It's OK, she knows my number.

NICK Hello?
MELANIE Hi, Nick. [7]__________ Melanie.
NICK Hi, Melanie!
MELANIE Sue says you [8]__________.
NICK Yes, that's right. Do you want to meet on Friday? We can go for a meal.
MELANIE Yes, I'd love to.

b Communication 6C Student A: Go to p. 131. Student B: Go to p. 132. Student C: Go to p. 130.

UNIT PROGRESS TEST

CHECK YOUR PROGRESS

You can now do the Unit Progress Test.

6D SKILLS FOR WRITING
Five months later, we got married

Learn to write a life story

W Linking ideas in the past

1 LISTENING AND SPEAKING

a Choose two important years in your life. Make notes about what happened in each year.

1999 – started school

b Tell your partner what happened in your two important years.

c 06.25 The years below were important in Eva's life. What do you think happened? Match the phrases with the years. Listen and check.

1 got a job as a teacher
2 went to live in the UK
3 moved to Germany
4 was born
5 met her husband

☐ 1992 ☐ 2005 ☐ 2014 ☐ 2017 ☐ 2019

Eva

d 06.25 Underline the correct answers. Listen again and check.

1 She was born in a *small* / *large* town in Sicily.
2 She went to the UK *alone* / *with her parents*.
3 She taught *young children* / *teenagers*.
4 She went to Germany *to get a job* / *to be near Niko*.

e Write two more important years in your life. Tell your partner the years. Guess what happened in your partner's years.

Noto, Sicily

2 READING

a Look at the timeline. Put sentences a–f about Okan in the correct order.

3 WRITING SKILLS Linking ideas in the past

a Complete sentence 2 so that it means the same as 1.

1 In 2002, we moved to Istanbul, and I went to school there.
2 _____ I was 11, we moved to Istanbul, and I went to school there.

b Complete the sentences with *in* or *when*.

1 I left school _____ I was 18.
2 _____ 2010, I went to university in Istanbul.
3 _____ I was in the UK, I worked as an engineer.

Which word (*in* or *when*) do we use … ?
a with years b in longer sentences

c Complete the sentences that are true for you. Write when you did each thing using *in* or *when*.

1 I started school …
2 I left school …
3 I went to university …
4 I met my wife / husband / friend …
5 I got my first job …
6 I first went on a plane …
7 I got my first phone / computer …

d Complete sentence 2 so that it means the same as 1.

1 I left school in 2009. In 2010, I went to university.
2 I left school in 2009. A year _____, I went to university.

e Change the underlined expressions using a time expression + *later*.

1 I left university in 2014. In 2015, I met Carolina.
2 I met Carolina in January 2015. In June 2015, we got married.
3 We got married in June 2015. In June 2019, we had our first child.

f Write two sentences in the past about you or someone in your family. Use *later* in the second sentence.

I came to the UK in January 2018. Three months later, I found a job.

g Read aloud your sentences, but stop after the word *later*. Can your partner guess how they end?

a When I was 11, we moved to Istanbul and I went to school there. ☐

b After university, I met Carolina and we got married a few months later. ☐

c A year later, I went to university in Istanbul and studied engineering. ☐

d I was born in 1991 in Ankara, Turkey. 1

e Then in 2016, I got a job as an engineer in the UK. ☐

f I left school in 2009 and I got a job in a bank. ☐

4 WRITING AND SPEAKING

a Think about someone in your family. Draw a timeline like Okan's and add notes.

b Write a life story from your notes using *he* or *she*. Don't write the name of the person or say what your relationship to the person is.

c Swap life stories with another student and guess who the people are.

d Read your partner's life story again. Check how ideas are linked in the past.

UNIT 6
Review and extension

1 GRAMMAR

a Complete the conversation with the correct form of the verb *be*. Use contractions if possible.

ANNA Hi, Jenny. How [1]______ you?
JENNY I [2]______ fine, thanks.
ANNA [3]______ you at the meeting yesterday?
JENNY Yes, I [4]______, but it [5]______ very useful.
ANNA What about Phil? [6]______ he at the meeting?
JENNY No, he [7]______. He [8]______ ill at home.
ANNA Oh dear, the poor guy. [9]______ he OK today?
JENNY Yes, I think so. He [10]______ here today.

b Complete the text with the correct past simple form of the verbs in brackets.

When I [1]______ (be) a child, I [2]______ (want) to be a truck driver. I [3]______ (love) big trucks and I [4]______ (have) a lot of toy trucks. But when I [5]______ (be) about twelve years old, I [6]______ (decide) that trucks were boring. After school, I [7]______ (study) business at university, but I [8]______ (find) that boring, too. Now I'm a chef and I love it.

c Complete the sentences with the present simple or the past simple form of the verbs in brackets.

1 Last night we ________ (stay) home and my husband ________ (cook) an amazing dinner.
2 I ________ (go) away with my family last weekend. We ________ (have) a really nice time together.
3 My sister ________ (play) volleyball on Tuesday nights. She usually ________ (get) home at about 7:30 pm, but tonight she ________ (get) back at 8:15 pm.
4 My brother and I ________ (spend) a lot of time together when we ________ (be) children, but now we almost never ________ (see) each other.

2 VOCABULARY

a Complete the text with the correct family words.

Peter and Barbara are my father's parents, so they are my [1]__________. I'm very close to my [2]__________ Barbara, and to my [3]__________ Peter, too. My father has only one sister, Helen, and she married Jonathan. My mother doesn't have any brothers or sisters, so Helen is my only [4]__________ and Jonathan is my only [5]__________. They have three children, so I have three [6]__________.

b Write the dates in words.

25/12/1982 – *the twenty-fifth of December, nineteen eighty-two*

1 19/10/2014	4 22/4/2008
2 12/6/1985	5 31/8/2020
3 3/9/1990	6 9/1/2012

3 WORDPOWER *go*

a Read the conversation and answer the questions.

SARAH I need to [1]**go home** now.
VIV I can drive you.
SARAH No, no. I can [2]**go by** bus.
VIV Are you sure?
SARAH Yes, I need to [3]**go shopping** on the way home. The supermarket is next to the bus stop.
VIV Do you want to [4]**go for** a swim later on?
SARAH Yes, that'd be nice.
VIV And after that, we could [5]**go out** to a restaurant.
SARAH Sounds like a good idea.

1 Who's got a car?
2 What plans do Sarah and Viv have for later on?

b Match the phrases in **bold** in 3a with meanings a–e.

a travel by
b leave and return to where I live
c buy some things
d leave home and do something fun
e do an activity

c Match 1–5 with a–e to make more phrases with *go*.

1 go to	a train
2 go for	b to the cinema
3 go	c a party
4 go out	d skiing
5 go by	e a run

d Correct the mistakes in the sentences.

1 They want to go to home now.
2 I need to go for shopping in town this afternoon.
3 I'd like to go the cinema this evening.
4 He usually goes to work for bus.
5 Would you like to go a coffee?

e Write sentences about your life using phrases with *go*.

1 every day / usually / go home
Every day I usually go home at 5:30 pm.
2 each week / go shopping
3 sometimes / go for a walk / in
4 this evening / would like / go out to

f Tell a partner your sentences in 3e. How similar are you?

REVIEW YOUR PROGRESS

How well did you do in this unit? Write 3, 2 or 1 for each objective.
3 = very well 2 = well 1 = not so well

I CAN ...	
talk about my family and my family history	☐
talk about past activities and hobbies	☐
leave a voicemail message and ask for someone on the phone	☐
write a life story.	☐

CAN DO OBJECTIVES

- Talk about past trips
- Talk about what you like and dislike about transport
- Say *excuse me* and *I'm sorry*
- Write an email about yourself

UNIT 7

TRIPS

GETTING STARTED

a Look at the picture and answer the questions.

1. These people are on a trip. What country do you think they're in? Why?
2. Who are the people in the photo: friends or family?
3. What do you think the people talk about?
   - directions
   - the weather
   - personal information
   - shopping
   - their families
   - something else

b In pairs, ask and answer the questions.

1. Where would you like to travel to?
2. Would you like to travel by ... ?
   - car
   - boat
   - plane
   - something else
3. What would you like to see and do there?

7A THE FERRY DIDN'T ARRIVE

Learn to talk about past trips

G Past simple: negative and questions

V Transport

1 READING

a Look at the pictures of the three holiday spots. Which countries do you think they are in? Which would you like to go to? Why?

b Read the blog post and match the stories with pictures 1–3 to find out where they are.

c Read the stories again. Who do you think said each sentence after their trip: Jessica (*J*), Ethan (*E*) or Kayla (*K*)?

1 It's not a good idea to buy something cheap.
2 You often see more with your own transport.
3 It's a good idea to look for transport information online.
4 It was quite cold on the water.
5 You sometimes meet interesting people on holiday.
6 If you're wearing nice clothes, maybe take a taxi.

d Which story did you like most? Why?

TRAVELBLOG

Every holiday is a story … tell us about yours!

1

Sometimes it's good to do something different …

It was our last day in Pattaya and my friends and I wanted to go to a beach on Koh Larn island. The receptionist at the hotel gave us a ferry timetable. We went to the pier, and there was another tourist – Lars, a guy from Denmark. He wanted to go to Koh Larn, too. We waited and we waited, but the ferry didn't arrive. So Lars checked an app and found out that you can catch a speedboat and get there in 15 minutes. We left the pier with Lars and got on a speedboat. It was a really exciting journey and so fast – much better than the ferry! We all had so much fun together that day. And, by the way, Lars is now my husband. –Jessica

How to miss the perfect moment …

I don't really like selfie sticks, but they're useful on holiday. I was in Alaska on holiday with three friends from university. They all had selfie sticks and I decided to buy one, too. But I didn't want to spend a lot of money, so I got a cheap one. The four of us went on a kayak trip to see Valdez Glacier. There we were – on the water, each person in their kayak – it was a great day. I wanted a memory of this perfect moment, so I put my phone on the selfie stick and … Well, I didn't buy a very good selfie stick and my phone fell off. Into the water! I felt so stupid.
My friends tried not to laugh, but it was funny and in the end I laughed too. –Ethan

Make-up danger …

Before we went on our holiday to Rome, some friends told us that there's a lot of traffic. They said a good way to get around the city is by scooter. So when my husband and I went to Rome, we didn't use public transport – we rented two Vespas, the famous Italian scooter. They were great to ride – we got around the city really easily. On the second evening, we decided to go to a nice restaurant for dinner. I put on some nice clothes and make-up – I chose a very red lipstick. But I didn't know about the insects. You see, when you wear lipstick on a scooter, flies and mosquitoes stick to your lips. When we got to the restaurant, my lips were covered with them. My husband thought it was very funny. I didn't wear make-up on the scooter again – just very cool sunglasses. –Kayla

2

3

2 VOCABULARY Transport

a Match the words in the box with pictures 1–9.

aeroplane (plane) scooter speedboat tram
coach cruise ship helicopter bus ferry train

1

2

3

4

5

6

7

8

9

10

b Which kinds of transport … ?

- do people often use to go on holiday
- do people normally use to get to work or school
- are unusual for people to use in your country
- do you normally use

c Now go to Vocabulary Focus 7A on p. 167.

3 GRAMMAR Past simple: negative

a Complete the sentences from Ethan's blog.

1 I ________ want to spend a lot of money.
2 I didn't ________ a very good selfie stick.

b Look at the sentences in 3a and complete the rule.

To make the past simple negative, we use:
________ + the base form

c Underline more examples of the past simple negative in Jessica's and Kayla's posts.

4 LISTENING

a 07.04 Carly and Scott talk about the blog stories and tell another story. Listen and answer the questions.

1 Which blog story did they like?
2 Who tells a story – Carly or Scott?
3 Is the story about transport or food?

b 07.04 Listen again. Underline the correct answers.

1 Carly went to *Mexico City / Juarez*.
2 She went with *a friend / two friends*.
3 They didn't understand the *waiter / menu*.
4 They used *pocket / smartphone* dictionaries.
5 The man ordered *food / drinks* for the women.
6 The man *left then paid / paid then left*.

c When was a stranger kind to you or someone you know? Tell your partner.

5 GRAMMAR Past simple: questions

a 07.05 Complete the questions from Carly and Scott's conversation. Listen and check.

1 ________ you go last year?
2 How ________ you travel there?
3 What ________ you choose?

b Look at the questions in 5a and complete the rule.

To make questions in the past simple, we use:
________ + subject + infinitive

c 07.06 **Pronunciation** Listen to the questions in 5a again. Notice the pronunciation of *did you* in each question. Can you hear both words clearly?

d Now go to Grammar Focus 7A on p. 150.

e 07.07 Kayla told a friend about her trip to Italy. Complete the conversation using the verbs in brackets. Listen and check.

MIKE How [1]______ (be) your trip to Italy?
KAYLA It [2]______ (be) amazing – incredible!
MIKE How many cities [3]______ you ______ (visit)?
KAYLA We [4]______ (go) to four: Rome, Florence, Siena and Venice.
MIKE How [5]______ you ______ (travel) around Italy?
KAYLA We [6]______ (take) trains, and in Tuscany we [7]______ (hire) a car for three days.
MIKE What [8]______ you ______ (enjoy) most?
KAYLA The art and the architecture were great, but I [9]______ (love) the food the most. It was delicious!

6 SPEAKING

a Imagine you went on a trip around your country last year. Write notes:

- your opinion of the holiday
- transport used
- places visited
- what you liked most

b Work in pairs. Have a conversation like the one in 5e. Ask and answer questions about your holiday.

c Work in groups. Tell each other about your partner's holiday.

7B I LIKE THE STATIONS

Learn to talk about what you like and dislike about transport

G *love / like / don't mind / hate* + verb + *-ing*

V Transport adjectives

1 READING

a Which cities do you know that have a metro or express buses?

b Read the article. Match the cities with pictures 1–3.

c Read the article again. Which city's transport system … ?

1 is more than 150 years old
2 is less than 20 years old
3 has good views of the city
4 has interesting stations
5 doesn't use trains
6 do you think is the best

d Underline two things in the article that surprise you. Tell a partner.

e Read *From the locals* and answer the questions.

- Which transport do you think each post is about?
- Which words tell you the answer?
- Who likes public transport? Who doesn't?

f In pairs, ask and answer the questions.

- Do you use public transport? Is it fast?
- What is the best way to get around where you live?

CityTripper.com

Fast City Transport … Around The World

London The London Underground – the 'Tube' – was the first underground (or metro) system in the world. It opened in 1863. It now has 270 stations, and you can go nearly everywhere in London. It's not cheap, and the trains are often full, but it's unusual because it's very deep under the ground (50 metres in some places). One station, Hampstead, has 320 steps!

Cape Town If you visit Cape Town, there isn't a metro, but you can go on an express bus system called MyCiTi. It opened in 2010, and there are now 36 routes through the city. The buses travel above ground along main roads. They have special lanes and bus stops, so the city traffic isn't a problem. The buses are very fast, and they're a great way to see the city. They're also very easy to use. You just put money onto a travel card and tap in when you get on the bus!

Moscow If you visit Moscow, go on the Moscow Metro. It opened in 1935, and the stations are very beautiful, with statues and lamps. Eight million people use it every day, so it can get very crowded. There are police at the stations so it's very safe, even at night. It's also very cheap – you can get across the city for 30 rubles. People on the trains are very polite. They always give their seat to an old person or to anyone with a baby.

1

2

3

From the locals

Sergei *'A good way to get around'*
Most of my friends drive in the city, but I always take the metro. The trains are good and it's a fast and comfortable way to get around. And I like the stations – they look like palaces!

Antonia *'So easy!'*
I use it to go to work every day and I love it. The buses come every few minutes, so I don't wait at all. They're clean and they're comfortable, too. And it's a safe way to travel when the roads are busy – I can leave my car at home!

Joanna *'Not much fun'*
I don't really enjoy it. I have to walk up and down over 300 steps because the stations are so deep. In the mornings, the trains are often full and it's uncomfortable.

2 VOCABULARY
Transport adjectives

a Find the opposite adjectives in the texts. Write them in the table.

fast	slow
	dangerous
empty	
comfortable	
	expensive
	dirty

b 07.08 **Pronunciation** Listen and check your answers. Practise saying the words.

c Which of the adjectives are positive? Which are negative?

d 07.09 **Pronunciation** Listen to the words and underline the stressed syllable in each word.

comfortable dangerous expensive

e With a partner, take turns being A and B.

A Make a sentence about transport with an adjective from 2a.

B Say you don't agree and use the opposite adjective.

Bill *'Good, but expensive'*

It's a fast way to get around such a big city, but it's pretty expensive when you use it every day. It's the only fast way to go to work. Sometimes I take a bus and it takes an hour, but on the underground you're there in 15 minutes.

3 GRAMMAR AND LISTENING
love / like / don't mind / hate + verb + *-ing*

a When you go to meet a friend, do you usually … ?

- go by car
- use public transport
- cycle
- walk

b 07.10 Svetlana and Alex live in Moscow and meet in the city centre. Listen and complete the table.

	She came by …	The journey took …
Svetlana		
Alex		

c 07.10 Listen again. Complete the notes.

	Svetlana thinks	Alex thinks
the metro is …		
the stations are …		
driving is …		
Alex's / Her car is …		

d 07.11 Can you remember what Svetlana and Alex said? Complete the sentences with *love*, *like*, *don't mind*, *don't like* or *hate*. Then listen and check.

1 **SVETLANA** I _____ going on the metro.
2 **ALEX** I _____ using the metro.
3 **SVETLANA** I _____ the stations.
4 **ALEX** I _____ driving in Moscow.
5 **SVETLANA** I _____ sitting in traffic.
6 **ALEX** I _____ it, it's not too bad.

e Which verb in 3d means … ?

1 I like it a lot.
2 I don't like it at all.
3 It's OK.

f Now go to Grammar Focus 7B on p. 150.

4 SPEAKING

a Tick (✓) three kinds of transport that you use.

☐ bus ☐ train ☐ metro ☐ speedboat ☐ scooter
☐ boat ☐ taxi ☐ plane ☐ tram ☐ coach

b Write notes about the transport you ticked. Use adjectives from 2a and verbs from 3d.

bus – hate, crowded, slow, dirty

c Tell your partner about your ideas from 4b. How similar are you?

I hate going on buses. They're always crowded …

7C EVERYDAY ENGLISH
Excuse me, please

Learn to say *excuse me* and *I'm sorry*

S Showing interest

P Emphasising what we say

1 LISTENING

a Ask and answer the questions.

1 Do you like going away for the weekend?
2 Where do you like going?
3 What do you like doing there?
4 Do you like going alone or with family and friends?

b Answer the questions about picture 1.

1 Where's Annie?
2 What do you think happened with Annie and the woman?
3 What do you think … ?
   a Annie says
   b the woman says

c 07.13 Watch or listen to Part 1 and check your answers in 1b.

d Answer the questions about picture 2.

1 Where are Annie and Leo?
2 How do you think Annie and Leo feel? Why?
3 What do you think happens next?
   a Leo gets off the train.
   b Leo gives Annie his seat.
   c Leo helps Annie put her bag on the shelf.

1

2

e 07.14 Watch or listen to Part 2 and check your answers in 1d.

f 07.14 Watch or listen to Part 2 again. Underline the correct answers.

1 *Annie / Leo* booked a seat.
2 *Annie / Leo* didn't check the seat numbers.
3 *Annie / Leo* takes a different seat.

2 USEFUL LANGUAGE
Saying *excuse me* and *I'm sorry*

a Match 1–2 with meanings a–b.

1 Excuse me, please.
2 Excuse me, but …

a She wants to say there's a problem.
b She wants to ask someone to move.

b 07.15 **Pronunciation** Listen to 1 and 2 in 2a. Notice how the intonation goes down ↘ in 1 but goes down and then up ↘↗ in 2.

c Look at 1 and 2 in 2a. What do you say when … ?

a you want to tell your teacher you don't understand something
b you want to leave the room but another student is in front of the door

d *Very*, *really* and *so* can all be added to the expression *I'm sorry*. Do you say the words before or after *sorry*?

I'm sorry I took your seat.

e 07.16 Match 1–5 with a–e. Listen and check.

1 I'm so sorry I walked into you.
2 I'm really sorry I'm late.
3 I'm sorry I didn't answer your call.
4 I'm sorry I didn't come.
5 I'm very sorry I broke your cup.

a I didn't feel well.
b I was in a meeting.
c I missed my bus.
d My hands were wet.
e I didn't see you.

f Tick (✓) the correct replies when people say they're sorry.

1 ☐ That's all right.
2 ☐ That's OK.
3 ☐ No problem.
4 ☐ Excuse me, please.
5 ☐ It doesn't matter.
6 ☐ Don't worry.

g 07.17 Put sentences a–f in order to make two short conversations. Listen and check.

a ☐ **A** No problem. They all look the same.
b 1 **A** Excuse me, but I think that's my coat.
c ☐ **B** Is it? I'm so sorry. I took the wrong one.

d ☐ **A** Don't worry. The seat numbers are hard to read.
e ☐ **B** Oh dear. I'm very sorry. I thought this was number 35.
f 1 **A** Excuse me, but I think this is my seat.

h In pairs, practise the two conversations in 2g.

3 PRONUNCIATION
Emphasising what we say

a 07.18 Listen to the sentences in 2e. Notice the stress on the underlined words.

1 I'm so sorry I walked into you.
2 I'm really sorry I'm late.
3 I'm sorry I didn't answer.
4 I'm sorry I didn't come.
5 I'm very sorry I broke your cup.

b Why are *so*, *very* and *really* stressed? Choose the best answer.

1 We don't want the other person to hear *sorry* clearly.
2 We want to sound more sorry.
3 We want to speak loudly.

c Practise saying the sentences in 3a.

4 CONVERSATION SKILLS
Showing interest

a 07.19 Watch or listen to Part 3. Are the sentences true (*T*) or false (*F*)? Correct the false sentences.

1 Annie and Leo are both on their way to Bristol.
2 Annie is visiting a friend in Bristol.
3 Leo went to university in Reading.

b Look at these parts of the conversation from Part 3. Two words aren't correct. Replace them with the words in the box.

Great!	Really?

ANNIE Are you on your way to Bristol?
LEO No, Reading. I went to university there.
ANNIE Right.

ANNIE My mum lives there. I go to see her every month.
LEO Oh.

07.19 Listen again and check your answers.

c Why do they say *Great* and *Really*?

1 to say something is true
2 to show they are interested

d 07.20 **Pronunciation** Listen to the sound of the letters in **bold** and answer the questions.

Gr**ea**t! R**ea**lly?

1 Do the letters make the same sound in both words?
2 Are the sounds long or short?

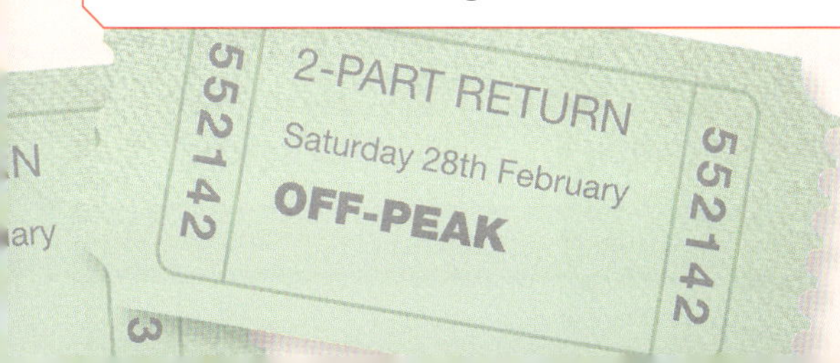

5 SPEAKING

a Work in pairs. Use the dialogue map to make a conversation in a café. Take turns being A and B.

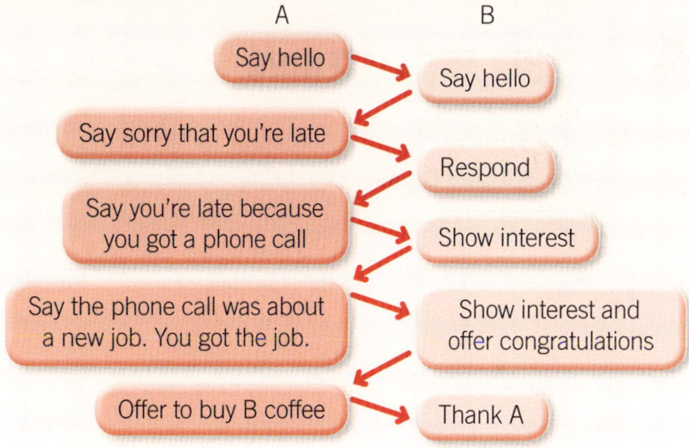

b In pairs, practise conversations like the one in 5a but with different reasons for being late. Take turns being A and B.

UNIT PROGRESS TEST

CHECK YOUR PROGRESS

You can now do the Unit Progress Test.

7D SKILLS FOR WRITING
It really is hard to choose

Learn to write an email about yourself

W Linking ideas with *after*, *when* and *while*

1 SPEAKING AND LISTENING

a You want to stay with a homestay family. What kind of family would you like to stay with? Tick (✓) three ideas and tell a partner.

1 ☐ quiet and friendly
2 ☐ friendly and fun
3 ☐ with young children
4 ☐ with no children
5 ☐ lives near a bus/train station
6 ☐ lives in the city centre
7 ☐ has wi-fi
8 ☐ has no TV

b Read the profiles of two Sydney homestay families. Which family would you like to stay with? Why?

c 07.21 Ahmed talks to his friend Finn about which family to stay with in Sydney. Does Finn tell Ahmed which family to choose?

d 07.21 Listen again. Tick (✓) the activities that are true for Ahmed.

1 ☐ enjoys gardening
2 ☐ likes watching sport
3 ☐ likes listening to pop music
4 ☐ wants to play rugby
5 ☐ loves going to the beach
6 ☐ wants to study a lot
7 ☐ likes playing football
8 ☐ wants to have fun

e Which family is good for Ahmed? Why?

I think the Philips family is good because they like doing sport.

HOMESTAY FAMILY PROFILES

NAME	Peter and Sharon Conway
CHILDREN	live away from home
PETS	Sam, our old cat
LIKES	gardening, going for walks, watching all sports
LOCATION	near city centre – you can walk to school

NAME	Joe and Annie Philips
CHILDREN	Kate (8), Ben (5) and Jacob (3)
PETS	no pets
LIKES	swimming, surfing, going to the cinema, listening to pop music
LOCATION	near a train station

2 READING

a Ahmed decided to stay with the Conways. Read his email to them. Tick (✓) the main reason he writes to them.

1 ☐ to ask about their house
2 ☐ to tell them about all the sports he likes
3 ☐ to tell them about himself
4 ☐ to explain how much he wants to study

b Read the email again. Number the information in the order you find it.

☐ his future plans ☐ his hobbies
☐ his family's jobs ☐ his home town

Subject: Homestay

Dear Mr and Mrs Conway,

My name is Ahmed Al Mansouri and I come from Dubai in the United Arab Emirates. Thank you for offering to be my homestay family when I'm in Sydney.

I am 23 years old and study biology at university. I live with my family in Dubai. My father is a businessman and my mother is a doctor. I've got one brother and one sister. They're university students too.

In my free time, I like playing football (I think you say 'soccer' in Australia!) and meeting my friends. I like watching different kinds of sports with them.

While I'm in Sydney, I really want to study hard and improve my English because I want to become a marine biologist after I finish university. I'd really like to work in a country like Australia.

I'm looking forward to meeting you when I arrive.

Best wishes,
Ahmed

3 WRITING SKILLS
Linking ideas with *after*, *when* and *while*

a Underline the word in each sentence that's different from Ahmed's email.

1 Thank you for offering to be my homestay family while I'm in Sydney.
2 I want to become a marine biologist when I finish university.
3 I'm looking forward to meeting you after I arrive.
4 When I'm in Sydney, I really want to study hard.

b Look at the sentences in 3a and complete the rules with the words in the box.

after	beginning	while

1 We use *when* and ________ to connect two activities that happen at the same time.
2 We use *when* and ________ to connect two activities that happen at different times.
3 If the linking word is at the ________ of the sentence, we use a comma (,) between the two parts.

c Underline the correct words. There is more than one possible answer.

1 *After / When / While* I finish my English class, I'd like to go to Canada for a holiday.
2 I'd like to go skiing in the mountains *after / when / while* I'm on holiday.
3 I often play basketball with my colleagues *after / when / while* I finish work.
4 *After / When / While* I watch a game of football, I usually want to play a game myself.
5 My English improved *after / when / while* I was in Sydney.

4 SPEAKING AND WRITING

a Make a list of English speaking countries you know.

b Which country in 4a would you like to visit? Why?

I'd like to go to …

I like warm places.

They say the people are friendly.

c Plan an email about yourself to a homestay family in that country. Write notes about:

- your age
- study / job
- what you'd like to do in that country
- free-time activities
- family

d Write your email. Tick (✓) each box.

☐ Start the letter with *Dear*
☐ Say thank you
☐ Say who you are
☐ Talk about study / work / free time
☐ Talk about your family
☐ Say what you want to do in the country
☐ Include *I'm looking forward …*
☐ Finish the letter with *Best wishes,*
☐ Use *after*, *when* and *while* to link your ideas

e Swap emails with another student and check the ideas in 4d.

UNIT 7
Review and extension

1 GRAMMAR

a Complete the text with the past simple positive or negative form of the verbs in brackets.

Paul [1]______ (call) a taxi, but it [2]______ (come), so he [3]______ (take) a bus to the airport. The plane [4]______ (be) late, so he [5]______ (wait) for three hours at the airport. The weather [6]______ (be) bad, so the plane [7]______ (land) in a different city. He [8]______ (arrive) at his hotel at 10 pm. The receptionist [9]______ (ask) him, 'Good journey?' 'No, I [10]______ (have) a good journey. It was terrible.'

b Write questions about a trip to Mumbai to match the answers.

1 When? — I went there last November.
When did you go there?
2 How? — I travelled by Air India from London.
3 a good time? — Yes, I had a very nice time.
4 Where? — I stayed in a hotel by the sea.
5 How long? — I only stayed a week. Then I went to Delhi.
6 hot? — Yes, it was about 35°.

c Work in pairs. Choose a place you've visited and ask and answer the questions in 1b. Ask more questions.

d Write sentences about what Clare likes doing. Use the words in the box and a verb + *-ing*.

~~loves~~ likes doesn't mind doesn't like hates

1 'Chinese food is fantastic!'
Clare loves eating Chinese food.
2 'I never listen to Mozart.'
3 'I sometimes take the metro. It's OK, but it's not great.'
4 'I don't want to watch the football – it's boring.'
5 'I speak good French – it's a nice language.'

2 VOCABULARY

a Complete the transport words.

1 b*us*
2 tr_i_
3 sh__
4 h__i___ter
5 f__ry
6 sc__ter

b Change the adjectives into their opposites so that the sentences are correct.

1 The bus was almost *full*. There were only three people on it. *empty*
2 I don't like the metro because the stations are so *clean*.
3 I couldn't sleep on the train. It was so *comfortable*.
4 The new train to the airport is very *slow* – only 15 minutes.
5 He's a very *safe* driver. He never looks in the mirror.
6 $100 for a ten-minute journey! That's very *cheap*!

3 WORDPOWER *get*

a Match questions 1–5 with answers a–e.

1 Is Bella still single?
2 What's the best way to get to the city centre?
3 Have a good journey.
4 Do you want milk in your coffee?
5 How's Susie?

a Thanks. I'll call you when I **get** home.
b Yes, please. Could you **get** some from the fridge?
c She's fine. I **got** an email from her last night.
d No. She **got** married last year.
e You can **get** the bus.

b Match the word *get* in a–e in 3a with meanings 1–5 below.

1 become
2 receive
3 travel on
4 arrive
5 take *or* bring

c Read the story and answer the questions.

> The next morning, Richard [a]got another email from the woman named Blanca. It said, [b]'Get $3,000 from your bank, put it in a black bag, and then [c]get the bus to Morton Street. When you [d]get there, walk towards the post office and leave the bag on the steps. Do as I say or things could [e]get very bad for you.' Richard knew this wasn't a joke – in fact, it was very serious.

1 What do you think happened next?
2 Match the word *get* in the story (a–e) to meanings 1–5 in 3b.

d Match the phrases in the box with a similar phrase in 1–5 below.

get a phone call get a taxi get an email get old get better get to the airport get a glass of water get the train get to school

1 get angry
2 get a letter
3 get the bus
4 get to work
5 get your coat

e Write four sentences about your life. Use phrases from 3d.

I never get a taxi to the airport.

f Tell a partner your sentences in 3e. How similar are you?

REVIEW YOUR PROGRESS

How well did you do in this unit? Write 3, 2 or 1 for each objective.
3 = very well 2 = well 1 = not so well

I CAN ...	
talk about past trips	☐
talk about what I like and dislike about transport	☐
say *excuse me* and *I'm sorry*	☐
write an email about myself.	☐

CAN DO OBJECTIVES

- Talk about past and present abilities
- Talk about sport and exercise
- Talk about the body and getting fit
- Talk about health and how you feel
- Write an article

UNIT 8

FIT AND HEALTHY

GETTING STARTED

a Look at the picture and answer the questions.

1 What country do you think these men are in?
2 What sport do you think this is?
3 Is the game for fun or for a competition?
4 Who do you think took this photo? Why?

b What other sports and exercise would these men like? Make a list.

c In pairs, share your list. Have you got any of the same sports and exercise?

8A THEY CAN DO THINGS MOST PEOPLE CAN'T

Learn to talk about past and present abilities
Learn to talk about sport and exercise

G *can / can't, could / couldn't* for ability
V Sport and exercise

1 READING

a Ask and answer the questions.

1 What famous sport events do you know?
2 Which sportspeople do you like? Why?
3 Look at the man in the pictures and answer the questions.
 a What sport does he do?
 b Where's he from?
 c Where is he in the pictures?
 d What would you like to know about him? Write two questions.

b Read the article and check your answers. Does it answer your questions?

c Read the article again. Answer the questions.

1 What was his life like until he was five?
2 How did his life change when he was five?
3 Why were his doctors, friends and parents surprised?
4 What does the text say about some of the Paralympic athletes?
5 Why is Jonnie famous?

d Underline the parts of the article that surprise you. Tell a partner.

e Are there any famous Paralympic athletes from your country?

2 GRAMMAR *can / can't, could / couldn't* for ability

a Complete the sentences from the article. Check your answers.

1 He ________ run around with the other children any more.
2 Only 18 months after he lost his leg, he ________ run, swim and play football again.
3 Some of the athletes in the Paralympics ________ walk.
4 But in their sports, they ________ do things that most people ________.
5 ________ you run that fast?

b Complete the rules with the words in the box.

past question present

1 To talk about ability, we use *can/can't* for the ________ and *could/couldn't* for the ________.
2 To make a ________, we change *You can …* to *Can you … ?*

c Look at the question. Which two answers are correct?

Can you run that fast?

a Yes, I do. b Yes, I can. c No, I can't. d No, I don't.

d 08.01 **Pronunciation** Listen to the sentences in 2a and answer the questions.

1 One word has a long sound. Which is it?
 a *can* b *can't* c *could* d *couldn't*
2 Can you hear an /l/ sound in *could* and *couldn't*?

e Now go to Grammar Focus 8A on p. 152.

Jonnie Peacock

CHAMPION RUNNER

When Jonnie Peacock was five, he was like most boys from his home town of Cambridge, England – he loved to play sports. Then suddenly his life changed when he became very sick with meningitis. Jonnie's parents took him to hospital and he nearly died. The doctors saved his life, but they couldn't save his right leg. He couldn't run around with the other children any more, and he couldn't play football, his favourite sport. In fact, he couldn't do any sports at all.

Then the doctors gave him a new, artificial leg. He could walk again, but he wanted to do more than that, so he started dancing and doing other sports. His doctors, his friends and his parents were all surprised that he could do so much. Only 18 months after he lost his leg, he could run, swim and play football again, but running was his best sport.

In 2010, Jonnie started to practise a lot. He wanted to go to the London 2012 Paralympics, the Olympic Games for disabled athletes. Some of the athletes in the Paralympics can't walk, and some can't see at all or can't see very well. But in their sports, they can do things that most people can't. Jonnie Peacock won a gold medal at the London 2012 Paralympic Games when he was only 19 years old. He ran the 100 metres in a time of 10.90 seconds! He won another gold medal at the 2016 Paralympic Games in Rio de Janeiro, Brazil, with an even faster time of 10.81 seconds! He still enjoys dancing as well. In 2017, Jonnie was the first amputee paralympian to compete on the TV show *Strictly Come Dancing*.

CAN YOU RUN THAT FAST?

3 LISTENING

a Talk to other students. Try to find a student who … .

1 often goes running
2 never goes running
3 once ran in a marathon or a half-marathon
4 exercises once a week or more

b Read the information about the podcast. What is your answer to the question in the title?

FOCUS ON SPORT

IS RUNNING GOOD FOR YOU?

This weekend, more than 40,000 people are running in the London marathon. But is running good for you? And how far is it safe to run? We talk to sports trainer Jayne Freeman.

LISTEN

c 08.03 Listen to the podcast. What does Jayne think … ?

1 is good for you
2 is not good for you

d 08.03 Listen again. Complete the notes below.

Rule No. 1: Don't ________.
At the start, run __________.
Rule No. 2: ________ a lot of ______.
When you run, you ________.
Rule No. 3: Listen ______________.
If you feel tired, ________.
If your foot hurts, ______.
Rule No. 4: __________!

e In groups, talk about other ways you know to stay fit. How many can you list?

4 VOCABULARY Sport and exercise

a Match the words in the box with the pictures 1–6.

do yoga play badminton ride a bike dance ice-skate ski

1 

2 

3 

4 

5 

6 

b Now go to Vocabulary Focus 8A on p. 167 for sport and exercise collocations.

c Read the sentences. Put them in order from good (*1*) to bad (*4*).

a ☐ I can play baseball quite well.
b ☐ I can't play baseball very well.
c ☐ I can play baseball really well.
d ☐ I can't play baseball at all.

d Ask and answer questions about the activities in 4a.

Can you ski?
Yes, I can ski very well.
I can't ski at all.

5 SPEAKING

a Think about sports or other free-time activities. Write sentences about … .

- one thing you can do well
  I can …
- one thing you can't do at all, but you'd like to learn
  I can't …
- one thing you could do well when you were a child
  I could …
- one thing you couldn't do very well as a child
  I couldn't …

b Ask other students if they can or could do the same things.

Can you dance the samba?
Could you swim well when you were a child?
No, I can't! Can you?
Quite well, yes.

c Who can or could do the same things? Who would like to do the same things?

Sachiko and I can do yoga quite well.
Mia and I would like to learn to snowboard.

8B HOW EASY IS IT TO GET FIT?

Learn to talk about the body and getting fit

G *have to / don't have to*

V Parts of the body; Appearance

1 READING

a Ask and answer the questions.

1 What do you think are good ways of getting fit?
2 What exercise do you do?
3 Would you like to do more or less exercise? Why?

b Read the first paragraph of the article. Answer the questions in the article.

c What do you think the new type of exercise is? Read the rest of the article to find out. Were you correct?

d Complete the HIIT fact sheet.

e Talk about the questions.

1 Would you like to try HIIT? Why / Why not?
2 Do you think it works? Why / Why not?

2 GRAMMAR *have to / don't have to*

a Complete the sentences from the text with the words in the box. Use some words more than once.

have	don't	to

1 You _____ _____ run as fast as you can.
2 You _____ _____ _____ spend hours and hours in the gym.
3 What do you _____ _____ do?

b Sentences a–c talk about the sentences in 2a. Underline the correct answers.

a In sentence 1, you *need to / don't need to* run as fast as you can.
b In sentence 2, you *need to / don't need to* spend hours in the gym.
c Sentence 3 asks what you *need to / don't need to* do.

HIIT: GET FIT IN FIVE! THE ROUTINE

warm up → _______ seconds of intense exercise → rest

Repeat ___ times

HOW LONG?
Time: _______ a day

GOOD FOR:
Getting fit, preventing diabetes and _______ disease

ONLY 5 MINUTES OF EXERCISE A DAY... AND YOU CAN GET FIT!

HOW EASY IS IT TO GET FIT? Do you think it's difficult to do enough exercise? Is having enough time to exercise a problem? Think you know the answers to these questions? Well, think again because a new type of exercise is here and it could change your life.

WHAT IS IT? This new, popular form of exercise is called High Intensity Interval Training (HIIT) and it means you don't have to spend hours and hours in the gym. A few minutes a day doing intense exercise is all you need. You can choose to do floor exercises, run or cycle.

WHAT DO YOU HAVE TO DO? Let's take the example of running – you begin with a short warm-up, then you have to run as fast as you can for 20 to 30 seconds and then rest. You repeat the routine twice and that's all you have to do!

SO HOW DOES HIIT WORK? No one is sure of the answer to this question. However, some sports scientists in Canada, Norway and the UK think that when we exercise intensely, we use more muscles than we do with normal exercise. This helps us get fit, which could also help prevent problems like diabetes and heart disease.

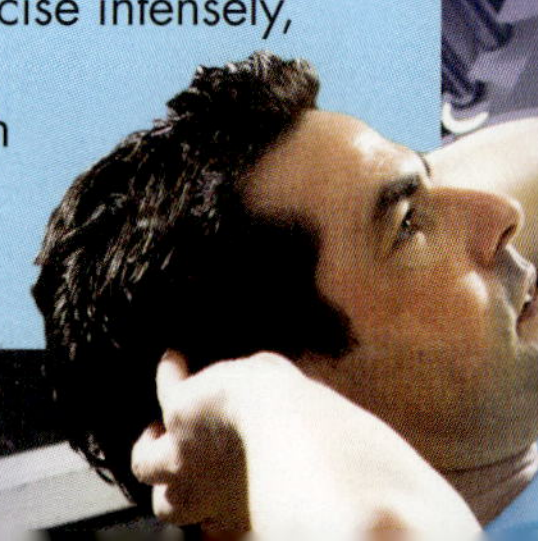

c 08.06 **Pronunciation** Listen to sentences 1 and 2 in 2a and answer the questions.

1 How does the speaker say *v* in *have*: /v/ or /f/?
2 How does the speaker say *to* – is it stressed or unstressed?

d Now go to Grammar Focus 8B on p. 152.

e Work on your own. Think about things you have to do in your life. Write four sentences. Think about:

- daily routine • work • study • family • pets

I have to take our family dog for a walk every morning.

f Tell a partner about things you have to do. Ask more questions.

I have to clean my flat every weekend.

Do you have to clean all the rooms?

3 LISTENING

a Look at pictures a and b and answer the questions with a partner.

1 What kind of exercise is this?
2 Do you think it's easy or difficult?

b 08.08 Listen to Stella and then Mariana talk about exercise. Match the speakers with pictures a and b.

c 08.08 Listen again. Are the sentences true (*T*) or false (*F*)? Correct the false sentences.

1 Stella thinks yoga is good for everyone.
2 Her favourite yoga exercise is easy to do.
3 She practised doing this exercise for a long time.
4 Mariana thinks beginner yoga is easy.
5 She has to think carefully when she does yoga.
6 She doesn't like the end of each yoga lesson.

4 VOCABULARY Parts of the body

a Match the words in the box with the parts of the body in the picture.

leg back foot head neck
stomach arm hand finger toe

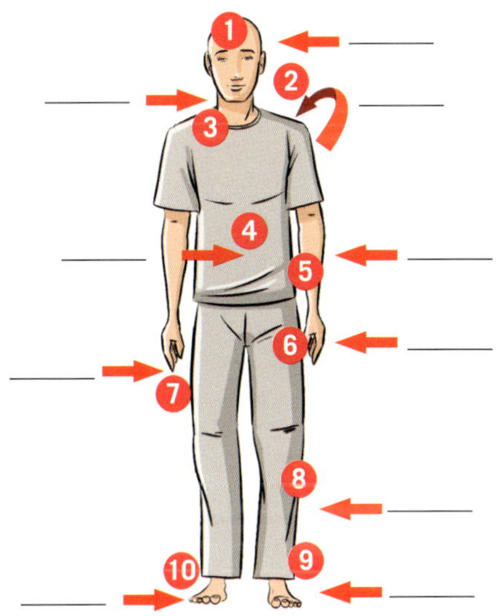

b Talk about the questions.

1 Which parts of the body can you break?
2 Which parts of the body often give people problems?

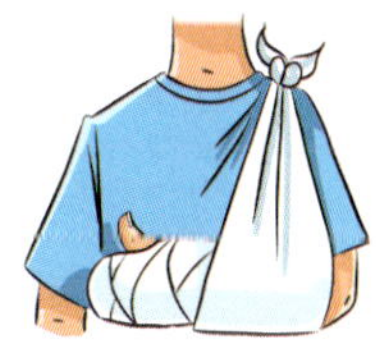

c Now go to Vocabulary Focus 8B on p. 168 for appearance vocabulary.

5 SPEAKING

a Look at activities 1–5 and choose one. Think of things people have to do and have to have if they want to do this activity. Make notes.

1 run a marathon
go running every day *have strong legs*
2 climb a mountain
3 swim a long way
4 dance for 24 hours
5 cycle across the country

b Tell your partner what people have to do to get ready for your activity and what they have to have. Don't tell them what your activity is. Can your partner guess?

You have to go running every day and you have to have strong legs.

8C EVERYDAY ENGLISH
I feel a bit tired

Learn to talk about health and how you feel

- **S** Expressing sympathy
- **P** Joining words

1 LISTENING

a Answer the questions about the pictures.

1. Where are Dan and Leo?
2. How do you think Dan feels?
3. Which picture do you think is last?
4. Imagine the conversation in picture b.

b 08.11 Watch or listen to Part 1. What does Martina tell Dan to do?

c 08.12 Watch or listen to Part 2 and answer the questions.

1. What's Dan's problem?
   - a He's got a headache.
   - b His back hurts.
   - c He needs to eat some food.
   - d He's got a temperature.
2. What do you think Dan wants to do?
   - a go to the aerobics class with Leo
   - b go home with Martina
   - c go on the running machine again

2 USEFUL LANGUAGE
Talking about health and how you feel

a Complete the mini-conversations. Use the words and phrases in the box.

the matter   feel well   look well   feel a bit tired   all right

MARTINA Are you [1]____________?
DAN I think so.

MARTINA You don't [2]____________.
DAN Yes, I [3]____________.

MARTINA What's [4]____________?
DAN I'm not sure. I don't [5]____________.

b 08.11–08.12 Watch or listen to Parts 1 and 2 again and check your answers in 2a.

c Look at some ways to say how you feel.

I feel **tired**.   I've got **a headache**.   My **back** hurts.

Which of the words in the box can you use instead of the words in **bold**?

stomach ache   a cold   sick   hungry   arm
ill   foot   toothache   a temperature

d In pairs, take turns asking about health and saying how you feel. Use the phrases from 2a and 2c.

c

d

e

3 CONVERSATION SKILLS Expressing sympathy

a Complete what Martina says with the words in the box.

poor	thing	dear

DAN Actually, I feel awful.
MARTINA Oh [1]_____. Come and sit down.

MARTINA You poor [2]_____. What's the matter?
DAN I'm not sure.

MARTINA So nothing to eat all day?
DAN I ... well ... um ... no. It was a busy day.
MARTINA [3]_____ you. Well, I'm not surprised you don't feel well.

b What do Martina's phrases in 3a mean?

1 I feel sorry for you. 2 I don't feel sorry for you.

c 08.13 Listen to the phrases in 3a. Answer the questions.

1 Which word has the main stress in each phrase?
a the first word b the last word
2 Does the intonation go up ↗ or down ↘ at the end?

d In pairs, take turns saying these sentences and giving sympathy using phrases from 3a.

1 I've got a cold.
2 I'm so tired.
3 My back hurts.
4 I feel really ill.
5 I lost all my money.
6 No one loves me.

4 PRONUNCIATION Joining words

a 08.14 Listen to the sounds of the letters in **bold** in these sentences. Then read the sentence below and underline the correct words.

1 Come and si**t** down.
2 I feel a bi**t** tired.
3 You don'**t** look well.
4 Goo**d** to see you.

The sound *joins* / *doesn't join* onto the next word, and there's *a* / *no* pause.

b In pairs, take turns saying the sentences in 4a and giving a reply.

Come and sit down.

OK, thank you.

5 SPEAKING

a Communication 8C Student A: Look at the information below. Student B: Go to p. 134.

Conversation 1. Read your first card. Think about what you want to say. Then start the conversation with Student B.

1 Student B doesn't look well. Ask him/her what's the matter. When he/she tells you, show sympathy using expressions like *Oh dear!* or *Poor you.*
Then ask if he/she has a temperature. Tell him/her what to do, e.g. *See a doctor. Go to bed.*

b **Conversation 2.** Now look at your second card. Think about what you want to say. Then listen to Student B and reply.

2 You're not feeling very well. You've got stomach ache and your eyes hurt. You don't feel hungry. When Student B asks you, tell him/her what's the matter.

UNIT PROGRESS TEST

CHECK YOUR PROGRESS

You can now do the Unit Progress Test.

8D SKILLS FOR WRITING
However, I improved quickly

Learn to write an article

W Linking ideas with *however*; Adverbs of manner

1 SPEAKING AND LISTENING

a Ask and answer the questions.

1 Which of these free-time activities are popular in your country? Which aren't popular in your country? Why not?
- playing chess
- going dancing
- cycling
- playing video games
- looking for interesting insects
- hiking

2 What other activities are popular in your country?

b Read the email Andy and Gina get at work and answer the questions.

1 What's the problem with the company blog?
  a There's too much information.
  b It's a bit boring.

2 What kind of information can staff put in their articles?
  a information about their free time
  b information about their day at work

c 08.15 Andy talks to Gina about his free-time activity. Listen and answer the questions.

1 Which activity in 1a does Andy talk about?
2 Does he want to write an article about it?

d 08.15 Listen again. Match 1–6 with a–f.

1 A year ago, …
2 Two weeks after his first bike ride, …
3 A couple of months ago, …
4 Last weekend, …
5 Almost every day, …
6 You always …

a he bought a bike.
b a car hit him.
c he goes cycling.
d he rode in the hills for two days.
e have to be careful in traffic.
f a friend invited him for a bike ride.

Our staff blog

From: The management team
To: All staff

We want to try to make the company blog more interesting. We would like to find out more about you – the people who work for this company. We'd love to hear about what you do in your free time. Write a short article and send it to us with a photo so we can put it on the blog.

e Think of something you do in your free time. Make notes. Use the questions to help you.

1 When did you start doing this activity?
2 What's something important you did when you started?
3 What do you normally do?
4 What is something interesting you did recently?

f Ask and answer questions about your activities.

I bought a chess set two months ago.

Was it expensive?

I found a very unusual stamp last month.

Where is the stamp from?

2 READING

a Read Dylan's article for the company blog. Tick (✓) what's the same about Dylan's and Andy's activities.

1 ☐ they do their free-time activities outdoors
2 ☐ they do their free-time activities every day
3 ☐ they get fit doing their free-time activities
4 ☐ they hurt their feet recently

b Read the article again. Are the sentences true (*T*) or false (*F*)? Correct the false sentences.

1 Three years ago, Dylan was lonely.
2 He liked the idea of hiking immediately.
3 Hiking was a little difficult at first.
4 He met his wife on a hike.
5 It's very difficult to learn how to go hiking.

OUR STAFF:

working hard, playing hard

Walking my way to love by Dylan Jones

Three years ago, I started working for this company. I didn't know anyone in the area, so I decided to do some exercise to meet new people. However, I was quite unfit. I tried doing different kinds of sports, but I did them all badly. I found an answer to all my problems by going for a walk.

A colleague of mine invited me to go on a hike in the mountains. I didn't say yes immediately because it didn't sound very interesting. However, I decided it could be good exercise for me, so I went along. This was the beginning of my love of hiking.

At first, I had to walk slowly because I wasn't very fit. However, I improved quickly and now I can walk pretty fast for hours. I began to feel so much better. While I was on a hike with a group of people one weekend, I met Marina. She's now my wife. We go hiking once or twice a month and we love it.

You don't have to do anything special to start hiking. You only have to know how to walk and most people can do that. However, you have to buy special boots so you don't hurt your feet. Hiking is a great way to enjoy our beautiful country. And you never know – perhaps you can find true love too!

Me on a hike!

3 WRITING SKILLS

Linking ideas with *however*; adverbs of manner

a Notice the underlined word that links the ideas in two sentences together.

I didn't say yes immediately because it didn't sound very interesting. However, I decided it could be good exercise for me, so I went along.

Is the idea in the second sentence surprising after reading the idea in the first sentence?

b Underline three more sentences in Dylan's article linked by *however*. What punctuation do we use after this word?

c Match the sentences. Link each pair with *however*.

1 I can only do very simple exercises.
2 I started doing yoga about six years ago.
3 I fell off my bike and hurt my leg.

a I didn't stop cycling.
b I can't do the difficult positions.
c I feel really fit.

d Notice the underlined adverb of manner in the sentence. Does it tell us what Dylan did or how he did it?

I tried doing different kinds of sports, but I did them all badly.

e Circle the adverbs in Dylan's article that go with these verbs.

1 walk (x2) 2 improve

f We make most adverbs of manner by adding *-ly* to an adjective.

clear + -ly = clearly

Which adverb in Dylan's article is different?

4 WRITING

a Plan an article about your free-time activity. Use your ideas in 1e. Think of:

- an interesting way to begin your article
- something you have to or don't have to do with your hobby

b Write your article. Use adverbs of manner.

c Swap articles with another student and check that:

☐ the beginning is interesting
☐ there's useful information about the hobby
☐ the article uses adverbs of manner

UNIT 8
Review and extension

1 VOCABULARY

a Complete the sentences with the words in the box.

yoga	dance	cycling	badminton	baseball	ski

1 When I went to the USA, I learnt to play ________. I wasn't very good at it because I could never hit the ball.
2 On my last winter holiday, I went to the mountains and learnt how to ________. It was great fun.
3 At weekends, my favourite form of exercise is to go ________ in the country.
4 I often meet my friend for a game of ________. We always play indoors.
5 I'd like to join a ________ class and learn the waltz and the tango. It's a fun way to keep fit and make friends.
6 The strange thing about ________ is that you have to stay in the same position for a long time.

b Complete the words for parts of the body.

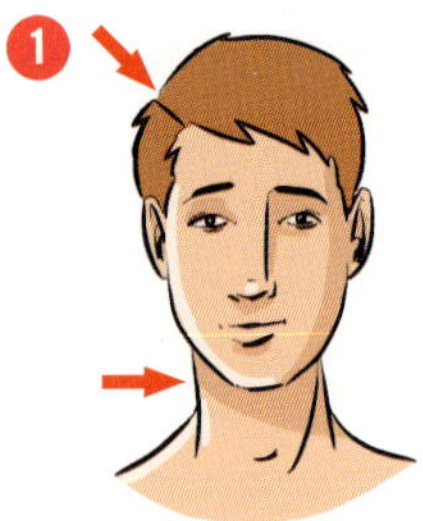

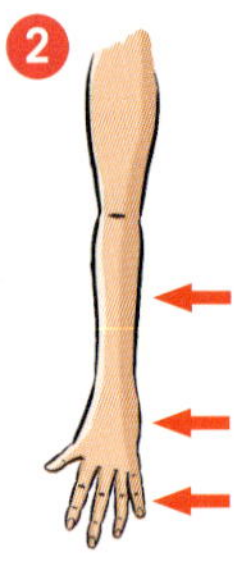

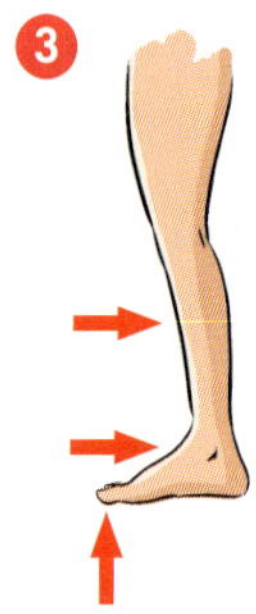

1 h______ and n______
2 a______, h______ and f______
3 l______, f______ and t______

2 GRAMMAR

a Complete the text with *can*, *can't*, *could* or *couldn't*.

In my family we love playing sport. I [1]______ play badminton well, and my sister [2]______ ski well. When we were children, we [3]______ both play football very well, but we're both a bit too slow now. The only sport I [4]______ do is swimming. I didn't learn to swim. My sister did and she [5]______ swim very fast – 50 metres in about 40 seconds. We also tried to learn musical instruments. I studied the guitar, but I [6]______ play well at all. I was always too busy playing sport.

b Complete the sentences with the correct form of *have to*.

1 If you want to go running, you ____________ buy comfortable running shoes.
2 You ____________ go to the gym every day – three times a week is enough.
3 ____________ I ____________ use the same machines every time I go to the gym?
4 You ____________ take a small towel with you when you go to the gym.
5 He ____________ be careful on his bike. Last year he had a bad accident.

3 WORDPOWER *tell / say*

a Match sentences 1–3 with pictures a–c.

1 My grandmother **told** us **stories** when we were children.
2 What did you **say** to me? I didn't hear you.
3 **Say hello** to your parents when you get there.

b Notice the words in **bold** in the sentences in 3a. Complete the phrases with *say* or *tell*.

1 ______ hello / goodbye / thank you / sorry
2 ______ a story / the truth / a joke

c Complete the sentences with *to* if it's necessary.

1 She told ______ me she doesn't feel well.
2 They said ______ me that they come from Argentina.
3 I'm sure he told ______ the truth.
4 We said thank you ______ them when we left.
5 Can you tell ______ me the time, please?

d Complete the sentences with the words in the box.

truth	you	sorry	thanks	me	story

1 Could you please tell the children a bedtime ______?
2 My wife told ______ she likes living here.
3 I don't think that's right. He didn't tell us the ______.
4 I just want to say ______ for a lovely dinner last night.
5 Please say ______ to Julia for not going to her party.
6 Yesterday I told ______ to arrive on time, but you're half an hour late.

e Complete the sentences with your own ideas.

1 When I was a child, ______ told me stories about ...
2 The last person I said sorry to was ______ because ...
3 I always say thank you to ...
4 ... tells really funny/bad jokes.

f Tell a partner your ideas from 3e.

REVIEW YOUR PROGRESS

How well did you do in this unit? Write 3, 2 or 1 for each objective.
3 = very well 2 = well 1 = not so well

I CAN ...	
talk about past and present abilities	☐
talk about sport and exercise	☐
talk about the body and getting fit	☐
talk about health and how I feel	☐
write an article.	☐

CAN DO OBJECTIVES

- Say where you are and what you're doing
- Talk about the clothes you wear at different times
- Shop for clothes
- Write a thank-you email

UNIT 9
CLOTHES AND SHOPPING

GETTING STARTED

a Look at the picture and answer the questions.

1 What are the boys doing?
2 What do these boys talk about? What questions do they ask?
3 Do you think these boys enjoy shopping?

b Where's the best place to go shopping in your town or city for … ?

- food
- clothes
- a present for someone

9A WE AREN'T BUYING ANYTHING

Learn to say where you are and what you're doing

G Present continuous

V Shopping; Money and prices

1 VOCABULARY Shopping

a Match pictures 1–6 with the words in the box.

a chemist   a department store   a fast food restaurant
a bookshop   a clothes shop   a café

Which of these shops is your favourite? Why?

b Look at the map of the shopping centre. Match the words with a–f in the map.

stairs   entrance   car park   bus stop
information desk   cash machine (*or* ATM)

c 09.01 **Pronunciation** Listen to the words. Which word is stressed: the first word or the second word?

- clothes shop
- information desk
- department store
- bus stop
- car park
- cash machine

d Where can these people go in the shopping centre?

1 'My son needs new jeans.'
2 'Let's get a new sofa.'
3 'I want something to read on the train.'
4 'I've got a headache. I need some medicine.'
5 'Can you take the shopping to the car?'
6 'Are you hungry? I need to eat!'
7 'I haven't got any money.'

e Now go to Vocabulary Focus 9A on p. 169.

2 LISTENING

a When you meet friends in town, what do you usually do? Here are some ideas:

- go shopping
- go to the cinema
- go to a café
- go for a walk

b A group of friends want to go to the cinema together. Look at the shopping centre. Where is a good place to meet?

c 09.03 Listen to Conversation 1. Where does Simon want to meet Susie? What do you think will happen?

d 09.04 Listen to the next two phone conversations. Underline the correct answers.

Conversation 2

1 Simon is *in the bookshop / in the café.*
2 Susie is *at the bus stop / in the car park.*

Conversation 3

3 Amy is *in the clothes shop / in the department store.*
4 Sandeep is *at the information desk / at the cash machine.*

e Look at the pictures and answer the questions with a partner.

1 Why do you think Simon is looking at his watch?
2 How do you think Susie feels? Why?

f 09.05 Listen to Conversation 4 and check your answers.

3 GRAMMAR Present continuous

a 09.06 Match the questions and the answers from the conversations. Listen and check your answers.

1 Where are you?
2 Are you having a coffee?
3 Where are you waiting for us?
4 Are you buying furniture?

a I'm standing by the entrance.
b I'm just getting some cash.
c No, we aren't buying anything.
d No, I'm just buying that new book.

b Choose the correct words to complete the rule.

We use *be* + verb + *-ing* to talk about … .   a now   b all the time

c Complete the tables with the correct form of the verbs in the box.

talk wait read park drink

Positive (+)		Negative (–)	
I'm We're He's She's	___ a magazine. ___ on the phone.	I'm not We aren't He isn't She isn't	___ coffee. ___ at the entrance.

Yes/No questions (?)	
Are you Is he/she	___ the car?

d 09.07 **Pronunciation** Listen to the sentences and notice the stress.

1 I'm standing by the entrance.
2 We're waiting for you.
3 We aren't buying anything.
4 Are you having a coffee?
5 Where are you waiting for us?

When is the word *are* stressed? Choose the correct answer.

a in positive sentences
b in negative sentences
c in *Yes/No* questions
d in *Wh-* questions

e Now go to Grammar Focus 9A on p. 154.

f Work on your own.

1 Think of three places in your town or city, but don't tell your partner.
2 Write a sentence to say what you are doing in each place.

g Listen to your partner's sentences. Guess where he/she is.

I'm eating a burger.

Are you in a fast food restaurant?

4 SPEAKING

a **Communication 9A** Student A: Go to p. 134. Student B: Go to p. 136.

9B EVERYONE'S DANCING IN THE STREETS

Learn to talk about the clothes you wear at different times

G Present simple or present continuous

V Clothes

1 READING

a Talk about when you go shopping for clothes, food and other things.

- before work/class
- at lunchtime
- at night
- at the weekend

b Lucas is from France and Diana is from the UK. Read the social media posts and answer the questions. Write Lucas (*L*), Diana (*D*) or both (*B*).

Who writes about ... ?

a studying
c work
b small shops
d shopping centres

c Read the posts again. Are the sentences true (*T*) or false (*F*)? Correct the false sentences.

1 Lucas only speaks Mandarin at work.
2 The Chinese people he knows like shopping.
3 Lucas would like to go to a party.
4 Diana doesn't like Venice in the winter.
5 She likes the shops in Venice.
6 It's very quiet in Venice at the moment.

d Read the messages below. Which one is Lucas's and which one is Diana's?

e Talk about the questions.

1 Which festival would you like to go to? Why?
2 Do you have festivals like these in your country? What do people do?

Friends Abroad

LUCAS Message posted: 18:36 Send Lucas a message

Hi everyone! I'm really enjoying life here in Shanghai. My new job is quite busy, but my colleagues are very friendly and they all speak English to me. In my free time, I sometimes study Mandarin and relax. I often go shopping because this is a popular 'hobby' here. I usually meet friends at a shopping centre. At the moment, it's Chinese New Year here. My friends told me there's a great street party this evening – I really want to go.

DIANA Message posted: 12:23 Send Diana a message

Hello to all my friends. I love it here in Venice! It's so beautiful – even in the winter. I have to spend a lot of time on my art history classes, but at the weekends I get some free time. I usually walk around and look at the old buildings, or when it's cold, I go to museums. There are so many interesting little shops here too – it's great. It's very different from going to a shopping centre. This week it's *Carnevale* and the whole city is like one big party. Yesterday my friends invited me to a big party in a *piazza* (that's Italian for a town square). It's tonight and I have to wear a long dress and mask. I need to go shopping!

1 We're all out in the street. We're watching a big, beautiful dragon go by. And everyone's wearing red – even me!

2 Everyone's dancing in the streets and having a great time. We're all wearing amazing clothes – I'm even wearing a dress!

2 GRAMMAR
Present simple or present continuous

a Read the sentences from Lucas's online post and message. Match them with meaning a or b.

1 I usually meet friends at a shopping centre.
2 We're watching a big, beautiful dragon.

a Lucas's normal routine b Happening to Lucas now

b Complete the rule with the correct tense.

present continuous present simple

1 We use the __________ to talk about things we usually do.
2 We use the __________ to talk about things that happen right now.

c Underline more examples of the present simple and present continuous in Diana's online post and message.

d Now go to Grammar Focus 9B on p. 154.

e 09.09 Complete the conversation with the correct form of the verbs in brackets. Listen and check.

LUCAS Hello?
JOHANNES Hi, Lucas! Are you busy?
LUCAS Hi! Yes, I [1]__________ (get) ready to go out to a street party.
JOHANNES Oh, sorry. I can call back.
LUCAS OK, thanks. I usually [2]__________ (not go) out much during the week, but it's New Year.
JOHANNES Of course.
LUCAS Sorry, Johannes. My friends [3]__________ (arrive). I have to go now. We can speak later.

3 LISTENING & VOCABULARY Clothes

a 09.10 Tina read Lucas's message and called him. Pete read Diana's message and called her. Listen to the conversations. Why are Tina and Pete surprised?

1 Tina thinks that Lucas doesn't like … .
  a parties
  b wearing red
  c going out at night
2 Pete thinks that Diana doesn't like … .
  a going out for dinner
  b being in photos
  c wearing dresses

b 09.10 Listen again and tick (✓) the clothes words you hear.

c Pronunciation The words in the table all have the letter *o* but have a different sound. Write *shoe* in the correct column.

Sound 1 /ɒ/	Sound 2 /uː/	Sound 3 /ʌ/	Sound 4 /əʊ/
sock	boot	glove	coat

d 09.11 Write these words in the table in 3c. Listen and check your answers.

come coffee shoe know mother
group box phone two

e Now go to Vocabulary Focus 9B on p. 168.

4 SPEAKING

a Think of someone in your family or a friend that you saw earlier today. What's this person wearing today? What colour are their clothes? Write notes.

b Tell your partner what this person is wearing.

Today my friend Louise is wearing dark blue jeans with brown boots.

My brother's at work today. He's wearing black trousers and an orange shirt. He's also wearing black shoes.

9C EVERYDAY ENGLISH
It looks really good on you

Learn to shop for clothes

- S Saying something nice
- P Joining words

1 LISTENING

a Ask and answer the questions.

1 How often do you buy clothes?
2 Which sentence a–c describes you best?
   a I love buying clothes. I buy something new every week.
   b I only buy clothes if I really need them.
   c I don't often buy clothes, but I like looking round clothes shops.

b 09.15 Watch or listen to Part 1. Who wants to buy clothes: Dan, Annie or both?

c 09.15 Change three incorrect things in the text below. Watch or listen to Part 1 again to check your answers.

> Dan's meeting Martina to go to a concert. He wants to wear new clothes as a surprise. Annie says she'll meet Dan at 5 pm. She isn't very happy about it.

d 09.16 Watch or listen to Part 2 and answer the questions.

1 What clothes does Dan want to buy?
2 What size does Dan wear?
3 Do you think Dan enjoys shopping?

e Do you ever ask friends or family to help you buy clothes? Who do you ask and why?

2 USEFUL LANGUAGE Choosing clothes

a Match 1–4 with a–d.

1 What are you looking for?
2 What size are you?
3 What colour would you like?
4 Why don't you try them on?

a In trousers? 32.
b Oh, I don't know. Something dark?
c A shirt and trousers.
d OK. Excuse me, where are the fitting rooms?

b 09.16 Watch or listen to Part 2 again and check your answers in 2a.

c In pairs, practise saying the questions and answers in 2a.

d Take turns helping your partner choose clothes.

A You want a jacket. B You want a pair of jeans.

3 LISTENING

a 09.17 Watch or listen to Part 3 and answer the questions.

1 Does Annie like the clothes Dan tries on?
2 What does Annie think about the last set of clothes Dan comes out in?

b 09.17 Watch or listen to Part 3 again and complete Dan's receipt.

4 USEFUL LANGUAGE Paying for clothes

a 09.18 Listen and correct a mistake in each sentence.

1 I take them.
2 How much they are?
3 Can I pay with card?

b Read this conversation in a clothes shop. Add one word in each gap.

A Can I [1]_____ you?
B Yes, how [2]_____ are these sunglasses?
A They're £29.99.
B OK, I'll [3]_____ them. Can I pay by credit [4]_____?
A No, sorry, only cash. But there's a cash machine just over there.
B OK, thanks. I'll be right back.

c In pairs, practise the conversation in 4b, but with different clothes. Take turns being A and B.

5 CONVERSATION SKILLS Saying something nice

a Read what Annie says. Add a verb to both sentences.

1 That _____ great.
2 It _____ really good on you.

b Which sentence could we use … ?
a about anything we see
b only about something someone's wearing

c Say something nice about what your partner's wearing.

I like your glasses. They look really good on you.

Thanks!

6 PRONUNCIATION Joining words

a 09.19 Listen to the sentences. Notice the words in **bold**. Is there a pause between them?

1 **Can I** help you?
2 What **size are** you?
3 Can I try **them on**?
4 How **much are** they?
5 The fitting rooms **are over** there.

b Notice how the words in **bold** in 6a are joined.

In 1–4, the consonant sound moves to the start of the next word:

1 Can I → Ca ni
2 size are → si zare
3 them on → the mon
4 much are → mu chare

In 5, we add the sound /r/ to join the words:

5 are over → are rover

c In pairs, take turns saying the sentences in 6a and giving a reply. Try to link the words in **bold**.

Can I help you?

Yes, I'm looking for a coat.

7 SPEAKING

a Look at this dialogue map. Make notes about what you want to say.

Shop assistant	Customer
Offer to help.	You want some jeans.
Size? Colour?	Reply.
Show some jeans.	Ask to try them on.
Say they look great!	Ask how much.
Say the price.	Buy them. Credit card?

b Work in pairs. Use the dialogue map and your notes in 7a to make a conversation in a clothes shop. Take turns being the shop assistant and customer.

c In pairs, practise conversations like the one in 7a but with different clothes. Take turns being the shop assistant and customer.

UNIT PROGRESS TEST

→ CHECK YOUR PROGRESS

You can now do the Unit Progress Test.

9D SKILLS FOR WRITING
Thank you for the nice present

Learn to write a thank-you email

W Writing formal and informal emails

1 LISTENING AND SPEAKING

a Look at the picture and answer the questions with a partner.

1 What kinds of presents do you like to get?
2 What kinds don't you like? Why?

b 09.20 What kinds of presents do you give your family and friends? Do you think you are more like Axel, Bob, Fernanda or Leila? Listen and check.

c 09.20 Who are these sentences about? Listen again to check.

1 They always buy their own presents. *Bob's children*
2 He likes to read. ______
3 They don't get expensive presents. ______
4 She loves expensive presents. ______
5 They go out for a meal on birthdays. ______

d Talk about the questions.

1 Who do you give presents to?
- a child in your family
- someone you visit
- grandparents
- someone who is ill in hospital
- a colleague

2 How do you thank people for presents?
- write an email
- send a text
- write a letter
- a phone call

2 READING

a It was Axel's 30th birthday last week and Molly gave him a present. Complete 1–5 in his thank-you email with sentences a–e.

To: mol@worldwide.net

1 Subject: ____________

2 ____________

3 ____________

4 ____________

5 ____________

a Hi Molly,
b Love, Axel
c Thanks very much for the cinema tickets. They're a really great present!
d Birthday present
e There's a film I want to see, so I'll use them this weekend.

b Read the email in 2a again. Answer the questions.

1 Who is Molly?
   a Axel's sister   b a colleague
2 How do you know?

c Read Molly's email to Mr Lewis and answer the questions.

1 Who is Mr Lewis?
   a someone she worked with   b a friend
2 Why did he give her a present?
   a It's her birthday.   b She's leaving the company.

d Read Molly's email again. Answer the questions.

1 How is her email different from Axel's email in 2a? Think about:
   - how she begins
   - how she ends
   - how she says thank you
2 Why do you think it's different?

Subject: Thank you

Dear Mr Lewis,

I just want to say thank you very much for the book you gave me on my last day. It's a very nice present.

I really enjoyed working for you and I wish you all the best.

Regards,

Molly

3 WRITING SKILLS

Writing formal and informal emails

a Sentences 1–4 all say thank you. Add one word to each sentence to make it correct.

1 Thank (you) for the nice present.

2 I'd just like to say thank you very for the beautiful flowers.

3 Thanks so for the chocolates. They're delicious!

4 Thank you the socks. They're a lovely colour.

b Which sentence in 3a is more formal than the others?

c Which of these phrases can you use in an email to someone you know well (1) or to someone you don't know well (2)?

Beginning	**Ending**
☐ Hello, Mrs Finch.	☐ Love,
☐ Hi there!	☐ Thanks,
☐ Hi Marie,	☐ Best wishes,
☐ Dear Mr Parker,	☐ Regards,
	☐ See you,

4 WRITING

a Think of a present for someone in the class. Write the word on a piece of paper, then give them the 'present'.

b Plan a thank-you email for the present. Think about:

- how to begin the email
- how to end the email
- what to say about the present.

c Write your email. Use the email in 2a to help you.

d Swap emails with another student and check:

☐ the beginning
☐ the sentence saying thank you
☐ the ending

e Write another email to someone you don't know well. What's different about it?

UNIT 9
Review and extension

1 GRAMMAR

a Write questions and answers for the people in the picture.

1 *What's he doing? He's listening to music.*

b Complete the conversation with the correct form of the present continuous or present simple.

SHARON Hi Jason. How are you? What [1]__________ (do)?
JASON Right now I [2]__________ (cook) dinner.
SHARON Really? But you never [3]__________ (cook).
JASON Well, I'm a bit bored with the meals at the school cafeteria. I [4]__________ (make) spaghetti with tomato sauce.
SHARON Great. Usually when I [5]__________ (make) it, I [6]__________ (put) in a lot of pepper.
JASON Pepper? OK, I [7]__________ (add) it now.
SHARON But not too much. Jason? Jason? What's that noise? Are you there?
JASON Sorry, I dropped the phone. I [8]__________ (try) to cook and talk to you at the same time.

2 VOCABULARY

a Read the sentences. Which place in a shopping centre is it?

1 Not feeling too well? We can help!
2 Come to us when you want something new to wear!
3 Feeling hungry? Try our cheeseburgers!
4 Read the best new books!
5 We have 20 kinds of tea!
6 We have everything for your home!

b Write the correct clothes word under each picture.

1  __________
2  __________
3  __________
4  __________
5  __________
6  __________

3 WORDPOWER *time*

a Look at the phrases in **bold** in sentences 1–5. Match the phrases with meanings a–e.

1 You can **save time** by shopping online.
2 **It takes time** to learn a second language.
3 I'd like to work less so I can **spend time** with my family.
4 How do you **find time** to take care of four children and work?
5 She always **wastes time** playing computer games when she really needs to study.

a have time together with people
b do things in a short amount of time
c use time badly
d you need a lot of time
e have enough time

b Read the conversations. Underline the adjectives that you can change with *spare* and *good*.

1 **A** See you later. I'm on my way to the cinema.
B OK. Have a nice time.
2 **A** What do you like doing in your free time?
B I really love reading.

c Complete the sentences with your own ideas.

1 It takes time to …
2 I save time by …
3 I can never find the time to …
4 I had a good time when I …
5 I sometimes waste time when I …

d Tell a partner your sentences in 3c. How similar are you?

REVIEW YOUR PROGRESS

How well did you do in this unit? Write 3, 2 or 1 for each objective.
3 = very well 2 = well 1 = not so well

I CAN …	
say where I am and what I'm doing	☐
talk about the clothes I wear at different times	☐
shop for clothes	☐
write a thank-you email.	☐

CAN DO OBJECTIVES

- Compare and talk about things you have
- Talk about languages
- Ask for help
- Write a post expressing an opinion

UNIT 10

COMMUNICATION

GETTING STARTED

a Look at the picture and answer the questions.

1 Who do you think these people are? Where are they?
2 Who are the children talking to?
3 What are the man and woman thinking?
4 What happened before this picture? What happens later?

b Which sentences are true for you?

1 I always have my phone with me.
2 If someone calls me, I always talk to them.
3 I never call people during meals.
4 I have my phone beside me when I sleep.

10A THEY'RE MORE COMFORTABLE THAN EARBUDS

Learn to compare and talk about things you have

G Comparative adjectives

V IT collocations

1 READING

a Ask and answer the questions.

1 Where do you listen to music and/or podcasts?
2 How do you listen?

b Read the posts about using headphones or earbuds. Who talks about ... ?

1 cost ____________
2 sound quality ____________
3 size ____________
4 where to use them ____________

c Read the posts again. Answer the questions.

1 How does Alyssa carry her earbuds?
2 How does Pedro carry his headphones?
3 Why does Kentaro feel OK about spending money?
4 Why doesn't Emily want to spend a lot of money?
5 Where does Monica use her earbuds?
6 How does Nils carry his headphones?
7 Why does Monica say the sound on headphones is clear?
8 What problem has Nils got with earbuds?

d Ask and answer the questions.

1 Do you prefer earbuds or headphones? Why?
2 What problems can you have when you use earbuds or headphones?

Lifestyle Chat

How do you like listening to music? Over-ear headphones or earbuds? Tell us which you prefer, and don't forget to vote!

Alyssa Yesterday
Earbuds are better than headphones. They are nice and small and they fit in my pocket. Headphones are too big!

Pedro Yesterday
Well, yeah, headphones are bigger than earbuds, but headphones aren't that big. Mine fold up and go in my bag, no problem!

Kentaro Yesterday
Most headphones are more expensive than earbuds, but I don't mind paying more for good sound.

Emily Yesterday
I do mind! I lose things all the time. If you're like me, it's better to buy something that's cheaper!

Monica Yesterday
Because they're smaller and lighter, you can use earbuds anywhere. I go to the gym and I always take my earbuds with me. Headphones aren't very comfortable if you're working out!

Nils Yesterday
Some people say you can only use headphones at home, but I take mine everywhere – around town, when I'm travelling. They're more comfortable than earbuds, and my headphones come with a case – that makes them easy to carry.

Kentaro 6 minutes ago
Headphones – absolutely. There's no question!

Monica 5 minutes ago
Well, I find the sound is clearer on headphones because they cover your ears. But if you buy a really good pair of earbuds – well, the sound is quite good.

Nils 2 minutes ago
I've got really small ears, so earbuds always fall out! If you want comfort and great sound quality, then headphones are definitely better.

Alyssa 1 minute ago
They're smaller, cheaper, easier to use and the sound quality is fine. I vote for earbuds – a winner for me in all categories.

2 GRAMMAR Comparative adjectives

a Underline the comparative adjectives in each sentence. Then circle the correct words to complete the rule.

1 Earbuds are better than headphones.
2 Headphones are bigger than earbuds.
3 Most headphones are more expensive than earbuds.
4 They're smaller, cheaper, easier to use.

The adjectives tell us how earbuds and headphones are *the same / different.*

b Underline more examples of comparative adjectives in the posts.

c Complete the rules about comparative adjectives.

1 Short adjectives (e.g. *small*) add ______
hard → ______
2 Adjectives that end in *-y* (e.g. *easy*) change *y* to ______ and add ______
happy → ______
3 Write ______ before long adjectives (e.g. *expensive*)
interesting → ______ interesting
4 Some adjectives are irregular (e.g. *good*, *bad*)
good → ______
bad → *worse*

d 10.01 Complete the sentences. Listen and check your answers.

a My new headphones are more comfortable ______ the old ones I had.
b Some headphones are cheaper ______ earbuds.

e 10.01 **Pronunciation** Listen again. Is the missing word in 2d stressed or not?

f Now go to Grammar Focus 10A on p. 156.

g **Communication 10A** Student A: Go to p. 134. Student B: Go to p. 137.

3 LISTENING

a 10.03 Listen to Ruby talk to her father, Greg. Answer the questions.

1 What does Greg want to change?
2 Does Ruby agree with him?

b 10.03 Listen again and put notes 1–4 in the correct place in the table.

1 they cost more
2 you can forget to charge them
3 good in emergencies, like a storm
4 you can do many things with them

	good	*bad*
Landline phones		
Smartphones		

c Do you and people in your family still have a landline? Why / Why not?

4 VOCABULARY IT collocations

a Complete the phrases from the conversation with the correct verbs. Listen and check your answers.

1 g_ online   2 c_ _ _ _ my emails   3 m_ _ _ calls

b Match verbs 1–6 with nouns a–f. Sometimes more than one answer is possible.

1 download	a a website
2 click on	b a document
3 visit	c a file
4 log into	d a phone
5 save	e a link
6 charge	f a computer

c Ask and answer questions using the phrases in 4a and 4b.

How often do you check your emails?

What kind of websites do you visit?

Do you use social media at work?

5 SPEAKING

a Choose idea 1 or 2.

1 something new you have compared to something old you had (e.g. smartphone / your first mobile phone)
2 two things that you use and are similar (e.g. desktop computer / laptop)

b Make notes about the two things.

- Is one better than the other? How?
  bigger, easier to carry around, …
- What can you do with each thing?
  go online, take photos, …

c Talk about the two things. Ask each other questions.

Are you happy with your new smartphone?

Which do you think is better, your computer or your laptop?

10B WHAT'S THE MOST BEAUTIFUL LANGUAGE IN THE WORLD?

Learn to talk about languages

G Superlative adjectives

V High numbers

1 LISTENING

a Ask and answer the questions.

1 Which languages can you speak?
2 Which languages would you like to learn?
3 Look at the languages in the box. Where do people speak these languages?

Greek ☐	Italian ☐	English ☐	French ☐
Arabic ☐	Turkish ☐	Japanese ☐	
Mandarin Chinese ☐	Portuguese ☐	Spanish ☐	

b 10.04 Listen to Professor Ryan Hunter talking about languages on the radio. Tick (✓) the languages in 1a that he talks about.

c 10.04 Match sentences 1–4 with the languages Professor Hunter talks about. Listen and check your answers.

1 He thinks it's a very beautiful language.
2 It's a difficult language for English speakers, but not for Mandarin Chinese speakers.
3 Many people think it's very easy.
4 Over 900 million people speak it.

d 10.04 Listen again and answer the questions.

1 What was the first language Professor Hunter learned?
2 How many languages can he speak?
3 Where do people speak Basque?
4 How much of the world's population speak Mandarin Chinese?

e Choose one thing Professor Hunter said which you think is ... .

a interesting b surprising

Professor Hunter

2 GRAMMAR Superlative adjectives

a 10.05 Complete the sentences with the words in the box. Listen and check your answers.

best easiest musical biggest hardest

1 Signora Monti was the ___________ teacher at my school.
2 Italian is the most ___________ language I know.
3 The ___________ language to learn is Basque.
4 Spanish is the ___________ language to learn.
5 China has the ___________ population in the world.

b Read the sentences below and put the languages in order (*1* = very easy, *4* = very difficult).

For me, **French** is easier than **Japanese**. But people say that **Spanish** is the easiest language in the world and **Basque** is the most difficult.

c Think about your own language. What number do you think it is (*1* = very easy, *4* = very difficult)?

d Look at the sentences in 2a. Then complete the rules and the examples.

1 Short adjectives (e.g. *hard*) add _____
small → _____
2 Write _____ before long adjectives (e.g. *musical*)
expensive → _____
3 Some adjectives are irregular (e.g. *good*, *bad*)
good → the _____
bad → the worst

e Now go to Grammar Focus 10B on p. 156.

f 10.07 **Pronunciation** Listen to these phrases. Notice how the words are stressed.

the biggest the easiest the hardest

g 10.08 **Pronunciation** Listen to these questions. Where's the main stress: on *most* or on the adjective?

What's the most beautiful language in the world?
What's the most useful language to speak?
What's the most difficult language in the world?

h Ask and answer the questions in 2g with other students.

3 READING

a Ask and answer the questions.

1 Do you read any blogs online? What are they about?
2 Do you use any language websites?
3 What do you think this blog is about?

b Read the blog post and check your answer to question 3 in 3a.

c Complete the blog post with the superlative forms of the adjectives in the box.

difficult (x2) fast heavy big long popular short expensive good

d Read the blog post again. Who or what are these people talking about?

1 'He could speak to people from many different countries.'
2 'It's a very popular indigenous language.'
3 'It takes a long time to learn the alphabet.'
4 'I'd love to have this book, but it costs too much.'
5 'She speaks too quickly! I can't understand her.'
6 'I can say the words, but I never know how to write them correctly.'

e Talk about the questions.

1 Which fact do you think is the most interesting? Why?
2 Do you know any other language facts?

Linguablog

FACTS OF THE WEEK

One Journalist Harold Williams was one of [1]______ language learners ever. He spoke 58 different languages.

Two Fran Capo of New York is [2]______ talker in the world. She can say 603 words in 54 seconds.

Three The Quechua language, from South America, has over 8 million speakers. It is [3]______ indigenous language that people still speak in the Americas today.

Four With over 600,000 words, the *Oxford English Dictionary* is one of the world's [4]______ dictionaries. It costs almost £1,000. Is this [5]______ dictionary in the world? It's certainly [6]______ – it has 20 books and weighs 62 kilograms!

Five Rotokas, a language in the Solomon Islands, only has 12 letters, so it has [7]______ alphabet in the world. Khmer, the language of Cambodia, has [8]______ alphabet. It has 74 letters.

Six Many people say English is [9]______ language for spelling. Some of [10]______ words to spell are *neighbour, foreign* and *awkward*.

4 VOCABULARY High numbers

a Find these numbers in 1c and the blog post. What do they refer to?

nine hundred million	
six hundred and three	
six hundred thousand	

b Now go to Vocabulary Focus 10B on p. 169 for more high numbers.

c Write down a high number for your partner to say.

5 SPEAKING

a Complete the questions with the superlative forms of the adjectives.

What or who is ... ?

1 ______ (nice) word you know in English
2 ______ (beautiful) word in your language
3 ______ (good) language learner you know
4 ______ (long) word you can think of in your language
5 ______ (hard) word to pronounce in English
6 ______ (difficult) word to spell in your language
7 ______ (interesting) book you've got

b Ask and answer the questions in 5a with other students.

I think the nicest word in English is *elbow*. I like the sound of it.

Who is the best language learner you know?

10C EVERYDAY ENGLISH

There's something I don't know how to do

Learn to ask for help

S Checking instructions

P Main stress and intonation

1 LISTENING

a Ask and answer the questions.

1 Are you good at learning how to use new things? Why / Why not?
2 You have a problem with something that you can't fix. What do you do? Why?
   a Read the instructions.
   b Ask someone in your family or a friend for help.
   c Take it to a shop for help.
   d Watch a video about it on the Internet.

b 10.10 Annie needs help with her tablet. Watch or listen to Part 1 and answer the questions.

1 Who does Annie want to help her at first?
2 Who can help her in the end?

c 10.10 Watch or listen to Part 1 again and answer the questions.

1 Why can't Dan help Annie?
2 What do Annie and Leo decide to do?

2 USEFUL LANGUAGE
Asking for help

a 10.11 Look at the different ways to ask for help. Which ones does Annie use? Listen and check your answers.

1 Could you help me?
2 Can you help me?
3 Would you mind showing me?
4 Do you mind showing me?

b 10.12 Tick (✓) the correct sentences. Correct the wrong sentences. Listen and check your answers.

1 ☐ Can you explain that?
2 ☐ Would you mind tell me?
3 ☐ Do you mind explaining it to me?
4 ☐ Could you showing me?
5 ☐ Would you mind helping me?

c Match the questions with the correct answers. One answer is correct for both questions.

1 Could you help me?
2 Do you mind helping me?

a No problem.
b Yes, of course.
c No, not at all.

3 PRONUNCIATION
Main stress and intonation

a 10.11 Listen for the question below and notice the main stress.

Do you mind <u>showing</u> me?

b What kind of word has the main stress when we ask for help?

c 10.11 Listen again. Does the intonation go up ↗ or down ↘?

d In pairs, practise saying the sentences in 2b and 3a.

e Think of a small problem you have with studying English. Think of a question to ask your partner for help.

f Take turns practising asking for help and agreeing to help each other. Use questions from 2a and 2b.

I don't understand this word. Would you mind explaining it to me?

No problem.

4 LISTENING

a 10.13 Annie and Leo have lunch together. Watch or listen to Part 2 and answer the questions.

1 What is Annie having problems with on her tablet?
2 Does Leo help her with the problem?

b 10.13 Watch or listen to Part 2 again. Leo tells Annie to do these things. Put them in the correct order.

a ☐ Open a new screen.
b ☐ Touch this button.
c ☐ Get into the email.
d ☐ Touch the 'Yes' box.

5 CONVERSATION SKILLS
Checking instructions

a Look at the sentences from the conversation. Who says them: Annie (*A*) or Leo (*L*)?

1 **So first** I touch this button?
2 And it takes me to a new screen. **Like this**?
3 And I touch 'Yes'. **Is that right**?

b Why does Annie ask these questions?

a She wants to be sure she understands the instructions.
b She wants Leo to repeat the instructions.

c Look at the words in **bold** in 5a. Which expression does Annie use when she's doing something?

d Put the instructions in the correct order.

a ☐ And next go to a new screen.
b ☐ And in the end save the photos here.
c ☐ Touch the word 'Open' here.

e In pairs, take turns practising giving and checking instructions. Use the instructions in 5d and these phrases. There is no correct answer.

So first Is that right? Like this?

6 SPEAKING

a Communication 10C Student A: Look at the information below. Student B: Go to p. 136.

Conversation 1. Read your first card.Think about what you want to say. Then start the conversation with Student B.

1 You bought a new phone, but you can't receive text messages on it. Ask Student B for help. Check the instructions he/she gives you.

b **Conversation 2.** Now look at your second card. Think about what you want to say. Then listen to Student B and reply.

2 Student B bought a new mouse for his/her computer, but it isn't working. When he/she asks for help, explain how the mouse works. Here are the instructions:

- Turn on the mouse and wait for the green light.
- Double click on the mouse.
- Wait ten seconds and click again. The mouse is working now.

UNIT PROGRESS TEST

CHECK YOUR PROGRESS

You can now do the Unit Progress Test.

10D SKILLS FOR WRITING

My friends send really funny texts

Learn to write a post expressing an opinion

W Linking ideas with *also*, *too* and *as well*

1 SPEAKING AND LISTENING

a Ask and answer the questions.

1 Do you send messages on your phone and on social media?
2 If you do, when do you send them?
- on holiday
- when you're travelling
- at work
- when you go out

Why do you send them?

3 If not, why not? How do you contact people?

b Match messages a–d with pictures 1–4. Where are the people and what are they doing?

c 10.14 Listen to three people talking about text messages. Which of texts a–d do you think they sent?

d 10.14 Listen again and complete the table.

	Sends texts to	Prefers to	Why?
Speaker 1			
Speaker 2			
Speaker 3			

e Which speaker's opinion is most similar to yours? In what way?

a Take-off not till 7:30, so home later than I thought. Maybe around 10. I'll text again when we land. xx

b Here's a pic of our first meal in Italy!

c Hungry! Anything for dinner? Train gets in 6:35. See you in a bit ;-)
Delivered

d Where are you? We're by the fountain. Can't see you.

2

1

3

4

2 READING

a Read the posts on the online discussion board. Tick (✓) who sometimes gets annoyed by people who use their phones.

☐ Genji ☐ MadMax ☐ Lars2
☐ Meepe ☐ AdamB ☐ Rainbows

b Read the posts again. Who thinks these things?

[1] I don't know anyone without a smartphone.

[2] It can be fun to send texts to friends.

[3] People shouldn't send texts when they're eating with other people.

[4] It's rude not to look at someone when they're talking to you.

[5] I don't like people who post photos in the middle of a conversation.

c Underline all the adjectives in the posts. Which three are negative?

d Look at the posts again and find … .

1 two ways to agree
2 one way to disagree

Things I hate!

Genji
I hate it when people look at their phone when they're talking to you. If you're talking to somebody, they should look at you, not at their phone. It's the worst thing you can do if you're with someone. I have a friend who does that.

Meepe
Yes, I agree. I've also got a friend like that. You're talking to him and he starts scrolling on his phone! It's so annoying.

MadMax
Yes, you're right, it's really rude. Some people post photos on social media in the middle of a conversation as well. I hate that.

AdamB
Yes, my sister does that too. We're having dinner and she starts sending texts to all her friends. I text my friends a lot too, but I try to put my phone down during dinner.

Lars2
Sometimes that's annoying, but I can also understand why people do it. Sometimes I want to send an important text before I forget about it. Everyone has a smartphone these days. We all use our phones for everything!

Rainbows
I don't agree with you, Genji. I don't mind when my friends are on their phones. Messaging is useful if you want to meet a friend. Also, my friends send really funny texts, so we laugh a lot.

3 WRITING SKILLS
Linking ideas with *also*, *too* and *as well*

a Look at the sentences and answer the question.

LARS2 Sometimes that's annoying, but I can also understand why people do it.
MEEPE I've also got a friend like that.
RAINBOWS Messaging is useful if you want to meet a friend. Also, my friends send really funny texts.

Where does the word *also* come in each sentence? Underline the correct answer.

1 *before* / *after* an auxiliary verb (*be*, *can* …)
2 *before* / *after* a main verb (*get*, *send*, *live* …)
3 at the *beginning* / *end* of a new sentence.

b Look at the sentences below and underline words or phrases that mean the same as *also*. Then answer the question.

1 **ADAMB** Yes, my sister does that too.
2 **MADMAX** Some people post on social media in the middle of a conversation as well.

Where do they come in the sentence: at the beginning, in the middle or at the end?

c Add *also*, *too* or *as well* to these sentences.

1 I've got a new PC and I have a new laptop.
2 We had satnav in the car and we took a street map.
3 She works for a mobile phone company and she knows a lot about computers.
4 Tablets are very light to carry. They have a large screen so they are easy to read.

4 WRITING AND SPEAKING

a Plan a post about something that annoys you. Use these ideas or your own. Write notes.

- another form of technology (not phones)
- people's bad habits
- an activity you hate doing

b Write your post. Use the ones on the discussion board to help you. Give your post to another student.

c Agree or disagree with another student's post, and try to add a sentence with *also*, *too* or *as well*. Then pass your post to the next student.

d Check the linking words in other students' posts. Did they use *also*, *too* and *as well* correctly?

e Compare posts. Which do you think is the most interesting? Why?

UNIT 10
Review and extension

1 GRAMMAR

a Complete the conversation with the comparative forms of the adjectives in brackets.

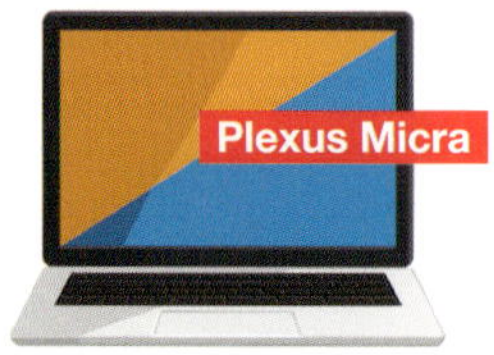

NEIL Which laptop is [1] _better_ (good)?
ASSISTANT Well, the Alba is [2]______ (powerful) than the Plexus – it has 16 gigabytes of RAM. It also has a [3]______ (big) screen. But it's [4]______ (expensive) than the Plexus – it's £1,000 more.
NEIL Which one is [5]______ (heavy)? The Alba?
ASSISTANT Yes. The Plexus is [6]______ (light) and [7]______ (thin) than the Alba. So the Plexus is a [8]______ (practical) laptop if you're travelling. And it's a little [9]______ (fast) than the Alba, too.

b Complete the questions with one word from each box. Use the superlative form of the adjectives.

long big expensive hot good

footballer country hotel room river place

1 **A** What's [a]__________ in the world?
B Death Valley in California. The highest temperature was 56°C.
2 **A** What's [b]__________ in Africa?
B The Nile. It's 6,695 kilometres long.
3 **A** What's [c]__________ in the world?
B One in the Palms Hotel in Las Vegas. It costs $100,000 for one night.
4 **A** Who's [d]__________ ever?
B Many people say it's Pelé from Brazil. He scored over 1,000 goals and won the World Cup three times.
5 **A** What's [e]__________ in the world?
B That's easy – Russia. It's 17 million km^2.

2 VOCABULARY

a Underline the correct words.

1 Don't forget to *click on* / *save* the document when you close it. You don't want to lose it.
2 He *visits* / *goes* online for hours every evening. He just goes from one *document* / *website* to the next.
3 How can I *log into* / *click on* your computer? I want to *visit* / *check* my emails.
4 *Click on* / *Visit* this link to download the *file* / *computer*.

b Write the numbers as words.

1 50,000,000 3 256 5 200,000
2 2,003 4 1,500 6 2,655

3 WORDPOWER *most*

a Read the text and answer the questions.

1 Which four languages does the family speak?
2 Which language does the writer prefer speaking? Which does her mother prefer speaking? Why?

One family – four languages

My mother is Mexican, my father is from Germany, we spent ten years in England and now we live in Italy. So we speak four languages in our family!

[1]**Most** of the people we know here are Italian, so when people come to our house, we speak Italian [2]**most** of the time, but [3]**most** of them understand English too, so we sometimes speak English and Italian together. I like speaking English [4]**most** of all because I was at school in London, and also because it's an international language and [5]**most** people speak it. But with my parents, I usually speak Spanish or German. My mother always prefers to speak Spanish with us – she says it's [6]**the most** beautiful language in the world.

b Look at the phrases with *most* in the text in 3a. Which of phrases 1–6 mean ... ?

a more than all the others
b nearly all (or about 70–80%)

c Look at the phrases *most of the people* and *most people* in the text. Which is about ... ?

a people in general
b a particular group of people

d Complete the sentences with the words in the box.

people of the way of the evening of my friends

1 I spent most ______ at a friend's flat, then I went home.
2 Most ______ in the USA speak English, but there are also more than 40 million Spanish speakers.
3 It's a lovely walk. You go along a river most ______.
4 I'm nearly 70, and most ______ don't work now.

e Write two sentences about your life. Choose two phrases.

most of the time most of all
most of my friends most days

f Tell a partner your sentences and ask and answer questions. How similar are you?

REVIEW YOUR PROGRESS

How well did you do in this unit? Write 3, 2 or 1 for each objective.
3 = very well 2 = well 1 = not so well

I CAN ...	
compare and talk about things I have	☐
talk about languages	☐
ask for help	☐
write a post expressing an opinion.	☐

CAN DO OBJECTIVES

- Ask and answer about entertainment experiences
- Talk about events you've been to
- Ask for and express opinions about things you've seen
- Write a review

UNIT 11

ENTERTAINMENT

GETTING STARTED

a Look at the picture and answer the questions.

1 What do you think these people are watching? Here are some ideas:

- a concert
- a film
- a music video
- homemade videos

2 What do you like to watch with your friends? Do you like the same things?

b Talk about films or TV programmes you enjoyed when you were a child. Say why.

11A I'VE HEARD SHE'S A GOOD ACTOR

Learn to ask and answer about entertainment experiences

G Present perfect

V Irregular past participles

1 READING

a Look at the pictures of the three actors. What do you think they have in common?

a They went to the same school.
b They all lived in Australia.
c They were models before they became actors.
d They also work as film directors.

b Read the fact files. Find the answer to 1a.

c Read the quiz questions about the actors. Guess the answers.

d Read the article and find out the answers to the quiz.

e Talk about the questions.

1 Who do you think is the most interesting actor? Why?
2 Do you know any other famous Australian actors?

FILM International

International Film Stars

Rose Byrne, Mia Wasikowska and Margot Robbie are three famous actors who work in Hollywood, and they have many things in common.

All three come from Australia and before they went to Hollywood, their first acting jobs were in Australian TV dramas and soap operas. They've acted in some very popular films. Rose was in *Bridesmaids* and the *X-Men* and *Peter Rabbit* film series. Mia was in *Jane Eyre* and *Alice Through the Looking Glass*. Margot was in *The Legend of Tarzan*; *I, Tonya* and *Mary Queen of Scots*. All three women have won awards in the USA and Australia for their acting.

They have also done some interesting and unusual things outside the film industry. Rose has worked for UNICEF in Australia. She's also a model and has been in TV advertisements for the make-up company Max Factor. Margot was in the film *The Legend of Tarzan*. Before she started making that film, she learned to swing on a circus trapeze. She also learned to ice-skate in order to play Tonya Harding in the film *I, Tonya*. Mia studied dance at school and has directed some short films. Now she really loves taking photos and won a national prize in Australia for one of her photos.

Rose, Mia and Margot are not just three amazing actors, they are three amazing people.

FACT FILE: MARGOT ROBBIE

Born	1990 Dalby, Australia
Childhood	Australia
Lives	Los Angeles

FACT FILE: MIA WASIKOWSKA

Born	1989 Canberra, Australia
Childhood	Australia & Poland
Lives	Sydney

FACT FILE: ROSE BYRNE

Born	1979 Sydney, Australia
Childhood	Australia
Lives	New York

THE QUIZ
Is Hollywood all they have in common?

Rose, Mia and Margot have also done some interesting and unusual things that you might not know about. Try our quiz. Can you guess which actor has done these things?

Which actor: … ?

1 has been in a make-up advertisement
2 can dance well
3 likes to use her camera a lot
4 can ice-skate well
5 has worked for a charity
6 learned to swing on a circus trapeze

2 GRAMMAR Present perfect: positive

a Complete the sentences. Check your answers in the article.

1 They ______ ______ in some very popular films.
2 Rose ______ ______ for UNICEF in Australia.
3 Mia ______ ______ some short films.

b Do we know when in the past the actors did these things?

c Complete the rule with the correct verb.

I / you / we / they + ________ *('ve)* *he / she / it* + ________ *('s)*	+ past participle (e.g. *worked*)

3 LISTENING

a 11.01 Maggie and Stephen answer the magazine quiz about the actors. Listen and answer the questions.

1 Did they both guess all the correct answers?
2 Tick (✓) the films they talk about:

a ☐ *Bridesmaids*
b ☐ *I, Tonya*
c ☐ *Mary Queen of Scots*
d ☐ *X-Men*
e ☐ *Jane Eyre*
f ☐ *The Legend of Tarzan*

b 11.01 Listen again. Tick (✓) if they've seen a film this actor is in. Then write the letter (a–f) of the film in 3a they've seen her in.

	Rose Dyrne	Mia Wasikowska	Margot Robbie
Maggie			✓ b
Stephen			

c What did Maggie and Stephen think about the actors in the films they've seen?

4 VOCABULARY Irregular past participles

a 11.02 Complete the sentences from the conversation with the words in the box. Listen and check your answers.

heard seen (x2) read

1 I've never ____________ any of Mia Wasikowska's films.
2 I've ____________ she's a good actor.
3 I've ____________ the book, I but haven't ____________ the film.

Do the verbs end in *-ed*?

b Go to Vocabulary Focus 11A on p. 170.

5 GRAMMAR Present perfect: negative and questions

a 11.05 Complete the sentences from the conversation with the words in the box. Listen and check your answers.

ever never seen

1 I haven't ______ any of her films.
2 I've ______ seen any of Mia Wasikowska's films.
3 Have you ______ seen any of her films?

b Complete the rules with the words *before* and *after*.

1 When we use *not*, *ever* and *never*, they come ______ *have* in the present perfect.
2 When we make a question in the present perfect, *have* comes ______ the subject.

c 11.05 **Pronunciation** Listen again to the sentences in 5a. Do we stress *have* or the past participle?

d Now go to Grammar Focus 11A on p. 158.

e 11.07 Complete the conversation with the present perfect form of the verbs in brackets. Listen and check your answers.

A [1]______ (you/see) the film *Crazy Rich Asians*?
B Yes, I have – it's so funny. What about you?
A I [2]______ (read) the book, but I [3]______ (not see) the film. [4]______ (you/read) the book?
B No, I haven't, but I want to. I [5]______ (hear) that there are three books.
A That's right.
B [6]______ (they/make) films of the other books?
A I'm not sure. I'll check online.

6 SPEAKING

a Think of some popular films, TV programmes and books. Write six questions about these things. Look at the questions in 5e to help you.

b Ask other students your questions from 6a.

Have you watched *Doctor Who* on TV?

Yes, I like it.

No, I haven't. Is it a good programme?

11B I BET YOU'VE NEVER BEEN TO THE OPERA

Learn to talk about events you've been to

G Present perfect or past simple

V Music

1 READING

a Look at pictures a–e. What kinds of music do they show?

b Look at *Budapest: City of Music*. Do you think it is about … ?

1 famous Hungarian bands
2 places to hear music
3 good places to eat out in Budapest

Read the article and check your ideas.

c Read the article again. Match pictures a–e with the places in the article.

d Read the article again and answer the questions. More than one answer may be possible.

1 Where can you hear typical Hungarian music and have a meal?
2 Which is a big event which you can go to every year?
3 Where can you go to hear famous international orchestras?
4 Where can you listen to music while you look at the river?

e You're in Budapest. Choose one place you'd like to go to, and one place you wouldn't like to go to. Why / Why not?

a

b

c

BUDAPEST CITY OF MUSIC

Budapest has beautiful buildings and great food, but did you know it's also a great city for music? Whatever kind of music you like, you can find it somewhere – it's a city of restaurants, cafés, clubs and music venues. Here are some of the places to go …

GO TO A CLASSICAL CONCERT

If you like classical music, go to the National Concert Hall. It's in a beautiful modern building right by the River Danube, which has a theatre and a museum as well as a concert hall. Top orchestras from all over the world play here and you can also see world-class operas and jazz concerts.

GO TO THE SZIGET FESTIVAL

Every August, Budapest has one of the best rock and pop music festivals in Europe. It's on an island in the river, close to the city centre! You can hear all kinds of pop and rock music here, as well as jazz and world music. It could be a chance to see your favourite rock star close up!

MUSIC IN THE RUINS

In an old part of the city, you can find ruined buildings which are now great places to hear live music. Try Szimpla Kert, which has a nice garden to sit in. They serve food and they often have live music so you can hear local bands and singers.

MUSIC ON THE RIVER

Another great venue in Budapest is the A38 Ship. It's an old ship where they have concerts and dance music. If it gets too hot inside, you can go out on the deck and look at the river!

OR GO FOR SOMETHING MORE TRADITIONAL …

It's easy to find restaurants in Budapest where you can listen to Hungarian folk music while you eat. Try the small streets in Óbuda, the old part of Budapest. They're not cheap, but the food's usually good and if you give the musicians some money, they will even play your favourite Hungarian song!

d

2 VOCABULARY Music

a ▶ 11.08 Underline words in the text for:

1 kinds of music: *classical* …
2 people who play music or sing: *an orchestra,* …
3 places where you go to hear music: *a concert hall,* …

Listen and check your answers.

b ▶ 11.09 **Pronunciation** Listen to these words again. Circle the number of syllables. Underline the stressed syllable in each word.

singer	1 ② 3		orchestra	1	2	3
musician	1 2 3		festival	1	2	3
classical	1 2 3					

c ▶ 11.10 Listen to five pieces of music. What kinds of music are they?

d Which kinds of music do you often listen to? Which kinds do you never listen to?

3 LISTENING

a ▶ 11.11 Max and Alana are students in Budapest. Listen to their conversation about *Budapest: City of Music*. How many places do they talk about? Which places have they been to?

b ▶ 11.11 Complete the table about Alana. Listen and check your answers.

Where?	When?	Did she like it?
1 Szimpla Kert		
2		
3		

4 GRAMMAR Present perfect or past simple

a ▶ 11.12 Match the questions with the answers. Listen and check your answers.

1 Have you ever been to these places?
2 Have you ever been to Szimpla Kert?
3 I bet you've never been to a concert at the National Concert Hall.

a Yes, I have actually. I went there last year.
b What places do you mean?
c Yes, I went there two weeks ago. They had a really good band.

b Answer the questions about 4a.

1 Which two tenses do the speakers use?
   a present simple c present continuous
   b past simple d present perfect
2 Which tense do we use … ?
   a if we don't say when something happened
   b if we say when something happened
3 Which tense do we use with … ?
   a *ever* and *never*
   b time expressions (*last weekend, a month ago*)

c Now go to Grammar Focus 11B on p. 158.

d ▶ 11.14 Put the conversation in the correct order. Listen and check your answers.

A ☐ Who did you go with?
A ☐ Did you enjoy it?
A 1 Have you ever been to a music festival?
A ☐ Where was it?
B ☐ It was in Novi Sad, in Serbia – the EXIT festival.
B ☐ I went with a group of friends from university.
B ☐ Yes, we all had a great time.
B ☐ Yes, I have. I went to one last summer.

e Practise the conversation in 4d.

5 SPEAKING

a Think of two things you've seen or places you've been to in your town or city. Here are some ideas:

- a concert or music event
- a film or play
- a theatre, cinema or club

Take notes.

City Theatre – Macbeth
football stadium – Rihanna concert

b Think of two things you haven't seen or places you haven't been to, but would like to. Write notes.

c Ask other students about the things and places in 5a and 5b. Ask for more information.

Have you been to Mombo's?
Who did you go with?
When did you go there?
Was it good?

11C EVERYDAY ENGLISH

I thought they were quite good

Learn to ask for and express opinions about things you've seen

S Responding to an opinion

P Main stress and intonation

1 LISTENING

a Ask and answer the questions.

1 When you go out in the evening, do you ... ?
- drive • walk • take a bus • take a taxi • other

2 When was the last time you took a taxi? Where did you go?

b Look at pictures 1 and 2. Write what you think Dan's saying.

c 11.15 Watch or listen to Part 1 and check your answers in 1b. Then choose the correct answers below.

1 Dan and Martina are *going out / on their way home.*
2 Their address is *50 Windsor Road / 15 Windsor Road.*

d 11.16 Dan and Martina are in the taxi. Watch or listen to Part 2 and answer the questions.

1 Where have they been?
2 Do they have the same opinion about what they saw?

e 11.16 Read the sentences and write *M* (Martina), *D* (Dan) or *B* (both). Watch or listen again to check your answers.

Who thinks ... ?

1 the concert was good
2 not all the bands were good
3 the first band was good
4 *Atlantis* are a good band
5 *Atlantis* were too loud

2 USEFUL LANGUAGE

Asking for and expressing opinions

a 11.17 Listen and put the conversation in the correct order.

a ☐ Did you enjoy it?
b ☐ How about you?
c ☐ I really liked it.
d ☐ So what did you think of it?
e ☐ Yeah, it was a good concert.

b In pairs, practise the mini-conversation in 2a.

c Now look at these ways to express an opinion. Match opinions 1–3 with reasons a–c.

1 I really liked the first band.
2 I didn't like the first band very much.
3 I didn't like the first band at all.

a I thought they were terrible.
b I thought the singer was great.
c I thought they played quite well, but their songs were boring.

3 LISTENING

11.18 What do you think's happening in picture 3? How does Martina feel? Watch or listen to Part 3 to check.

4 CONVERSATION SKILLS
Responding to an opinion

a Read the mini-conversations. Which replies mean … ?

a I agree b I don't really agree

1 **MARTINA** I didn't like all the bands.
DAN No, me neither.

2 **MARTINA** I really liked it, how about you?
DAN Yeah, me too.

3 **MARTINA** I thought they were quite good.
DAN Did you?

4 **DAN** Really great music.
MARTINA Do you think so?

5 **MARTINA** They were too loud.
DAN Yeah, maybe.

b Complete the table with *do* or *did*.

Present	Past
A I think they**'re** good. **B** **Do** you?	**A** I thought they **were** good. **B** 1_____ you?
A Their music **is** interesting. **B** 2_____ you think so?	**A** The concert **was** boring. **B** **Did** you think so?

c In pairs, practise the mini-conversations in 4b. Take turns being A and B.

5 PRONUNCIATION
Main stress and intonation

a 11.19 Listen to these replies. Notice that both words are stressed in each one.

1 Do you? 2 Did you? 3 Me neither. 4 Me too.

b 11.19 Listen again and answer the questions.

1 Does the intonation go up ↗ or down ↘ at the end of each reply?
2 In 1 and 2, do you think the speaker sounds … ?
a angry b surprised c happy

c 11.19 Listen again and repeat.

d In pairs, take turns responding to these opinions. You can agree or disagree.

1 I thought the concert was boring.
2 I didn't enjoy the concert.
3 I think the band play very interesting music.
4 I thought the concert was too long.
5 I think she's a fantastic singer.

You did? I thought it was really good.

6 LISTENING

a Look at picture 4. Answer the questions with a partner.

1 Where do you think Dan and Martina are now?
2 What do you think Dan says?

b 11.20 Watch or listen to Part 4 and check your answers in 6a.

7 SPEAKING

a **Communication 11C** Student A: Go to p. 134. Student B: Go to p. 136.

UNIT PROGRESS TEST

CHECK YOUR PROGRESS

You can now do the Unit Progress Test.

11D SKILLS FOR WRITING
It was an interesting film

Learn to write a review

W Structuring a review

1 SPEAKING AND LISTENING

a Ask and answer the questions.

1 Have you seen any of the films on these pages?
2 Have you ever watched a film more than once?

b 11.21 Melissa and John talk about a film. Listen and answer the questions.

1 What film are they talking about?
2 Did John like it? Did Melissa like it?

c 11.21 Listen again. Write John (*J*) or Melissa (*M*). Who … ?

1 thinks James Bond films are always the same
2 thinks James Bond films are just for fun
3 thinks the special effects were good
4 is going to see the film again

d Choose a film you've seen and a film you haven't seen. Write notes. Think of … .

- why you liked or didn't like the film
- why you'd like to see the other film

e Talk about the two films from 1d.

1 Have other students seen them?
2 What did they think of them?

2 READING

a Ashley watched the film *Roma*. Read her review. Is it positive or negative?

b Read Ashley's review again and answer the questions.

1 How many times has she watched the film?
2 What are two things she says about Alfonso Cuarón?
3 What are two things she says about Yalitza Aparicio?

c Oscar also watched *Roma*. Read his review. Is it positive or negative?

d Read Oscar's review again and answer the questions.

1 Why did he watch it?
2 What are the good and bad things he says about the film?

e Anna also watched *Roma*. Read her review. Is it positive or negative?

f Read Anna's review again and answer the questions.

1 Where did she watch it?
2 What new information does she give about the film?

3 WRITING SKILLS Structuring a review

a Read Ashley's and Oscar's reviews again. Write the numbers of the sentences that answer the questions below.

a [4] Who are the actors and are they good?
b [ ] When did you see the film?
c [ ] Did you like it?
d [ ] Do you recommend it?
e [ ] Who wrote or directed it?
f [ ] What is the film about?

b Read Anna's review again. Does it answer the questions in the same order?

c Look at some comments about different films. Which questions in 3a do they answer?

1 I loved it!
2 I heard it was good, so I went to see it at the weekend.
3 I thought the story was quite interesting.
4 Emma Stone is brilliant.
5 It's by Korean director Bong Joon-ho.
6 Don't go to see it. It's terrible!
7 The film is about a boy who grows up in a small town in the desert.

ROMA

'I thought it was an interesting and very beautiful film. So try to see it if you can.'

Ashley

[1]I saw *Roma* at the cinema last year and then I watched it again on Netflix. [2]So I've watched it twice now, and it was even better the second time. [3]It's by the Mexican director Alfonso Cuarón, and it's based on his own childhood growing up in Mexico City. [4]All the actors are excellent, but I liked Yalitza Aparicio the best. She was completely unknown when Cuarón gave her the part, but she's great. [5]She plays the role of a maid who works for a middle-class family, and the film is the story of her relationship with the parents and the children of the family. [6]I thought it was an interesting and very beautiful film. So try to see it if you can.

d Look at the reviews again. How are sentences 1–3 different from the ones in the reviews?

1 I watched *Roma* on Netflix a few weeks ago. A friend recommended *Roma*, and we usually like the same films, so I decided to watch *Roma*.
2 I liked Yalitza Aparicio the best. Yalitza Aparicio was completely unknown when Cuarón gave Yalitza Aparicio the part, but Yalitza Aparicio is great.
3 So I didn't think the film was a great film, but maybe it's OK to watch the film if you have nothing better to do.

e Answer the questions with a partner.

1 How many times did the three people write the name of the film in their reviews?
2 What words did they use in place of the name of the film?

4 WRITING AND SPEAKING

a Plan a review of a film you've seen. Write notes using the questions in 3a and the comments in 3c to help you.

b Write your review. Use Ashley, Oscar and Anna's reviews to help you.

c Swap reviews with another student and check. Does your partner's review answer the questions in 3a?

d Read other students' reviews. Which film would you like to see?

'OK to watch it if you have nothing to do one evening.'

Oscar

[1]I watched *Roma* on Netflix a few weeks ago. [2]A friend recommended it, and we usually like the same films, so I decided to watch it, but I was disappointed. [3]Alfonso Cuarón, who also made the film *Gravity*, wrote and directed it. [4]The acting was good (Marina de Tavira is great in the role of the mother), but I found the story a bit boring. [5]The film is about a family and their maid. All the characters in the film just do ordinary things and nothing exciting happens. [6]So I didn't think it was a great film, but maybe it's OK to watch it if you have nothing better to do.

'A very interesting film, but it was also very sad.'

Anna

[1]I watched *Roma* at a friend's house last week. [2]I thought it was a very interesting film, but it was also very sad and the ending made me cry. [3]The film is by the Mexican director Alfonso Cuarón, and it's in black and white. [4]The film is about a family in Mexico City and their life with their maid, who comes from a village. [5]The acting is very good, especially the actors who play the maid and the mother. [6]I can recommend this film, but only watch it if you enjoy sad films!

UNIT 11
Review and extension

1 VOCABULARY

a Underline the correct words.

1 I don't like *classic* / *classical* music.
2 He likes *rock* / *rocker* music like Coldplay.
3 After years of playing the violin, he finally got a job with an *orchestral* / *orchestra*.
4 In my opinion, Taylor Swift is the most famous *popular* / *pop* music singer in the world.
5 Bill only plays his guitar on the street for money. But listen to him – he's a very good *musician* / *musical*.
6 Would you like to come and see *Così fan tutte*? It's a very famous *opera* / *operatic* by Mozart.

b Write the past participle of the verbs.

1 be
2 do
3 go
4 hear
5 read
6 see
7 win
8 write

2 GRAMMAR

a Write sentences and questions with the correct form of the present perfect.

1 I / be to South Africa twice.
2 She / meet a lot of famous actors.
3 you / see the latest James Bond film?
4 He / not / work in an office before.
5 We / never / win the lottery.
6 they / read all the Harry Potter books?
7 I / not / hear a lot of jazz music.

b Tick (✓) the correct sentences. Change the verb form in the sentences that are not correct.

1 ☐ We've been to Brazil only once.
2 ☐ He's read a book in English last week.
3 ☐ I never saw a *Star Wars* film.
4 ☐ They've won a pop music competition two years ago.
5 ☐ I saw three films last weekend.
6 ☐ She's never been to Argentina.
7 ☐ I didn't read a book by Stephen King.

c Complete the conversation with the correct present perfect or past simple form of the verbs in brackets.

A 1 ______ (you/be) to Australia?
B No, I haven't, but I 2 ______ (be) to New Zealand.
A Have you? I 3 ______ (never/be) there, but I would love to go.
B We 4 ______ (go) about four years ago in the summer.
A How long 5 ______ (you/stay)?
B About three weeks, but it 6 ______ (not be) long enough. I 7 ______ (do) a bungee jump when I 8 ______ (be) there. 9 ______ (you/ever/try) anything like that?
A No. I'm too afraid!

3 WORDPOWER Multi-word verbs

a Match 1–6 with a–f to make conversations.

1 Sorry, Mike, I have a meeting now.
2 Here's my photo ID.
3 Are you from London?
4 Here's a very nice shirt in blue.
5 You're looking a little tired.
6 I have nothing to do this evening.

a Yes, I think I need to **lie down** for a while.
b Well, I was born in Manchester, but I **grew up** here.
c That's OK. I can **call** you **back** this afternoon.
d Well, would you like to **come over** for dinner?
e Thank you. Now can you **fill** this form **out**, please?
f Could I **try** it **on**?

b Match the multi-word verbs in **bold** in 3a with meanings 1–6.

1 return a phone call
2 put on clothes to check that the size is right
3 complete
4 take a rest on a sofa or bed
5 visit a person's home
6 go from being a child to an adult

c Complete the sentences with the correct form of a multi-word verb from 3a.

1 She never wants to ______ things ______ in the shop and often gets the wrong size.
2 You need this form at the airport. Can you ______ ______ your details here?
3 I've always lived in Toronto. I ______ ______ here.
4 She finally ______ me ______ this morning and told me she was away all last week.
5 Why don't you ______ ______ and read your book?
6 My brother ______ ______ last night and brought a cake for my birthday.

d Work in pairs. Ask and answer the questions.

1 How often do friends or family come over to your place?
2 Do you sometimes forget to call people back?
3 Where did you grow up?
4 Do you usually try on clothes before you buy them?
5 What was the last form you had to fill out?
6 Do you sometimes lie down during the day?

REVIEW YOUR PROGRESS

How well did you do in this unit? Write 3, 2 or 1 for each objective.
3 = very well 2 = well 1 = not so well

I CAN ...	
ask and answer about entertainment experiences	☐
talk about events I've been to	☐
ask for and express opinions about things I've seen	☐
write a review.	☐

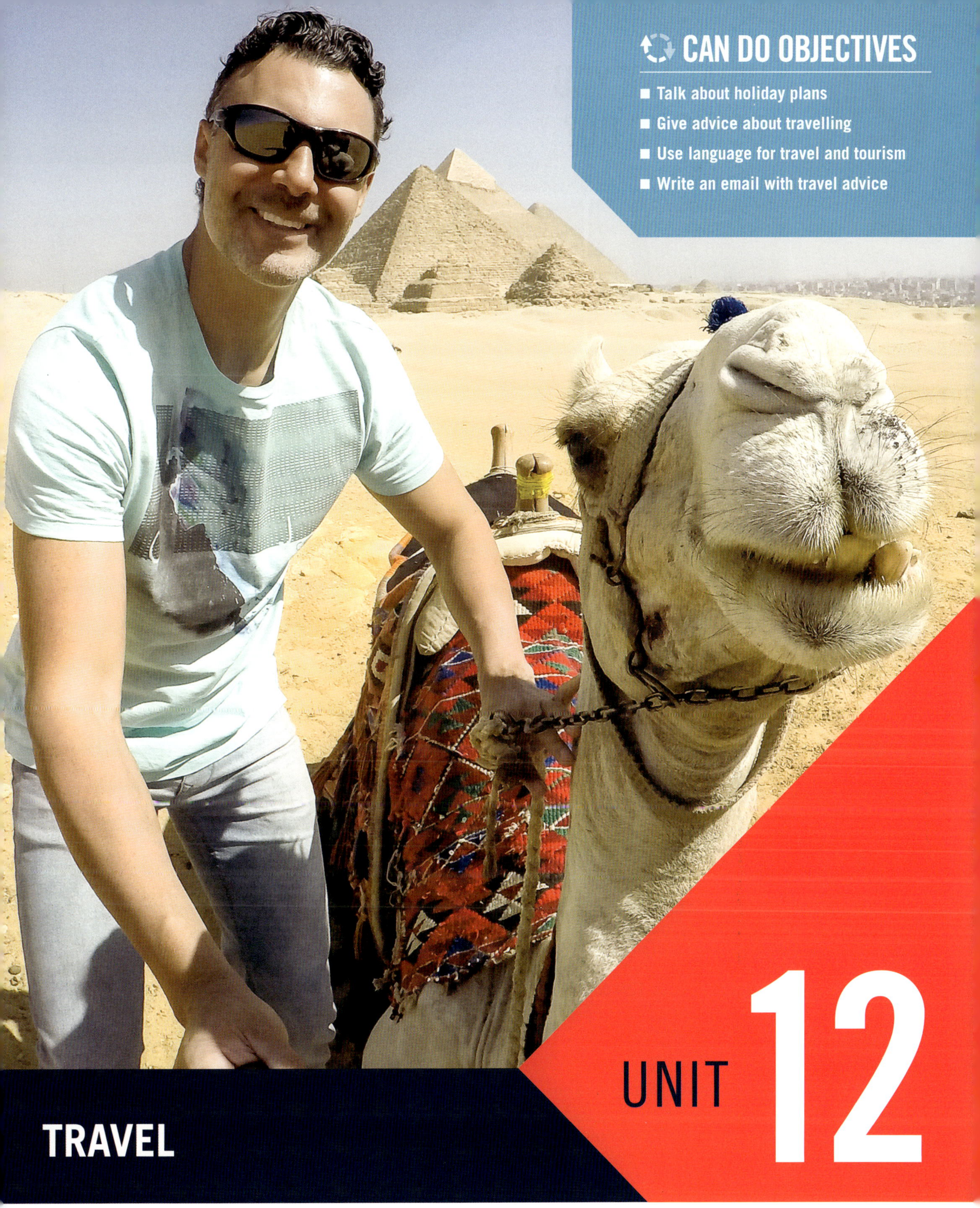

CAN DO OBJECTIVES

- Talk about holiday plans
- Give advice about travelling
- Use language for travel and tourism
- Write an email with travel advice

UNIT 12

TRAVEL

GETTING STARTED

a Look at the picture and answer the questions.

1 Where do you think this man is on holiday? Why?
2 What other things has he planned to do there?
3 Who do you think took this picture?

b In pairs, ask and answer the questions.

1 Do you take photos of friends and family on holiday or other special days?
2 What other things do you take photos of?
3 What do you do with your photos after you've taken them?
4 What's your favourite photograph?

12A WHAT ARE YOU GOING TO DO?

Learn to talk about holiday plans

G *be going to*

V Geography

1 VOCABULARY Geography

a Match words 1–10 with pictures a–j.

1 island
2 mountain
3 forest
4 waterfall
5 beach
6 desert
7 lake
8 glacier
9 rainforest
10 river

b 12.01 **Pronunciation** Listen and check your answers in 1a. Then answer the questions.

1 Which two words have only one syllable?
2 Which syllable is stressed in all the other words?

c Work in pairs. Look at pictures a–j and answer the questions.

1 Which places would you like to live near?
2 Have you been to any of these places?
3 Which place would you like to go to on holiday? Why?

d Now go to Vocabulary Focus 12A on p. 170.

2 READING

a What's important for you when you're on holiday? Why?

- nothing – just relax
- meet new people
- do a lot of sightseeing
- understand a new culture
- try a new sport
- eat local food

b Read the web page. Which ideas in 2a can you do on *Work Around the World* holidays?

c Read the web page again. What is a good job for someone who likes … ?

- swimming and dancing
- drawing
- outdoor sports

d Talk about the questions.

1 Would you like to do one of these jobs? Why / Why not?
2 Order the three jobs from hard work (1) to not very hard work (3). Say why.

WAW

WORK AROUND THE WORLD

What are Work Around the World holidays?

They're holidays where you work for a few hours every day and you get your accommodation and food for free.

Why go on a Work Around the World holiday?

Because it's fun, you help other people and you also make a lot of interesting new friends.

Here are some examples of great Work Around the World holidays.

Summer work in a small hotel in the Åland Islands, Finland.

- Jobs include cleaning and taking reservations.
- Great for people who love cycling and kayaking.

1

3 LISTENING

a ▶12.03 Listen to two conversations about holiday plans. Which *Work Around the World* holidays are Emily and Chloe interested in?

b ▶12.03 Listen again to the two conversations. Answer the questions.

Conversation 1

1 Why doesn't Emily want to go to university?
2 What does she like about the job she is interested in?
3 Why doesn't Zoe want her to go?

Conversation 2

1 Why does Chloe want to leave her job?
2 What does she like about the job she is interested in?
3 Does Frank think it's a good job for Chloe?

c Talk about the questions.

1 Do you think it's a good idea for Emily and Chloe to do a Work Around the World holiday? Why / Why not?
2 What are the good things and the bad things about going on one of these holidays?

4 GRAMMAR *be going to*

a ▶12.04 Complete the sentences from the conversations. Listen and check your answers.

1 I'm ________ to email and ask about it.
2 I'm ________ to leave this job.

b Look at the sentences in 4a. Underline the correct words to complete the rule.

We use *be* + *going to* + infinitive when we want to describe *a future plan / a present action.*

c ▶12.05 Complete the sentences with the correct forms of *be going to* and the verbs in brackets. Listen and check your answers.

\+ I ________ (find out) more about it.
– I ________ (not go) to university next year.
? What ________ (do)?

d ▶12.05 **Pronunciation** Listen to the sentences in 4c again. How is *going to* often pronounced? Which is stressed: *going* or the main verb?

e Now go to Grammar Focus 12A on p. 160.

f ▶12.07 Complete the conversation with *be going to* and the verbs in brackets. Listen and check your answers.

A I [1]________ (spend) six months travelling and working next year.
B Great. Where are you [2]________ (go)?
A I [3]________ (travel) around South Africa.
B What jobs [4]________ (do)?
A Cleaning, cooking, working in restaurants – things like that. I [5]________ (not do) anything difficult.
B And what about after your trip?
A I [6]________ (look) for a job at home.

5 SPEAKING

a Talk about which of the three working holidays you would like to do.

b **Communication 12A** Student A: Go to p. 135. Student B: Go to p. 137.

12B YOU SHOULD LIVE LIKE THE LOCAL PEOPLE

Learn to give advice about travelling

G *should / shouldn't*

V Travel collocations

1 READING

a Ask and answer the questions.

Would you like to live in a different country? Why / Why not? If yes, which country would you choose?

b Read the article and name the people in pictures 1–4.

c Read the sentences. Who do you think wrote each one: Tom (*T*), Oliver and Kirsten (*OK*) or Maya (*M*)?

1 Saw some beautiful fish yesterday. Fantastic!
2 We've got a job taking photos for a local newspaper.
3 I think they liked the music I played last night.
4 I'm going to work on the island of Koh Tao – the sea is so clear there.
5 We're going to find a local school for our daughter next week.

d Would you like to go travelling and never stop? Why / Why not?

Why not go travelling ... and never stop?

In 2010, Tom sold everything, packed a small bag and left his home in London to travel abroad. He was 30. Ten years and 15 countries later, he's still travelling and he says he's never going to go back home. Last year he arrived in Portugal. To earn money, Tom works as an English teacher. He's also a DJ in some local nightclubs.

***TOM SAYS:* You can use English in most places, but you should try to learn the local language, too.**

1

4

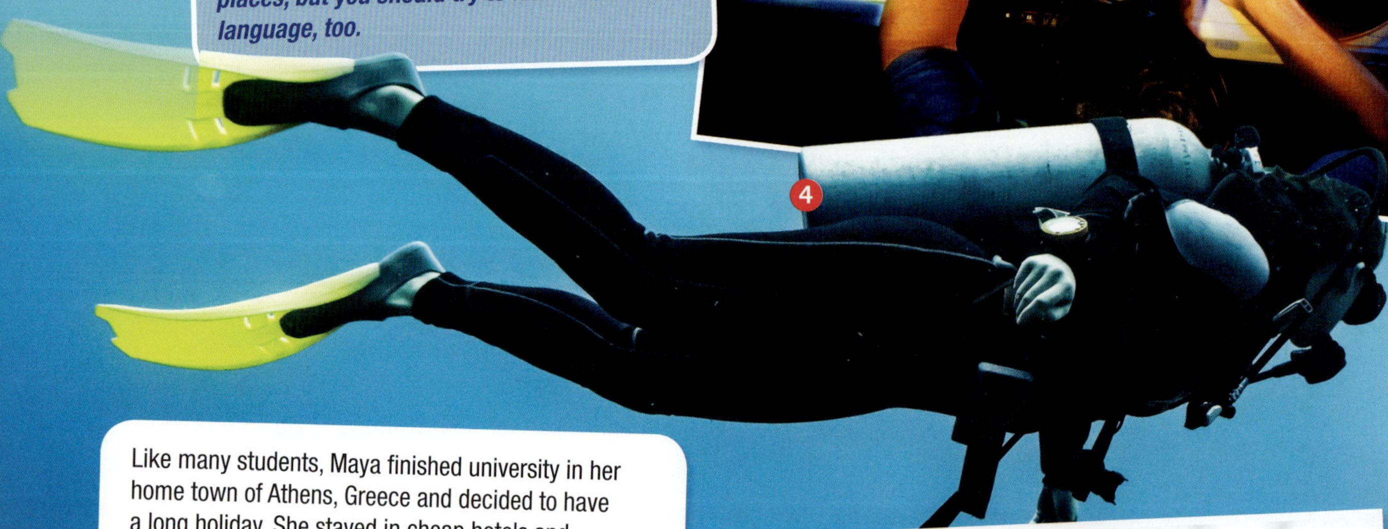

Like many students, Maya finished university in her home town of Athens, Greece and decided to have a long holiday. She stayed in cheap hotels and with friends in different countries. Five years later, she is still enjoying that holiday. When she was in Australia, she learned how to dive. She loved it and she decided to do a course and learn to teach other people how to dive. Now she works all over the world teaching tourists to dive.

***MAYA SAYS:* It's a big, wide world out there. I don't want to spend my life in just one place.**

2

2 VOCABULARY Travel collocations

a Match pairs of verbs 1–6 with a word or phrase in the box. Use the texts in 1b to help you.

a hotel   a bag   home   abroad   plans   holiday

1 make / change ______
2 travel / live ______
3 stay at / go back ______
4 plan a / go on ______
5 book / stay in ______
6 pack / unpack ______

b 12.08 Six people talk about travelling and holidays. Complete the sentences with verbs in 2a. Listen and check your answers.

1 I always ________ my holidays carefully. I read about the place before I go there.
2 I don't want to ________ abroad. It's better to go on holiday in my own country.
3 I never ________ a hotel. I want to see my room before I decide to stay there.
4 I usually ________ my bags about an hour before I go on holiday. I hate doing it!
5 After a week away, I'm always happy to ________ home and see my family again.
6 When I'm on holiday, I never ________ plans. I just see what happens when I get there.

c Which speakers in 2b do you agree with? Why / Why not?

3 GRAMMAR *should / shouldn't*

a Look at the sentences. Underline the correct words. Then check in the texts.

1 You *should / shouldn't* try to learn the local language, too.
2 You *should / shouldn't* forget your family back home.
3 You *should / shouldn't* live like the local people.

3

Oliver and Kirsten Foster left the UK in 2013. In three years, they travelled to Mexico, Peru, the USA, Thailand, China, Dubai and Germany before arriving at their latest home in Egypt in 2016. They're both photographers, so they can work anywhere in the world. They've now got a three-year-old daughter, Liona, so they have to make plans more carefully. But they don't want to change their lives. Next year they are going to live in Ecuador and then South Africa.

***OLIVER SAYS:** I love meeting new people, but you shouldn't forget your family back home. I call my mum every week.*

***KIRSTEN SAYS:** You should live like the local people and try to make friends with people from the country.*

b Choose the correct answer to complete the rules.

1 *You should* means ... .
a you have to do it   b it's a good idea
2 After *should* and *shouldn't* we use ... .
a *to* + infinitive   b infinitive without *to*

c 12.09 **Pronunciation** Listen to sentences 2 and 3 in 3a.

1 Is there an /l/ sound in *should* and *shouldn't*?
2 Is the vowel long or short?

d Now go to Grammar Focus 12B on p. 160.

e Read the advice about living abroad. Change the verbs in blue by adding *should* or *shouldn't*.

WOULD YOU LIKE TO LIVE ABROAD? TAKE OUR ADVICE!

1 **Don't stay** at home all the time.
Go out and meet people.
You shouldn't stay at home all the time. You should ...
2 **Try** to visit a new place every weekend.
Don't wait until the last few weeks of your stay.
3 **Read** about the country before you go there.
4 **Don't get** angry when things go wrong.
5 **Remember** that things work differently in other countries.

4 LISTENING AND SPEAKING

a What do you think these people mean?

I'm quite a sporty person.   I'm not really a city person.   I'm a beach person.

What about you and other students? Are you the same?

b Quickly read the information again about Tom and Maya. Which things below do you think Tom likes and which do you think Maya likes? Why? Write *T* (Tom) or *M* (Maya).

☐ the sea   ☐ noise   ☐ big cities
☐ cafés   ☐ beaches   ☐ dancing
☐ sport   ☐ music
☐ shopping   ☐ the countryside

c 12.11 Listen to Tom and Maya. Check your answers in 4b.

d Tom and Maya are going to visit your country. Talk about where they should and shouldn't go, what they should do, and why.

You should go to the city centre. There are a lot of good cafés.

You shouldn't go to the National Museum. It's very boring!

e Work with a student you don't know very well. Find out what they like and don't like doing on holiday.

f Give your partner some advice about what to do and what not to do in a city you know.

12C EVERYDAY ENGLISH

Is breakfast included?

Learn language for travel and tourism

- S Showing surprise
- P Consonant clusters

1 LISTENING

a Ask and answer the questions.

1 When you go on holiday, where do you usually stay? Choose one or more places.

- hotel
- hostel
- camping in a tent
- flat / house
- with friends
- another place

2 Why do you like staying in this / these place(s)?

b 12.12 Watch or listen to Part 1 and answer the questions.

1 Who has won a competition?
2 Can Dan and Martina use the prize?

c 12.12 Watch or listen to Part 1 again. Complete the email. Put a word or number in each gap.

Dear [1] ________

Congratulations! You have won a weekend for [2] ________ people in the city of [3] ________. All your travel and hotel expenses are included in the prize.

You can only use your prize on the weekend of [4] ________ [5] ________ July. Enjoy!

2 CONVERSATION SKILLS Showing surprise

a Look at the conversation. Underline the two ways that Dan shows surprise.

MARTINA I've won a competition!
DAN Have you? Fantastic! What's the prize?
MARTINA A weekend for two in Bath …
DAN Really? That's great.

b Which question in 2a can you use to reply to any news?

c 12.13 Match 1–4 with a–d. Listen and check your answers.

1 I'm getting married.	a Do you?
2 I really like grammar.	b Have you?
3 I went to New York for the weekend.	c Are you?
4 I've eaten an insect.	d Did you?

d 12.13 **Pronunciation** Listen again. Does the intonation in a–d in 2c go up ↗ a little or a lot?

e Think of two surprising things. They don't have to be true! Make notes.

f In pairs, take turns telling each other your surprising things and showing surprise. Use expressions from 2a and 2c.

3 LISTENING

a 12.14 Who do you think Dan and Martina gave the prize to? Watch or listen to Part 2 and check.

b 12.14 Watch or listen to Part 2 again. Complete the guest information card.

WELCOME TO THE
IMPERIAL
HOTEL

Your room number is [1] ______.
Please join us for breakfast in the dining room from [2] ______ to [3] ______.
Your checkout time is [4] ______.

ENJOY YOUR STAY.

4 USEFUL LANGUAGE
Checking in at a hotel

a Below are useful expressions for hotel guests. Which two expressions did Annie use?

1 I've got a reservation for a double room for two nights.
2 Is there a car park?
3 Is breakfast included?
4 Is there wi-fi in the room?
5 What time is checkout?
6 Is there a safe in the room?

b Which four questions in 4a do we use to ask about things hotels can offer?

c 12.15 Complete the conversation between a guest and a hotel receptionist with sentences from 4a. Listen and check your answers.

RECEPTIONIST Hello, how can I help you?
GUEST Hello. I [1]__________.
RECEPTIONIST A double room? Your name, please?
GUEST Morton.
RECEPTIONIST Thank you. So, that's two nights?
GUEST Yes. Is [2]__________?
RECEPTIONIST Yes, it's from 6:30 am until 9:30 am in the dining room.
GUEST Is [3]__________?
RECEPTIONIST Yes, there is.
GUEST And what [4]__________?
RECEPTIONIST It's 11 o'clock on the day you leave.

5 PRONUNCIATION
Consonant clusters

a 12.16 Listen to these sentences. Notice how the consonant clusters with /t/ in **bold** are pronounced.

1 I've got a reservation for a double room for two ni**ghts**.
2 So, tha**t's** two ni**ghts**?
3 Is breakfa**st** included?
4 **It's** from 6:30 am until 9:30 am.

b 12.17 Listen to these sentences below. Underline consonant clusters with /t/.

1 We're away next weekend.
2 I'd like some tourist information.
3 The kitchen is on your left.
4 Can I buy two tickets, please?

c In pairs, practise conversations like the one in 4c. Use your own name and change some of the questions about things in the hotel. Take turns being the receptionist and guest.

6 LISTENING

a 12.18 Watch or listen to Part 3. Complete the information on city bus tours.

Bath City
BUS TOURS

Leaves from [1]__________
Price [2]__________
Buy tickets at [3]__________
Pay by cash or [4]__________

b After the bus tour Annie goes to a museum. What do you think happens next?

c 12.19 Watch or listen to Part 4 and check your answer to 6b. Then answer the questions.

1 Did Dan and Martina tell Annie their plan?
2 Why do you think they did / didn't?

7 USEFUL LANGUAGE
Asking for tourist information

a 12.20 Match 1–5 with a–e to complete the questions. Listen and check your answers.

1 Can you	a for a ticket?
2 Is there a city bus tour	b a ticket, please.
3 How much is it	c help me?
4 Can I buy	d I can go on?
5 I'll have	e a ticket here?

b You are on holiday and go to a Tourist Information Office to ask about an interesting museum to visit. Answer the questions.

1 Can you use all the questions in 7a?
2 Which one(s) do you have to change?
3 Write a new question for the example(s) you need to change.

c Work in pairs. Use your answers in 7b to make a conversation at the Tourist Information Office about visiting a museum. Take turns being the tourist and an assistant who works in the office.

8 SPEAKING

a **Communication 12C** Student A: Go to p. 135. Student B: Go to p. 137.

UNIT PROGRESS TEST

CHECK YOUR PROGRESS

You can now do the Unit Progress Test.

12D SKILLS FOR WRITING
You should explore the River Douro

Learn to write an email with travel advice

W Paragraph writing

1 SPEAKING AND LISTENING

a How much do you plan your holidays before you leave? Choose an answer and say why.

1 I like to plan everything as much as possible so I know what I'm going to do.
2 I plan my travel and accommodation, but nothing else.
3 I only buy tickets. I organise everything else when I arrive.

b Look at the pictures of places in Porto and answer the questions.

1 What do you know about Porto and Portugal?
2 What can you see in the pictures?

c 12.21 Fred tells Louise about a holiday he's planned. Listen and underline the correct answers.

1 Fred booked his holiday *online* / *at a travel agency*.
2 He's going to go to Porto for a *weekend* / *week*.
3 He's going to stay in a *hostel* / *hotel*.
4 He's going to go at the end of *this* / *next* month.
5 *Louise* / *Fred* has a friend named Fabiana in Porto.

d You want to visit Porto. What questions could you ask Fabiana?

What should I see in Porto?

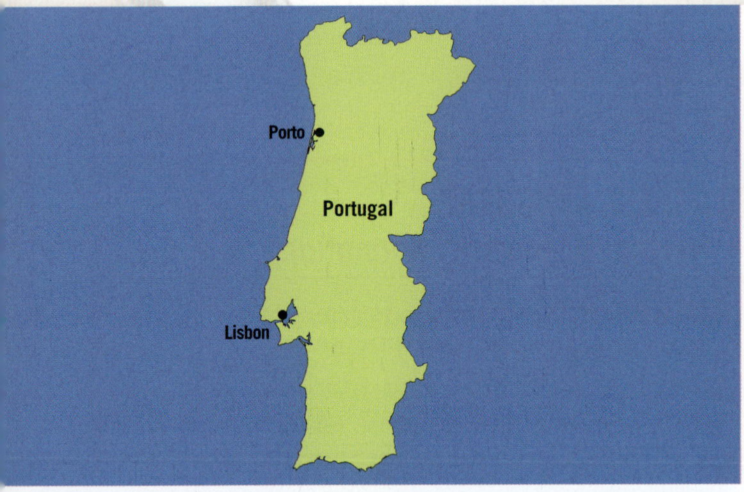

2 READING

a Fred sent Fabiana an email. Read Fabiana's reply. What *doesn't* she talk about?

a places to visit b the hostel c the weather

Re: Porto

Hi, Fred,

[1]Thanks for your email. [2]I'm really happy to help you plan your holiday in Porto. [3]I've been here for two years now, and I just love it. [4]I'm sure you're going to have a great time here. [5]You asked me about the three top tourist things to do in Porto, so here are some ideas. [6]First, you should visit my favourite part of the city: Aliados & Bolhão. [7]It's a mix of cool shops, amazing buildings and cafés. You can visit the Lello bookshop – it's really popular with Harry Potter fans like you! [8]And secondly, you should explore the River Douro – there are beautiful walks on both sides. [9]Finally, the third place you should go to is the tiny village of Afurada – it's just down the river. [10]Catch a ferry and stay for an afternoon. [11]It's really lovely, with wonderful fish restaurants, and there's a lot of interesting history and culture you can learn about. [12]But you can also spend time just walking around the centre of Porto. [13]You said you were going to come at the end of next month. [14]It's autumn then and it's not too hot or too cold, so it's really nice doing things outdoors. [15]It's a city with so much to see and do – I'm sure you're going to love it! [16]I hope these ideas help you. [17]Let's meet and get a cup of coffee when you come.

Best wishes,

Fabiana

b Read Fabiana's email again and complete the table.

Place to visit	Reason to visit
Aliados & Bolhão	cool shops & [1]_____ buildings and [2]_____
River Douro	beautiful [3]_____ on both [4]_____
Afurada	interesting history and [5]_____

3 WRITING SKILLS Paragraph writing

a Read Fabiana's email again. Make four paragraphs.

Paragraph 1 answers Fred and talks about Porto in general: Sentences 1 to ___

Paragraph 2 talks about things to do: Sentences ___ to 12

Paragraph 3 talks about the weather: Sentences 13 to ___

Paragraph 4 finishes the message: Sentences ___ to ___

b Look at Paragraph 2. Underline three linking words that order the information.

c Read the email from Alice to you and answer the questions.

1 What is she going to do?
2 What does she want to know?

Hi

Hi there,

[1]My name is Alice, and I'm going to visit your home town soon. [2]A friend told me that you can give me useful information, so I have some questions if that's OK. [3]I would like to do some sightseeing. [4]What are some interesting things to see? [5]I'd also like to do some kind of sports activity. [6]What are some interesting things to do? [7]I hope you can help me!

Kind regards,

Alice

d Make three paragraphs in Alice's email in 3c.

4 WRITING

a Plan an email to Alice.

- answer both her questions
- use paragraphs for different parts of your message
- use linking words to order your ideas

b Write your email. Use Fabiana's email to help you.

c Swap emails with another student and check.

☐ Are the paragraphs clear?
☐ Are there good ideas of things to see and do?
☐ Are there linking words to order ideas?

UNIT 12
Review and extension

1 GRAMMAR

a Complete the sentences with the correct form of *be going to* and a verb from the box.

travel move wear have

1 He's 30 next week. He ____________ a big party.
2 When we're older, we ____________ to a cottage in the country.
3 I ____________ my new suit and a tie for my interview.
4 She's got two months' holiday before she starts university, so she ____________ around Europe with a friend.

b Write the conversation using the prompts with the correct form of *be going to*.

PAULINA 1What / you / do after university?
What are you going to do after university?
NATALIA 2I / go to New York.
PAULINA New York? Sounds great. 3What / you / do there?
NATALIA Well, my brother lives there.
PAULINA Oh, right. 4you / stay / with / him?
NATALIA Yes. He says 5he / find / me / a job.
PAULINA Oh, really? 6How long / you / stay?
NATALIA Just a month. But 7I not / book my flight back. Who knows? If I find a good job, I may stay longer!

c Read the travel advice to people going to Kenya in East Africa. Complete the text with *you should* or *you shouldn't*.

It's very hot in Kenya, so 1__________ stay in the sun for too long and 2__________ drink a lot of water. 3__________ buy bottled water and 4__________ drink water from lakes or rivers.

Most people speak English, but 5__________ try to learn a few words of Swahili, the local language.

2 VOCABULARY

a Underline the correct words.

1 We went to a Greek *island* / *mountain*. We just sat on the *forest* / *beach* and swam in the sea. It was very relaxing.
2 I went across the Gobi *Desert* / *Lake* on a camel.
3 I watched birds in the Brazilian *desert* / *rainforest*.
4 The Iguazu Falls are big *waterfalls* / *mountains* between Argentina and Brazil.
5 I climbed *rivers* / *mountains* in Norway and we crossed a *glacier* / *beach*. It was very cold on the ice.

b Put the words in the correct order to make questions.

1 you / abroad / lived / ever / have ?
2 you / planned / your next holiday / have ?
3 in a hotel / last / stay / you / did / when ?
4 always / you / your own bags / pack / do / for a holiday ?
5 this weekend / you / at home / are / staying ?

c Ask and answer the questions in 2b.

3 WORDPOWER *take*

a Match sentences 1–6 with pictures a–f. What do you think the people are talking about?

1 You can take the number 23.
2 Please take care!
3 It will only take five minutes.
4 Then you take the first left.
5 Let me take your suitcase for you.
6 Take one three times a day before meals.

a

b

c

d

e

f

b Match the sentences in 3a with the uses of *take* in a–f.

a to give street directions
b to talk about time
c to tell someone to be careful
d to talk about using transport
e to talk about medicine
f to talk about carrying something

12.22 Listen to the conversations and check.

c Complete the sentences with *take* and a word or phrase in the box.

a taxi the first left hours
my medicine my laptop care

1 I've got two essays to write. It will ______ to finish my homework.
2 There aren't any buses. Why don't we ______?
3 Have a lovely holiday and ______.
4 Go straight until you come to a supermarket, then ______.
5 I'll carry the bags, but could you ______?
6 Oh, it's six o'clock. Time to ______.

d Choose two of the uses of *take* in 3b. Write a short conversation using examples of both uses.

e Practise your conversations in 3d.

REVIEW YOUR PROGRESS

How well did you do in this unit? Write 3, 2 or 1 for each objective.
3 = very well 2 = well 1 = not so well

I CAN ...	
talk about holiday plans	☐
give advice about travelling	☐
use language for travel and tourism	☐
write an email with travel advice.	☐

Phonemic symbols

Vowel sounds

Short

/ə/	/æ/	/ʊ/	/ɒ/	/ɪ/	/i/	/e/	/ʌ/
breakf**a**st	m**a**n	p**u**t	g**o**t	ch**i**p	happ**y**	m**e**n	sh**u**t

Long

/ɜː/	/ɑː/	/uː/	/ɔː/	/iː/
sh**ir**t	p**ar**t	wh**o**	w**a**lk	ch**ea**p

Diphthongs (two vowel sounds)

/eə/	/ɪə/	/ʊə/	/ɔɪ/	/aɪ/	/eɪ/	/əʊ/	/aʊ/
h**air**	n**ear**	t**our**	b**oy**	n**i**ne	**ei**ght	wind**ow**	n**ow**

Consonants

/p/	/b/	/f/	/v/	/t/	/d/	/k/	/g/
picnic	**b**ook	**f**ace	**v**ery	**t**ime	**d**og	**c**old	**g**o
/θ/	/ð/	/tʃ/	/dʒ/	/s/	/z/	/ʃ/	/ʒ/
think	**th**e	**ch**air	**j**ob	**s**ea	**z**oo	**sh**oe	televi**s**ion
/m/	/n/	/ŋ/	/h/	/l/	/r/	/w/	/j/
me	**n**ow	si**ng**	**h**ot	**l**ate	**r**ed	**w**ent	**y**es

Irregular verbs

Infinitive	Past simple	Past participle
be	was / were	been
become	became	become
begin	began	begun
break	broke	broken
bring	brought	brought
buy	bought	bought
catch	caught	caught
choose	chose	chosen
come	came	come
cost	cost	cost
cut	cut	cut
do	did	done
drink	drank	drunk
drive	drove	driven
eat	ate	eaten
fall	fell	fallen
feel	felt	felt
find	found	found
fly	flew	flown
forget	forgot	forgotten
get	got	got
give	gave	given
go	went	gone
grow	grew	grown
have	had	had
hear	heard	heard
hold	held	held
know	knew	known
learn	learned / learnt	learned / learnt
leave	left	left

Infinitive	Past simple	Past participle
lose	lost	lost
make	made	made
meet	met	met
pay	paid	paid
put	put	put
read	read	read
ride	rode	ridden
ring	rang	rung
run	ran	run
say	said	said
see	saw	seen
sell	sold	sold
send	sent	sent
sing	sang	sung
sit	sat	sat
sleep	slept	slept
speak	spoke	spoken
spell	spelled / spelt	spelled / spelt
spend	spent	spent
stand	stood	stood
swim	swam	swum
take	took	taken
teach	taught	taught
tell	told	told
think	thought	thought
throw	threw	thrown
understand	understood	understood
wear	wore	worn
win	won	won
write	wrote	written

COMMUNICATION PLUS

1A STUDENT A

a Read this social media profile. Answer Student B's questions about Robert.

Hi! My name's Robert. I'm from Nice. It's a lovely city by the sea in the south of France. I'm a student at Manchester University in the UK.

b Ask Student B your questions. Write their answers.

1 What's her name? ___Lora___
2 What's her nationality? ________
3 What's her home town? ________
4 Where is she now? ________

c Now go back to p. 11.

2A STUDENT A

a Read about the job. Complete the sentences with the correct forms of the verbs.

Shop assistant
1 She ______ (start) work at 8:00 am.
2 She ______ (not work) on Sunday.
3 She ______ (like) her job because she ______ (meet) people.
4 She ______ (not wear) a uniform.
5 People ______ (buy) things from her.
6 She ______ (work) in a small shop in the city centre.

b Read your sentences out loud. Student B tries to guess the job after each sentence.

c Listen to Student B's sentences and guess the job.

d Now go back to p. 21.

6C STUDENT C

a **Conversation 1.** Read your first card. Then listen to Student B and reply.

1
- You return home. Student B has a message for you from Student A.
- Call Student A back. Have a conversation.

b **Conversation 2.** Now look at your second card. Start the conversation with Student B.

2
- Student B calls and you answer the phone.
- He/She wants to speak to Student A, who isn't there. Take a message.
- Student A returns. Give him/her Student B's message.

c **Conversation 3.** Now look at your third card. Think about what you want to say. Then call Student B.

3
- Think of a reason to call Student B.
- You call Student B, but he/she isn't there. Leave a message with Student A.
- Student B calls you back. Have a conversation.

4A STUDENT A

a **Conversation 1.** Look at the picture. Answer Student B's questions about what's on your stall. Look at the examples.

Have you got any apples on your stall?

I'd like some cheese, please.

Yes, I have.

I'm sorry, I haven't got any cheese.

b **Conversation 2.** You want to buy food to cook dinner. You visit Student B's market stall. Ask about the things in the box. Look at the examples.

lamb eggs one lemon fruit tomatoes mushrooms cheese pears vegetables bread one onion apples

Have you got any eggs on your stall?

I'd like some mushrooms, please.

2C STUDENT A

a **Conversation 1.** Read your first card. Think about what you want to say. Then start the conversation with Student B.

1
You're at Student B's home for the weekend. You'd like to do the following things:
- have something to eat
- use your friend's computer
- watch TV

b **Conversation 2.** Now look at your second card. Listen to Student B and reply.

2
Student B's at your home for the weekend. You're good friends, but you don't like it when other people use your things, especially your new phone.

5A STUDENT A

a Look at your picture. Student B has a similar picture. Ask and answer questions to find six differences.

Is there a park in your picture?

Yes, there is. / No, there isn't.

b Now go back to p. 51.

1C STUDENT A

a **Conversation 1.** Read your first card. Think about what you want to say. Then start the conversation with Student B.

> ① You want to ask about beginner guitar lessons. Talk to the receptionist at the music school.
> - Say what you would like to do.
> - Ask when the first lesson is.
> - Ask where the lesson is.
> - Sign up for lessons.

b **Conversation 2.** Now look at your second card. Listen to Student B and reply.

> ② You're a receptionist in a language school. Here's some information about an English course:
> - *Time*: 6:20 pm next Tuesday
> - *Place*: Room 12
> - To sign a student up, you need the student's name.

6C STUDENT A

a **Conversation 1.** Read your first card. Think about what you want to say. Then call Student C.

> ①
> - Think of a reason to call Student C.
> - You call Student C but he/she isn't there. Leave a message with Student B.
> - Student C calls you back. Have a conversation.

b **Conversation 2.** Now look at your second card. Listen to Student C and reply.

> ②
> - You return home. Student C has a message for you from Student B.
> - Call Student B back. Have a conversation.

c **Conversation 3.** Now look at your third card. Start the conversation with Student C.

> ③
> - Student C calls and you answer the phone.
> - He/She wants to speak to Student B, who isn't there. Take a message.
> - Student B returns. Give him/her Student C's message.

4B SPEAKING 5c

Healthy food

Every day you can eat these food quantities:

bread – 4 pieces	rice or pasta – 2 cups
vegetables – 5 pieces	fruit – 2 pieces
cheese – 2 pieces	meat/fish – 1 piece

5C STUDENT A

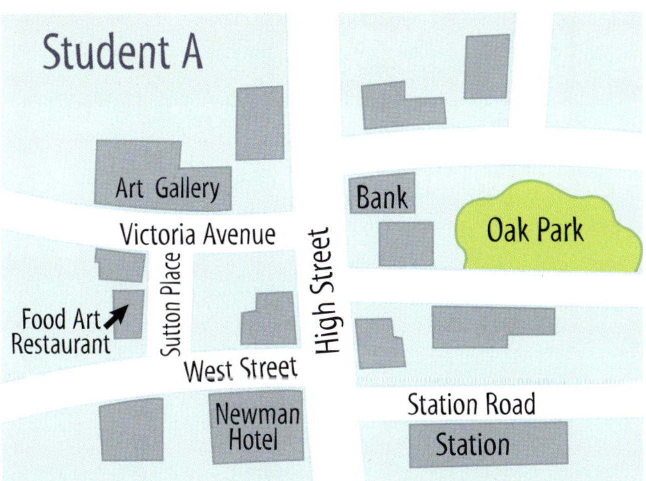

a **Conversation 1.** Read your first card. Think about what you want to say. Then start the conversation with Student B.

> ① You're at the station with your friend, Student B. The map on your phone isn't clear. You need to go to:
> - the supermarket
> - Dash Café
>
> Student B's map is clear. Ask him/her how to get to these places. Someone told you Dash Café is in James Street, but you're not sure.

b **Conversation 2.** Now look at your second card. Think about what you want to say. Then listen to Student B and reply.

> ② You're at the station with your friend, Student B. The map on his/her phone isn't clear. You want to go to:
> - the art gallery
> - Food Art Restaurant
>
> Use your map to tell Student B how to get there. A lot of people think that Food Art Restaurant is on the corner of Sutton Place and West Street, but that isn't correct.

5C STUDENT B

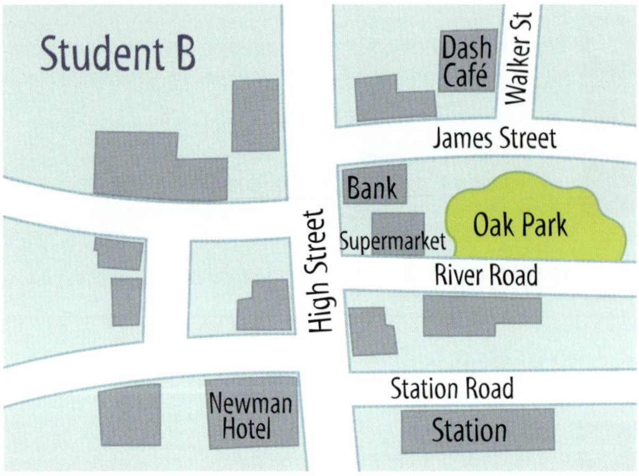

a **Conversation 1.** Read your first card. Think about what you want to say. Then listen to Student A and reply.

1
You're at the station with your friend, Student A. The map on his/her phone isn't clear. You need to go to:
- the supermarket
- Dash Café

Use your map to tell Student A how to get there. A lot of people think that Dash Café is in James Street, but that isn't correct.

b **Conversation 2.** Now look at your second card. Think about what you want to say. Then start the conversation with Student A.

2
You're at the station with your friend, Student A. The map on your phone isn't clear. You want to go to:
- the art gallery
- Food Art Restaurant

Student A's map is clear. Ask him/her how to get to these places. Someone told you that Food Art Restaurant is on the corner of Sutton Place and West Street, but you're not sure.

6C STUDENT B

a **Conversation 1.** Read your first card. Start the conversation with Student A.

1
- Student A calls and you answer the phone.
- He/She wants to speak to Student C, who isn't there. Take a message.
- Student C returns. Give him/her Student A's message.

b **Conversation 2.** Now look at your second card. Think about what you want to say. Then call Student A.

2
- Think of a reason to call Student A.
- You call Student A, but he/she isn't there. Leave a message with Student C.
- Student A calls you back. Have a conversation.

c **Conversation 3.** Now look at your third card. Listen to Student A and reply.

3
- You return home. Student A has a message for you from Student C.
- Call Student C back. Have a conversation.

3C STUDENT B

a **Conversation 1.** Read your first card. Listen to Student A and reply.

1
You aren't free this Saturday because you work at the weekends. You'd like to go out to the cinema on Friday.

b **Conversation 2.** Now look at your second card. Think about what you want to say. Then start the conversation with Student A.

2
You want to meet Student A for coffee. You think next Friday after work/school is a good time. Decide the following and invite Student A:
- where to have coffee
- what time
- something to do after

c ≫ Now go back to 5c on p. 35.

5A STUDENT B

a Look at your picture. Student A has a similar picture. Ask and answer questions to find six differences.

b ≫ Now go back to p. 51.

1A STUDENT B

a Read this social media profile. Answer Student A's questions about Lora.

> Hi, my name's Lora. I'm from Berlin, Germany, but now I'm in England with my family. I'm a teacher in London.

b Ask Student A your questions. Write their answers.

1 What's his name? ___Robert___
2 What's his nationality? ________________
3 What's his home town? ________________
4 Where is he now? ________________

c Now go back to p. 11.

2A STUDENT B

a Read about the job. Complete the sentences with the correct forms of the verbs.

Nurse
1 He sometimes ________ (work) at night.
2 He ________ (not make) a lot of money.
3 He ________ (wear) a uniform at work.
4 He ________ (like) his job because he ________ (help) people.
5 He ________ (give) people medicine.
6 He ________ (work) in a big hospital in the city centre.

b Listen to Student A's sentences and guess the job.

c Read your sentences out loud. Student A tries to guess the job after each sentence.

d Now go back to p. 21.

1C STUDENT B

a **Conversation 1.** Read your first card. Think about what you want to say. Listen to Student A and reply.

1 You're a receptionist at a music school. Here is some information about beginner guitar lessons:
- *Time*: 6:30 pm next Thursday
- *Place*: Room 2
- To sign a student up, you need the student's full name.

b **Conversation 2.** Now look at your second card. Think about what you want to say. Then start the conversation with Student A.

2 You want to ask about English classes. Talk to the receptionist at the language school.
- Say what you would like to do.
- Ask when the first class is.
- Ask where the class is.
- Sign up for the class.

4A STUDENT B

a **Conversation 1.** You want to buy food to cook dinner. You visit Student A's market stall. Ask about the things in the box. Look at the examples.

steak one lemon beans fruit tomatoes mushrooms cheese pears vegetables bread one onion apples

Have you got any apples on your stall?

I'd like some pears, please.

b **Conversation 2.** Look at the picture. Answer Student A's questions about what's on your stall. Look at the examples.

Have you got any eggs on your stall?

Yes, I do.

I'd like some mushrooms, please.

I'm sorry, I haven't got any mushrooms.

2C STUDENT B

a **Conversation 1.** Read your first card. Think about what you want to say. Listen to Student A and reply.

1 Student A's at your home for the weekend. You're good friends, but you don't like it when other people use your things, especially your computer.

b **Conversation 2.** Now look at your second card. Think about what you want to say. Then start the conversation with Student A.

2 You're at Student A's home for the weekend. You'd like to do the following things:
- have something to drink
- use your friend's phone
- have a shower

9A STUDENT A

a Look at your picture for two minutes. What are the people doing? Make notes.

b Student B has a similar picture. Ask and answer questions to find five differences.

11C STUDENT A

a **Conversation 1.** Read your first card. Think about what you want to say. Then listen to Student B and reply about the concert.

1 You went with Student B to a concert last night. You thought the band were really good. You like their music and you thought the singer was good.

b **Conversation 2.** Now look at your second card. Think about what you want to say. Then start a conversation about your meal with Student B.

2 You went with Student B to *Al Dente*, an Italian restaurant, last weekend. You didn't like it. You had fish, but it wasn't very good and it was expensive. You thought the waiters were unfriendly.

10A STUDENT A

a Ask Student B about his/her smartphone. You can use these questions:

How long is your smartphone?
How wide is your smartphone?
How big is the screen?
How much does it weigh?

b Look at the picture of your new smartphone. Compare your phone with Student B's.

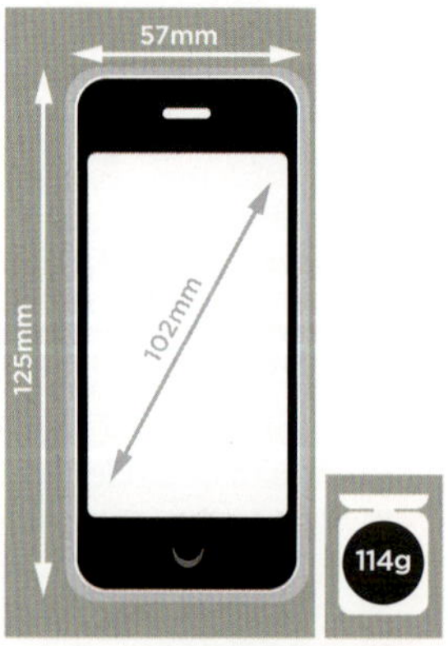

c Now go back to p. 101.

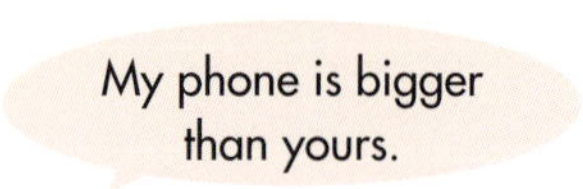

8C STUDENT B

a **Conversation 1.** Read your first card. Think about what you want to say. Then listen to Student A and reply.

1 You're not feeling very well. You're very tired and your back hurts. You haven't got a temperature. When Student A asks you, tell him/her what's the matter.

b **Conversation 2.** Now look at your second card. Think about what you want to say. Then start the conversation with Student A.

2 Student A doesn't look well. Ask him/her what's the matter. When he/she tells you, show sympathy using expressions like *Oh dear!* or *Poor you.*
Then ask if he/she feels hungry. Tell him/her what to do, e.g. *See a doctor. Take some medicine. Have some soup.*

12A STUDENT A

a You're going to go on a working holiday. Look at your plans.

< Notes 28 Nov 15:46

WHERE: Australia and Pacific islands

WHY: see beautiful beaches, visit the desert in Australia

HOW LONG: three months

POSSIBLE JOBS: hotels and restaurants

BEFORE TRIP: look online for jobs

AFTER TRIP: study at university

b Student B is planning his/her own working holiday. Write questions you can ask him/her about the trip. Use 4f on p. 121 to help you.

c Have a conversation with Student B about his/her holiday.

d Listen to Student B's questions about your holiday and reply.

e »» Now go back to p. 121.

12C STUDENT A

a **Conversation 1.** Read your first card. Think about what you want to say. Then start the conversation with Student B.

1 You're a guest at a hotel. You've got a reservation for a double room for two nights. Check with the receptionist about:

- the breakfast time
- wi-fi in the room

Ask about this tourist information:

- interesting local markets near the hotel

b **Conversation 2.** Now look at your second card. Then listen to Student B and reply.

2 You're a hotel receptionist. Check the guest's name and let him/her know they have a reservation. Here is other information you need:

- checkout: 10:30 am
- safe in the room
- free box of chocolates in the room

Some important tourist information about Central Park:

- on the same street as the hotel
- only half a kilometre away from the hotel
- large and beautiful park

10C STUDENT B

a **Conversation 1.** Read your first card. Think about what you want to say. Then listen to Student A and reply.

1. Student A bought a new phone, but he/she can't receive any text messages on it. When he/she asks for help, explain how it works. Here are the instructions:
   - Touch the box that says *Messages*.
   - Wait for a blue screen.
   - Touch the box that says *Receive*. It can receive messages now.

b **Conversation 2.** Now look at your second card. Think about what you want to say. Then start the conversation with Student A.

2. You bought a new mouse for your computer, but it isn't working. Ask Student A for help. Check the instructions he/she gives you.

11C STUDENT B

a **Conversation 1.** Read your first card. Think about what you want to say. Start a conversation about the concert with Student A.

1. You went with Student A to a concert last night. You didn't like the band very much. You thought they played badly and the music was boring.

b **Conversation 2.** Now look at your second card. Think about what you want to say. Then listen to Student A and reply about your meal.

2. You went with Student A to *Al Dente*, an Italian restaurant, last weekend. You liked it. You had a very good pizza and you thought the food was delicious and not too expensive.

9A STUDENT B

a Look at your picture for two minutes. What are the people doing? Make notes.

b Student A has a similar picture. Ask and answer questions to find five differences.

Is Ken eating a sandwich in your picture?

Yes, he is. / No, he isn't. He's …

10A STUDENT B

a Ask Student A about his/her smartphone. You can use these questions:

How long is your smartphone?
How wide is your smartphone?
How big is the screen?
How much does it weigh?

b Look at the picture of your new smartphone. Compare your phone with Student A's.

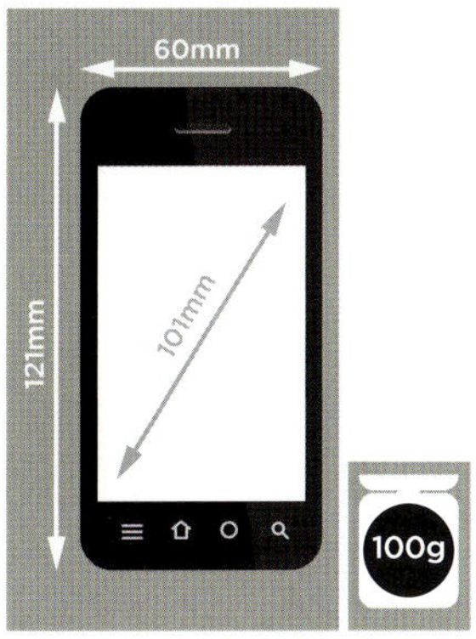

c Now go back to p. 101.

My screen is wider than yours.

12A STUDENT B

a You're going to go on a working holiday. Look at your plans.

< Notes 18 Dec 15:46

WHERE: Central America
WHY: see rainforests, old Maya and Aztec buildings
HOW LONG: four months
POSSIBLE JOBS: looking after children, tour guide
BEFORE TRIP: send emails to friends
AFTER TRIP: find a new job

b Student A is planning his/her own working holiday. Write questions you can ask him/her about the trip. Use 4f on p. 121 to help you.

c Listen to Student A's questions about your holiday and reply.

d Have a conversation with Student A about his/her holiday.

e Now go back to p. 121.

12C STUDENT B

a **Conversation 1.** Read your first card. Then listen to Student A and reply.

1 You're a hotel receptionist. Check the guest's name and let him/her know they have a reservation. Here is other information you need:

- breakfast 7–9:30 am
- free wi-fi in the room
- free dinner at the hotel tomorrow night

Some important tourist information about a local market:

- in a car park opposite the hotel
- biggest market in town
- clothes, paintings, old furniture

b **Conversation 2.** Now look at your second card. Think about what you want to say. Then start the conversation with Student A.

2 You're a guest at a hotel. You've got a reservation for a single room for three nights. Check with the receptionist about:

- checkout time
- safe in the room

Ask about this tourist information:

- nice parks and gardens to visit near the hotel

1A *be*: positive and negative

01.07

Positive (+)	
Full form	**Contraction**
*I **am** a student.*	*I**'m** a student.*
*You **are** a good cook.*	*You**'re** a good cook.*
*He **is** my friend.*	*He**'s** my friend.*
*She **is** Spanish.*	*She**'s** Spanish.*
*It **is** sunny.*	*It**'s** sunny.*
*We **are** sisters.*	*We**'re** sisters.*
*They **are** from Japan.*	*They**'re** from Japan.*

Negative (-)	
Full form	**Contraction**
*I **am not** a student.*	*I**'m not** a student.*
*You **are not** a good cook.*	*You **aren't** a good cook.*
*He **is not** my friend.*	*He **isn't** my friend.*
*She **is not** Spanish.*	*She **isn't** Spanish.*
*It **is not** sunny.*	*It **isn't** sunny.*
*We **are not** sisters.*	*We **aren't** sisters.*
*They **are not** from Japan.*	*They **aren't** from Japan.*

Remember to use the verb *be* to give information with a noun, adjective, preposition or adverb.
*My name**'s Hamid**.* (NOT ~~*My name **Hamid***~~.)
*My teacher **is nice**.* (NOT ~~*My teacher **nice***~~.)
*I**'m from China**.* (NOT ~~*I **from China***~~.)
*We **are here**.* (NOT ~~*We **here***~~.)
Always use a noun or a pronoun before positive and negative *be*:
He's** my teacher.* (NOT ~~Is** my teacher*~~.)
They're** Spanish.* (NOT ~~Are** Spanish*~~.)

Tip
you is the same when we talk to one person or two or more people.
***You're a** good **cook**.* = one person
***You're** good **cooks**.* = two or more people

We use contractions to help us speak quickly. In contractions, the apostrophe (') shows a letter is missing:
*You **are not** old.* → *You **aren't** old.*
There are two different contractions for *is not* and *are not*.
is not → *isn't* / *'s not* — *He **isn't*** = *He**'s not***
are not → *aren't* / *'re not* — *We **aren't*** = *We**'re not***

Tip
We can use *'s* after one name, but we don't use *'re* after two names:
***Tom is** my friend.* → ***Tom's** my friend.*
Tom and Jo are** my friends.* (NOT *Tom and* ~~Jo're***~~ *my friends.*)

1B *be*: questions and short answers

In questions with the verb *be*, we change the word order:
***They are** Turkish.* → ***Are they** Turkish?*
***Our teacher is** from Rome.* → ***Is our teacher** from Rome?*

01.14

	***Yes/No* questions**		**Short answers**	
I	***Am** I*	*late?*	*Yes,* *No,*	*I **am**.* *I**'m not**.*
you / we / they	***Are** you*	*ready?*	*Yes,* *No,*	*you **are**.* *you **aren't**.*
he / she / it	***Is** it*	*cold?*	*Yes,* *No,*	*it **is**.* *it **isn't**.*

In *Wh-* questions, we use a question word before *be*.
***Where are** you from?*
***What is** your name?*

Tip
With positive short answers, we don't use contractions:
*Yes, I **am**. Yes, he **is**. Yes, we **are**.*
(NOT ~~*Yes, I'm. Yes, he's. Yes, we're.*~~)

Tip
We can use the contraction of *is* with question words:
***What is** your name?* → ***What's** your name?*
***Where is** he from?* → ***Where's** he from?*

1A *be*: positive and negative

a Write the correct form of *be* (*am*/*is*/*are*) in these sentences.

1 We ___are___ very happy.
2 My father ________ a taxi driver.
3 My parents ________ not old.
4 Carl and Michael ________ brothers.
5 I ________ not a good driver.
6 She ________ at work today.
7 Cambridge ________ not a big city.
8 Our cats ________ hungry.

b Write the sentence again with positive and negative contractions. More than one negative contraction may be possible.

1 She is Brazilian.
___She's Brazilian.___
___She isn't Brazilian.___
2 It is a beautiful city.
____
____
3 We are from Ankara.
____
____
4 They are at a party.
____
____
5 I am tired.
____
____
6 You are right.
____
____

c Complete the sentences with the correct positive (+) or negative (–) form of *be*. Use contractions if possible.

1 We ___'re___ (+) at a concert.
2 She ___isn't___ (–) Japanese.
3 I ________ (+) from Mexico City.
4 He ________ (–) at home.
5 It ________ (+) a big hotel.
6 Lena and Thomas ________ (–) friends.
7 My city ________ (+) very beautiful.
8 Hi, my name ________ (+) Michael.
9 My parents ________ (–) at the match.
10 You ________ (+) very nice.

d Write the correct sentences.

1 ~~Spanish~~ → French
She's Spanish. ___She isn't Spanish. She's French.___
2 ~~a doctor~~ → a student
He's a doctor. ________
3 ~~brothers~~ → friends
They're my brothers. ________
4 ~~London~~ → Bangkok
We're from London. ________
5 ~~good cook~~ → very bad cook
I'm a good cook. ________

e Now go back to p. 11.

1B *be*: questions and short answers

a Put the words in the correct order to make questions.

1 her / what / name / 's ? ___What's her name?___
2 from / are / you / where ? ________
3 American / are / you ? ________
4 she / popular / is ? ________
5 names / are / what / your ? ________
6 friends / you / are ? ________
7 is / cold / it / very ? ________
8 from / he / is / France ? ________

b Match questions 1–7 with short answers a–g.

1 [d] Is she Italian?
2 [ ] Are you teachers?
3 [ ] Are Robert and Helen here today?
4 [ ] Is it a beautiful city?
5 [ ] Am I late?
6 [ ] Is he on holiday?
7 [ ] Are you from England?

a No, he isn't.
b No, they aren't.
c No, you aren't.
d Yes, she is.
e No, I'm not.
f Yes, we are.
g Yes, it is.

c Complete the conversations with the correct form of *be*. Use contractions if possible.

1 **A** Hi, I ___'m___ Manuel.
B Hi, Manuel. Where ______ you from?
A I ______ from Lima, Peru.

2 **A** See that footballer? What ______ his name?
B He ______ Timo Werner.
A Where ______ he from?
B He ______ from Germany.

3 **A** Excuse me, where ______ you from?
B We ______ from Japan. We ______ here for the World Cup.

4 **A** Hi, my name ______ Alice, and this ______ my sister, Marta.
B Hi, Alice. Hi, Marta. ______ you from England?
A No, we ______. We ______ American. We ______ from New York.
B Oh really? My cousins ______ from New York.

d Now go back to p. 13.

2A Present simple: positive and negative

We use the present simple to talk about things that are generally true in daily life:

- habits and routines
  *I **drive** to work every morning.* *My sister **doesn't eat** breakfast.*
- facts and feelings
  *They **have** a fast car.* *The children **don't like** coffee.*

02.04

	+		–	
I / you / we / they	*I*	***work**.*	*We **don't***	***work**.*
he / she / it	*She*	***works**.*	*It **doesn't***	***work**.*

SPELLING: verb + *-s*

most verbs → add *-s*	*start → start**s*** *work → work**s*** *play → play**s***
verb ends in consonant + *-y* → change *-y* to *-i* then add *-es*	*tr**y** → tr**ies*** *stud**y** → stud**ies***
verb ends in *-sh*, *-ch*, *-x*, *-ss* → add *-es*	*wa**sh** → wash**es*** *cat**ch** → catch**es***

Tip
Don't add *-s* to the verb in negative sentences:
*He doesn't **work** hard.* (NOT ~~*He doesn't **works** hard.*~~)

2B Present simple: questions and short answers

02.11

	***Yes/No* questions**		**Short answers**	
I / you / we / they	***Do** you*	***study**?*	*Yes,* *No,*	*I **do**.* *I **don't**.*
he / she / it	***Does** she*	***work**?*	*Yes,* *No,*	*she **does**.* *she **doesn't**.*

	***Wh-* questions**		
I / you / we / they	*Where*	*do you*	***work**?*
he / she / it	*Where*	*does she*	***work**?*

Tip
Don't add *-s* to the verb in questions:
*Does he **work** hard?* (NOT ~~*Does he **works** hard?*~~)

2A Present simple: positive and negative

a Write the -*s* form of each verb.

1 fly ___flies___
2 finish ______
3 relax ______
4 buy ______
5 want ______
6 miss ______
7 say ______
8 teach ______
9 worry ______
10 watch ______

b Complete the sentences with the correct present simple form of the verbs in brackets. The verbs are all positive.

1 I ___work___ (work) in an office. I ______ (start) work at 9 o'clock.
2 Lisa ______ (finish) school at 5 o'clock every day. She ______ (do) her homework on the bus.
3 Phil ______ (go) to work by train. The train ______ (leave) at 8:35 am.
4 Marta ______ (watch) TV in the evening. She ______ (try) to go to bed before 11:00 pm.
5 My parents ______ (get) up very early. My father ______ (make) their breakfast.
6 My brother ______ (have) a fast car. He ______ (love) it.
7 We ______ (study) English after work. We ______ (enjoy) our classes.

c Complete the sentences with the correct present simple form of the verbs in brackets.

1 Allan ___doesn't like___ (not like) his job.
2 My parents ______ (not drive) fast.
3 I ______ (not cook) at home.
4 She ______ (not have) a car.
5 We ______ (not worry) about work.
6 The bus ______ (not go) to my house.
7 You ______ (not do) the housework.

d Correct one mistake in each sentence.

1 I ~~studies~~ every evening. ___study___
2 Eva don't work in a hospital. ______
3 My brother gos to university. ______
4 Tom haves a very big house. ______
5 We no like this book. ______
6 I am love animals. ______

e »» Now go back to p. 21.

2B Present simple: questions and short answers

a Put the words in order to complete the questions.

1 like / she / does
___Does she like___ this class?
2 you / do / go
______ shopping at weekends?
3 want / does / he
______ a new computer?
4 where / you / play / do
______ football?
5 they / what / do / wear
______ to school?
6 they / lunch / what time / do / have
______?

b Complete the sentences with *do*, *does*, *don't* or *doesn't*.

1 What ___do___ you do in your free time?
2 ______ Anne study hard for exams?
3 Yes, she ______. She studies very hard.
4 ______ students at your school have a lot of exams?
5 No, they ______. They just have one big exam at the end of the year.
6 Where ______ you study?
7 ______ Patrick listen to music while he studies?
8 No, he ______. He prefers to study quietly.

c Use the words in brackets to write complete present simple questions.

1 **A** Where ___do you live___? (you / live)
B I live in Adelaide.
2 **A** What ______? (she / study)
B French and Italian.
3 **A** What time ______? (the shop / open)
B At 10:00 am.
4 **A** What ______ for lunch? (you / want)
B I want a sandwich.
5 **A** Where ______? (the bus / go)
B The bus goes to the city centre.
6 **A** How many times a week ______? (you / go to the gym)
B We go to the gym every day.
7 **A** How many hours a day ______? (they / work)
B They work seven hours a day.

d »» Now go back to p. 23.

3A Position of adverbs of frequency

We often use adverbs of frequency with the present simple. Adverbs of frequency tell us how often something happens.

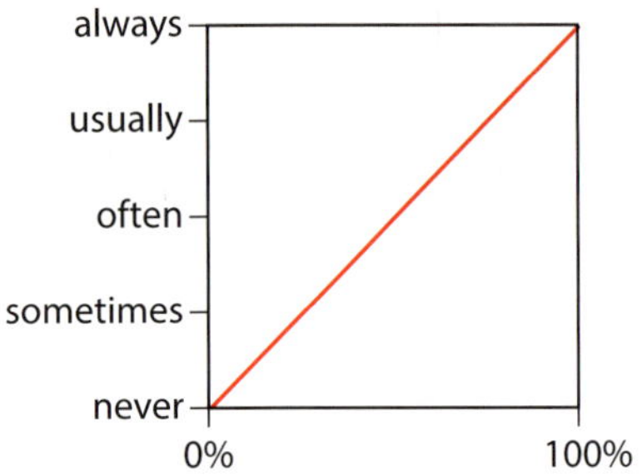

Adverbs of frequency go <u>after</u> the verb *be*.
*I'm **never** late.*
*She **isn't always** happy.*
***Are** they **usually** at home?*

Adverbs of frequency usually go <u>before</u> other main verbs.
*I **always arrive** at 8:45 am.*
*I **never** call my friends. I **always** text them.*

In negatives, the adverbs go <u>between</u> *don't/doesn't* and the main verb.
*I **don't usually get** up early.*

Sometimes, usually and *often* can go before the verb or at the beginning or end of a sentence.
***Sometimes** we go dancing on Saturdays.*
*My brother cooks for me **often**.*

We can ask questions with *How often*:
***How often** do you come here?*
***How often** is the bus late?*

03.01

Statements with the verb *be*
*I'm **sometimes** late for work.*
*I'm **always** tired.*
Statements with other verbs
*I **often play** tennis in the morning.*
*I **usually go** shopping in the afternoon.*
*I **never do** any sport in the evening.*

Questions
***How often** do you go to the cinema?*
*When do you **usually** see your friends?*

I **often play** tennis in the morning.

I **usually go** shopping in the afternoon.

I **never do** any sport in the evening. I'**m always** tired.

3B *have got*

03.13

have got means *have*.
*I'**ve got** a new phone. = I have a new phone.*
*It **hasn't got** a camera. = It doesn't have a camera.*

We can use *have got* to talk about possessions, appearance and work:
*We **haven't got** a big house.*
*I'**ve got** blue eyes.*
*He'**s got** a lot of homework this week.*

We don't use ***have got*** for actions:
*I **have** a shower before work.*
NOT ~~*I **have got** a shower before work.*~~
*I always **have** breakfast with my family.*
NOT ~~*I always **have got** breakfast with my family.*~~

	+		–	
I / you / we / they have got	*I've*	***got** a car.*	*They **haven't***	***got** a car.*
he / she / it has got	*She's*	***got** a car.*	*He **hasn't***	***got** a car.*

Tip
The full form of *'ve* is *have*.
The full form of *'s* is *has*.

	Yes/No questions		Short answers	
I / you / we / they have got	***Have** you*	***got** a car?*	*Yes,* *No,*	*I **have**.* *I **haven't**.*
he / she / it has got	***Has** she*	***got** a car?*	*Yes,* *No,*	*she **has**.* *she **hasn't**.*

3A Position of adverbs of frequency

a Put the adverbs in brackets in the correct places in each sentence. Use them in the order given.

1 I ^never^ miss a visit to my parents at weekends – I go and see them. (~~never~~, always)

2 I'm late for work, but my boss gets angry. (sometimes, never)

3 He comes here for coffee at 10 o'clock – he's late. (usually, never)

4 We have lunch together and talk. It's good to see him. (often, always)

5 They're away on holiday – they're at home. (never, always)

b Write sentences using the information in the table and adverbs of frequency. always = ✓✓✓✓✓, never = ✗✗✗✗✗

	Monday	Tuesday	Wednesday	Thursday	Friday
Paul / have breakfast	✓	✓	✗	✓	✓
My parents / eat in a restaurant	✗	✓	✓	✗	✗
I / play tennis	✓	✗	✓	✗	✓
Natasha / late for work	✗	✗	✗	✗	✗
We / watch TV in the evening	✓	✓	✓	✓	✓

1 *Paul usually has breakfast.*
2 ______
3 ______
4 ______
5 ______

c Put the words in the correct order to make questions.

1 often / how / cinema / do / you / to / go / the ?
How often do you go to the cinema?
2 to work / do / walk / you / usually ?
______
3 always / are / tired / you / why ?
______
4 you / where / usually / at weekends / go / do ?
______
5 football / do / how / they / play / often ?
______
6 often / is / late / for work / he ?
______
7 me / you / never / do / write / to / why ?
______

d Now go back to p. 30.

3B *have got*

a Correct one mistake in each sentence.

1 Have she got a laptop?
Has she got a laptop?
2 Do you have got 4G on your phone?
______
3 We not got a car.
______
4 They got a TV but they haven't got a tablet.
______
5 My brother haven't got a digital camera.
______
6 My parents haven't a printer.
______

b Use the words to write questions and short answers.

1 you / a fast car
Have you got a fast car? No, I haven't.
2 your grandparents / a digital camera
______ Yes, ______
3 your mum / a smartwatch
______ No, ______
4 your teacher / blue eyes
______ No, he ______
5 your dad / a satnav
______ Yes, ______
6 you / a lot of homework
______ No, ______

c Complete the conversations with the correct form of *have got*. Use the words in brackets to help you.

TOM [1] *Have you got* (you) a laptop?
EMILY No, we [2] ______ . But we [3] ______ a tablet.
TOM Oh cool! We [4] ______ a tablet, but I really want one.
EMILY Yes, it's great. It [5] ______ the Internet, a digital camera, everything.
TOM [6] ______ (you) lots of good games on your computer?
EMILY Yes, we [7] ______ . But I never play games. My brother plays games all the time. He [8] ______ lots of video games.

LEO What car [9] ______ (your parents)?
ROB They [10] ______ (not) a car. They don't need a car. My mum [11] ______ a bike – she rides to work every day.
LEO What about your dad? [12] ______ (he) a bike?
ROB No, he [13] ______ . He travels by bus.

d Now go back to p. 33.

4A Countable and uncountable nouns: *a / an, some / any*

Countable and uncountable nouns

We can count some things (e.g. *one lemon, eight grapes*). These things (e.g. *lemon, grape*) are **countable** nouns. They can be singular (e.g. *lemon*) or plural (e.g. *lemons*).

We can't count some things (e.g. *cheese* NOT ~~*one cheese*~~; *pasta* NOT ~~*two pastas*~~). These things (e.g. *cheese, pasta*) are **uncountable** nouns. They can only be singular (e.g. *cheese*), not plural (~~*cheeses*~~).

a / an

We use *a/an* with singular nouns. *a/an* means *one*. We can't use them with plurals or uncountable nouns.

We use *a* before a consonant sound:

***a l**emon, **a p**otato*

We use *an* before a vowel sound (*a, e, i, o, u*):

***an o**nion, **an e**gg*

some / any

We use *some/any* with plural and uncountable nouns. We use *some/any* when we do not need to say the exact amount.

We use *some* in positive sentences:

*I'd like **some** potatoes.*

We use *any* in negative sentences and questions:

*We haven't got **any** potatoes.*

*Have you got **any** potatoes?*

04.08

Countable	**singular**	**a/an** *I've got **a lemon**.* *I don't need **an onion**.*
	plural	**some/any** *We'd like **some grapes**.* *We don't want **any potatoes**.*
Uncountable		**some/any** *They've got **some pasta**.* *Do you want **any cheese**?*

These common nouns are uncountable:

money *music* *hair* *furniture* *fruit* *water* *cheese*
butter *bread* *rice* *meat* *chicken* = meat *fish* = meat

4B Quantifiers: *much, many, a lot of*

How much? / How many?

We use *How much? / How many?* to ask about quantities.

04.14

We use *How many?* with countable nouns:

***How many eggs** have we got?*

We use *How much?* with uncountable nouns:

***How much milk** have we got?*

When we ask about a price, we can just ask *How much?*

***How much** does it cost?*

Large and small quantities

04.15

	Countable	Uncountable
Large quantity	***a lot of*** *I buy **a lot of grapes**.*	***a lot of*** *I cook **a lot of pasta**.*
Medium quantity	***quite a lot of*** *I eat **quite a lot of grapes**.*	***quite a lot of*** *I eat **quite a lot of pasta**.*
Small quantity	***a few*** *I eat **a few grapes** every evening.*	***a little*** *I've got **a little pasta**.*
	not many *We have**n't** got **many grapes**.*	***not much*** *I have**n't** got **much pasta**.*
One	***a / an*** *Would you like **a grape**?*	–
Zero quantity	***not any*** *We have**n't** got **any grapes**.*	***not any*** *I have**n't** got **any pasta**.*

a lot of / much / many

We use *a lot of / much / many* to talk about large quantities.

We use *a lot of* in positive sentences:

*I need **a lot of** potatoes.*

We often use *much/many* in negative sentences and questions:

*We haven't got **many** potatoes.*

*I don't eat **much** chocolate.*

*Have you got **many** potatoes?*

*Do you eat **much** chocolate?*

Tip

Only use *a lot of* before a noun (e.g. *chocolate*) or a pronoun (e.g. *it*). Use *a lot* at the end of a sentence.

*I eat **a lot of chocolate**.*

*I eat **a lot of it**.*

*I eat **a lot**.* (NOT ~~*I eat **a lot of**.*~~)

I don't eat **much chocolate** – just **a little** after every meal.

4A Countable and uncountable nouns: *a / an, some / any*

a Are these countable (*C*) or uncountable (*U*) nouns?

1 bread ___U___
2 carrot ______
3 cheese ______
4 chocolate ______
5 fruit ______
6 furniture ______
7 lemon ______
8 money ______
9 egg ______
10 meat ______

b Complete the conversation between a customer and a shop assistant with *a, an, some* or *any*.

CUSTOMER Hello, have you got [1] ___any___ fruit?
SHOP ASSISTANT Yes, of course. This is [2] ______ shop and I sell fruit.
CUSTOMER Oh, good. I'd like [3] ______ grapes, please.
SHOP ASSISTANT Ah, sorry, we haven't got [4] ______ grapes.
CUSTOMER Really? OK, I'd like [5] ______ orange.
SHOP ASSISTANT Just one?
CUSTOMER Yes, please, and [6] ______ lemon.
SHOP ASSISTANT Um ... no, sorry, we don't have [7] ______ lemons. But we've got [8] ______ lovely bananas.
CUSTOMER But I don't want [9] ______ bananas. Well, that's all then, thank you.
SHOP ASSISTANT OK, so one orange. That's 50 cents, please.
CUSTOMER Oh, no! Sorry, I haven't got [10] ______ money.

c Correct one mistake in each sentence.

1 I haven't got some tomatoes.
___I haven't got any tomatoes.___
2 He hasn't got furnitures.
______
3 Have you got any moneys?
______
4 I'd like a onion and a carrot, please.
______
5 We need a cheese.
______
6 I don't want some meat.
______
7 She's got long hairs.
______
8 Do you want any apple?
______

d ≫ Now go back to p. 41.

4B Quantifiers: *much, many, a lot of*

a Complete the sentences about the pictures.

1 We've got ___a lot of___ apples.

2 We've only got a ______ milk.

3 We've got quite ______ pasta.

4 We've got a ______ lemons.

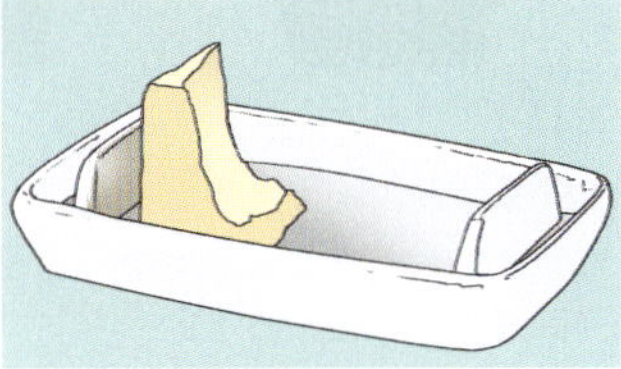

5 We haven't got ______ butter.

6 That's ______ sugar!

b Complete the questions with *much* or *many*.

1 How ___many___ carrots do you want?
2 How ______ money has she got?
3 How ______ do those grapes cost?
4 How ______ tomatoes do you want?
5 How ______ cheese do we need?
6 How ______ apples have you got?
7 How ______ do postcards cost?
8 How ______ salt do you eat?

c Underline the correct answers.

1 I don't eat *many / much* chocolate.
2 How *many / much* butter do we need?
3 How *many / much* onions do you want?
4 I just need *a few / a little* salt.
5 She hasn't got *many / much* money.
6 He eats quite *a lot of / a lot* vegetables.
7 Do you drink *many / much* coffee?
8 We have *a few / a little* good restaurants in my town.

d ≫ Now go back to p. 43.

5A *there is / there are*

We use *there is / there are* to say that something exists in a place.
We often use *there is / there are* with *a/an, some* and *any*.
We use *some* and *any* with uncountable nouns and plural nouns.
We use *some* in positive sentences and *any* in negative sentences and questions.

05.03

	+		–	
Singular	***There's***	*a river.*	***There isn't***	*a theatre.*
Plural	***There are***	*some restaurants.*	***There aren't***	*any cafés.*

	***Yes/No* questions**		**Short answers**	
Singular	***Is there***	*a square?*	*Yes,* *No,*	***there is.*** ***there isn't.***
Plural	***Are there***	*any shops?*	*Yes,* *No,*	***there are.*** ***there aren't.***

	***Wh-* questions**		
Countable	*How* ***many***	*people*	***are there****?*
Uncountable	*How* ***much***	*pasta*	***is there****?*

Tip
Use *There's* (NOT ~~*There are*~~) to talk about a list of singular things:
There's a *book, a phone and a laptop on the table.*

5B Possessive pronouns and possessive *'s*

Possessive pronouns

05.09

Subject	Possessive adjective	Possessive pronoun
I	*my* *Those are my shoes.*	***mine*** *Those are* ***mine****.*
you	*your* *These are your pens.*	***yours*** *These are* ***yours****.*
he	*his* *This is his shirt.*	***his*** *This is* ***his****.*
she	*her* *That's her bag.*	***hers*** *That's* ***hers****.*
it	*its* *Those are its wheels.*	–
we	*our* *They're our cats.*	***ours*** *They're* ***ours****.*
they	*their* *They aren't their cats.*	***theirs*** *They aren't* ***theirs****.*

05.10
We use possessive adjectives (e.g. *my, your*) before nouns:
Is this ***your*** *hat?*
We use possessive pronouns (e.g. *mine, yours*) in the place of a possessive adjective and a noun:
Is this ***yours****?*
We can ask about possession with the word *whose*:
Whose *hat is this? /* ***Whose*** *is this hat?*

Tip
- Be careful with *it's* (= *it is / it has*) and *its* (= possessive adjective).
- Be careful with *who's* (= *who is / who has*) and *whose*.

Possessive *'s* 05.11

We add an apostrophe (') + *s* to a singular noun or a name to show possession:
*My sister has a car. It's my sister****'s*** *car.*
If a plural noun already ends in *-s*, we just add an apostrophe after the *-s*:
My grandparents have a house. It's my grandparents' house.

Other uses of *'s*

- We also use *'s* as a contraction of *is* or *has got*:
  He**'s** (= He is) very lucky. He**'s** got (= He has got) four brothers.

5A *there is / there are*

a Write sentences about a small town using the information in the table.

airport	✗		parks	four
cafés	six		schools	not many
stadium	✗		river	✓ (one)
shops	a lot		bridges	two

1 There isn't an airport.
2 ______
3 ______
4 ______
5 ______
6 ______
7 ______
8 ______

b Write questions and short answers about the town, using the information in the table in **a**.

1 Is there an airport in the town? No, there isn't.
2 How many ______
3 ______
4 ______
5 How many ______
6 ______
7 ______
8 How many ______

c Write sentences about the things in the table in **a** that are true for your town.

1 There isn't an airport.
2 There aren't a lot of cafés.
3 ______
4 ______
5 ______
6 ______
7 ______
8 ______

d ⋙ Now go back to p. 51.

5B Possessive pronouns and possessive *'s*

a Complete the sentences with the correct possessive pronouns.

1 It's my pen.

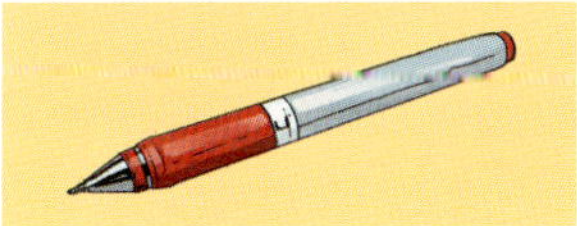

It's mine.

2 They're her shoes.

They're ______.

3 It's their ball.

It's ______.

4 It's his hat.

It's ______.

5 It's our car.

It's ______.

6 He's your dog.

He's ______.

b Underline the correct words.

1 Excuse me. Is this *your* / *yours*?
2 *Its* / *It's* a very interesting book.
3 *Our* / *Ours* flat is quite small.
4 That's my *parent's* / *parents'* room.
5 Don't touch that lamp – it's *my* / *mine*!
6 *Whose* / *Who's* book is this?
7 *Anita's* / *Anitas* house is in the city centre.
8 What colour are *your* / *yours* curtains?

c Underline the *'s* in the conversation. Write *P* (possessive) or *C* (contraction). Then write the full form of the contractions.

ALEXIS Hello. I think I know you. You're in my brother's (P) class at school.
NADIA What's your brother's name?
ALEXIS Paul.
NADIA Paul? Yeah, he's in my class. So, you're Paul's sister.
ALEXIS That's right. Well, in fact, Paul's got two sisters.
NADIA Oh, yes, I remember. My name's Nadia. What's your name?
ALEXIS I'm Alexis.
NADIA Hi, Alexis. It's nice to meet you.

d ⋙ Now go back to p. 53.

6A Past simple: *be*

My grandparents **were** at school together, but they **weren't** friends then.

We use *was/were* to talk about the past.
Was/were are the past forms of *am/is/are*.
We often use past time expressions with *was/were*, e.g. *yesterday*, *last year*, *in 2012*.

06.05

	+		–	
I / he / she / it	*I* ***was***	*at home yesterday.*	*He* ***wasn't***	*at home yesterday.*
you / we / they	*They* ***were***	*at home yesterday.*	*We* ***weren't***	*at home yesterday.*

	Yes/No questions		Short answers	
I / he / she / it	***Was*** *she*	*at home yesterday?*	*Yes,* *No,*	*she* ***was****.* *she* ***wasn't****.*
you / we / they	***Were*** *you*	*at home yesterday?*	*Yes,* *No,*	*we* ***were****.* *we* ***weren't****.*

	Wh- questions		
I / he / she / it	*Where*	***was*** *he*	*yesterday?*
you / we / they	*Where*	***were*** *you*	*yesterday?*

We can also use *there was / there were*:
There was *a computer on the table.*
There were *some chairs in the garden.*

6B Past simple: positive

Past simple

We use the past simple to describe completed actions in the past.
We often use past time expressions with the past simple, e.g. *yesterday*, *last week*, *when I was a child*.

06.13

I ***arrived*** *last night.*
I ***bought*** *a new car last week.*
I often ***visited*** *my grandmother when I was a child.*
I sometimes ***went*** *to the theatre when I* ***lived*** *in London.*
I ***liked*** *sweets a lot when I was young.*
I ***had*** *a lot of friends at school.*

My parents **bought** me a guitar when I was 12. I **loved** it.

Regular and irregular verbs

Past simple verbs are the same for all persons: *I / you / we / they / he / she / it.*
I *worked.* ***She*** *worked.* ***They*** *worked.*
You *went.* ***He*** *went.* ***We*** *went.*
Some verbs are regular. We add *-ed* to make the past simple:
work → *work**ed***   help → *help**ed***
Some verbs are irregular, and you will need to learn their past forms:
meet → ***met***   buy → ***bought***
There is a list of irregular verbs on p. 129.

SPELLING: regular verbs

most verbs → add *-ed*	*start* → *start**ed*** *watch* → *watch**ed***
verb ends in *-e* → add *-d*	*live* → *live**d*** *die* → *die**d***
verb ends in consonant + *-y* → change *-y* to *-i* then add *-ed*	*try* → *tr**ied*** *cry* → *cr**ied***
verb ends in one vowel (*a, e, i, o, u*) and one consonant (*g, n, t*, etc.) → double the consonant and add *-ed*	*stop* → *sto**pped*** *plan* → *pla**nned***
never double the consonants *w, x* or *y* → add *-ed* only	*show* → *show**ed*** *play* → *play**ed***

6A Past simple: *be*

a Underline the correct word.

1 I <u>*was*</u> / *were* on holiday last week.
2 Where *were* / *was* you born?
3 *Wasn't* / *Weren't* there any eggs in the fridge?
4 I *wasn't* / *weren't* at school yesterday. I was ill in bed.
5 There *were* / *was* a lot of people in the queue.
6 Why *was* / *were* your friends late?
7 *Was* / *Were* there a laptop on the desk?
8 When *was* / *were* your children born?

b Rewrite the sentences so that they are about the past.

1 My father's a manager. My father was a manager.
2 They aren't friends. ___
3 **A** Is your grandfather rich? **B** No, he isn't.
___
4 We're at school together. ___
5 It's a beautiful day. ___
6 My teacher's name's Miss Smith. ___
7 She isn't at home. ___
8 There are 20 people in my class. ___
9 I'm not tired. ___
10 **A** Are you happy? **B** Yes, I am. ___

c Put the words in the correct order to make questions.

1 born / you / where / were ?
Where were you born?
2 good / film / was / the ?
___
3 a lot of / there / party / were / people / at / the ?
___
4 grandmother's / was / name / your / what ?
___
5 school / at / were / yesterday / you ?
___
6 was / your hotel / a pool / at / there ?
___

d Now go back to p. 61.

6B Past simple: positive

a Write regular (*R*) or irregular (*I*) next to each verb. Use the list on p. 129 to help you.

1 arrive	11 have
2 become	12 like
3 buy	13 plan
4 come	14 play
5 cook	15 spend
6 decide	16 tell
7 enjoy	17 try
8 find	18 win
9 finish	19 work
10 go	20 write

b Write the past simple forms of the regular verbs in **a**. Be careful with spelling!

1 arrived
2 ___
3 ___
4 ___
5 ___
6 ___
7 ___
8 ___
9 ___
10 ___

c Complete the sentences with the past simple forms of the verbs in brackets.

1 When I was a child, we had an old computer. (have)
2 They ___ good friends in 1996, and they stayed friends for many years. (become)
3 I lost my phone for about a week, but then I ___ it under my bed! (find)
4 She ___ me an amazing story about Steve Jobs. (tell)
5 It was a very difficult game, but in the end we ___. (win)
6 My uncle was a famous writer. He ___ books for children. (write)
7 I ___ my first computer in 1995. (buy)
8 I ___ for a walk yesterday. (go)
9 When I ___ home, I checked my emails. (get)

d Correct one spelling mistake in each sentence.

1 He <u>plaied</u> volleyball when he was young.
played
2 I buyed a new bed yesterday, and it cost £450.
___
3 I really liket the concert on Saturday.
___
4 She eated a piece of cake with her coffee.
___
5 They gotten an email about the new course.
___
6 We dicide to stay at home last weekend.
___

e Now go back to p. 63.

7A Past simple: negative and questions

07.06

	+		–	
I / he / she / it / you / we / they	I I	***enjoyed*** *the trip.* ***took*** *the train.*	*He* ***didn't*** *He* ***didn't***	***enjoy*** *the trip.* ***take*** *the train.*

	Yes/No **questions**		**Short answers**	
I / he / she / it / you / we / they	***Did*** *they* ***Did*** *they*	***enjoy*** *the trip?* ***take*** *the train?*	*Yes,* *No,*	*they* ***did****.* *they* ***didn't****.*

	Wh- **questions**		
I / he / she / it / you / we / they	*Where*	***did*** *you*	***go****?*

Tip

Remember, don't change the main verb in questions and negatives:
I didn't **enjoy** it. (NOT ~~I didn't **enjoyed** it.~~)
Did you **enjoy** it? (NOT ~~Did you **enjoyed** it?~~)

7B *love / like / don't mind / hate* + verb + *-ing*

07.12

☺☺☺	*I* ***love*** *driving!*
☺	*I* ***like*** *driving.*
😐	*I* ***don't mind*** *driving.*
☹	*I* ***don't like*** *driving.*
☹☹☹	*I* ***hate*** *driving!*

After *like*, *love*, *hate* and *don't mind*, we can use a noun or a verb + *-ing*.

I love ***my car****.* *I love* ***driving****.*

SPELLING: verb + *-ing*

most verbs → add *-ing*	*watch → watch**ing*** *go → go**ing*** *see → see**ing***
verb ends in consonant (*g, n, t,* etc.) + *-e* → take away the *-e* then add *-ing*	*drive → driv**ing*** *use → us**ing***
verb ends in one vowel (*a, e, i, o, u*) and one consonant (*g, n, t,* etc.) → double the consonant and add *-ing*	*run → run**ning*** *sit → sit**ting***
never double the consonants *w, x* or *y* → add *-ing* only	*know → know**ing*** *play → play**ing***

7A Past simple: negative and questions

a Complete the sentences with the past simple forms of the verbs in brackets.

1 We ___didn't travel___ (not travel) by plane to Denmark – we took trains.
2 I ____________ (not take) an umbrella today, so I got wet.
3 Marion and Neil ____________ (not want) a big wedding.
4 He ____________ (not answer) the telephone because he was busy.
5 When I was a child, I ____________ (not like) chocolate.
6 We ____________ (not see) any wild animals when we went to Egypt.
7 She ____________ (not get) back home on time, so I was really worried.

b Change the positive past simple verbs to negative verb forms in these sentences.

1 We went by tram.
___We didn't go by tram.___
2 They travelled across the country.
____
3 We had a good time.
____
4 The tickets cost a lot of money.
____
5 She visited China.
____
6 They stayed in hotels.
____
7 The people spoke English, so I understood them.
____

c Complete the questions and answers.

1 **A** ___Did___ you ___go___ (go) through Eastern Europe?
B Yes, I ___did___.
2 **A** ____________ you ____________ (start) your journey in Turkey?
B No, I ____________.
3 **A** ____________ he ____________ (enjoy) his trip?
B No, he ____________.
4 **A** ____________ they ____________ (travel) by train?
B Yes, they ____________.

d Write the questions to complete the conversation.

A 1 ___How did you travel?___ (how)
B We travelled by train.
A 2 ____________ (how much)
B The trip cost £750.
A 3 ____________ (how many)
B We visited five countries.
A 4 ____________ (where)
B We stayed in hotels.
A 5 ____________ (when)
B We arrived home yesterday.

e Now go back to p. 71.

7B *love / like / don't mind / hate* + verb + *-ing*

a Write the *-ing* form of the verbs.

1 wait ___waiting___
2 drive ____________
3 walk ____________
4 get ____________
5 fly ____________
6 relax ____________
7 be ____________
8 have ____________
9 speak ____________
10 sit ____________
11 stand ____________
12 stay ____________
13 run ____________
14 try ____________
15 use ____________
16 agree ____________

b Write sentences about Jamie and Lisa.

	eat in restaurants	cook	get pizza	try new food
Jamie	☹	😐	😐	☺☺☺
Lisa	☺	☹☹☹	☹	☺☺☺

1 Jamie ___doesn't like eating in restaurants.___
He ____________
____
____
2 Lisa ____________
She ____________
____
____

c Circle the correct symbols and write sentences that are true for you.

1 wait for buses
☺☺☺ / ☺ / (😐) / ☹ / ☹☹☹
___I don't mind waiting for buses.___
2 sit in traffic
☺☺☺ / ☺ / 😐 / ☹ / ☹☹☹
____
3 play video games
☺☺☺ / ☺ / 😐 / ☹ / ☹☹☹
____
4 fly in aeroplanes
☺☺☺ / ☺ / 😐 / ☹ / ☹☹☹
____
5 cook dinner
☺☺☺ / ☺ / 😐 / ☹ / ☹☹☹
____

d Now go back to p. 73.

8A *can / can't, could / couldn't* for ability

We use *can/can't* to talk about present abilities:
I ***can*** *read English, but I* ***can't*** *speak it.*
We use *could/couldn't* to talk about past abilities:
When I was young, I ***could*** *dance, but I* ***couldn't*** *sing.*

08.02

		+		–	
I / he / she / it / you / we / they	Present	*I* ***can***	***run*** *fast.*	*They* ***can't***	***run*** *fast.*
	Past	*He* ***could***	***run*** *fast.*	*We* ***couldn't***	***run*** *fast.*

		Yes/No questions		Short answers	
I / he / she / it / you / we / they	Present	***Can*** *you*	***run*** *fast?*	*Yes,* *No,*	*I* ***can****.* *I* ***can't****.*
	Past	***Could*** *you*	***run*** *fast?*	*Yes,* *No,*	*I* ***could****.* *I* ***couldn't****.*

Tip
There is no *-s* on *can* for *he / she / it*:
He ***can*** *swim.*
(NOT ~~*He* ***cans*** *swim.*~~)

Tip
The full form of *can't* is *cannot*.

8B *have to / don't have to*

We use *have to* + infinitive to talk about things we need to do:
I ***have to drink*** *a lot of water when I go running.*
She ***has to get up*** *at six every day.*
We can use *have to* to talk about rules:
We ***have to take off*** *our shoes before we go inside.*
We ***have to get to*** *school by nine.*
Don't have to means we don't need to do something.
I ***don't have to pay*** *for my lunch at work.* (My lunch is free.)
Our teacher ***doesn't have to wear*** *a suit.* (There is no rule.)

Tip
Sometimes, *you* means *everybody* or *people* generally.
A *Do* ***you*** *have to be fit to run a marathon?*
(= *Do* ***people*** *have to be fit … ?*)
B *Yes,* ***you*** *do.* (NOT ~~*Yes, I do.*~~)

08.07

	+		–	
I / you / we / they	*I*	***have to work*** *hard.*	*I* ***don't***	***have to work*** *hard.*
he / she / it	*She*	***has to work*** *hard.*	*He* ***doesn't***	***have to work*** *hard.*

	Yes/No questions		Short answers	
I / you / we / they	***Do*** *you*	***have to work*** *hard?*	*Yes,* *No,*	*I* ***do****.* *I* ***don't****.*
he / she / it	***Does*** *he*	***have to work*** *hard?*	*Yes,* *No,*	*he* ***does****.* *he* ***doesn't****.*

If you're tired, you don't **have to** run any more. You can walk.

8A *can / can't, could / couldn't* for ability

a Complete the sentences with *can/can't, could/couldn't*.

1 I ___can___ play the guitar. I want to learn the drums next.
2 I ________ drive last year, but I passed my test six weeks ago!
3 She ________ cook really well. Her food is always great.
4 He isn't on the football team, because he ________ run very fast.
5 When I was in school, I ________ do maths. But now I'm much better.
6 My husband ________ speak French, Spanish and Portuguese. It's useful when we travel!
7 I ________ climb trees when I was a child, but I'm too old now.

b Write sentences about what Rob *could/couldn't* do in the past and what he *can/can't* do now.

When he was a boy	Now
swim 1,000 metres ✗	swim 1,000 metres ✓
cook a meal ✗	cook a meal ✓
ride a bike ✓	ride a bike ✗
run 25 km ✗	run 25 km ✓
speak Spanish ✗	speak Spanish ✓

1 Rob couldn't swim 1,000 metres when he was a boy. He can swim 1,000 metres now.
2 ________
3 ________
4 ________
5 ________

c Find and correct a mistake in each sentence.

1 I don't can play the guitar. I can't play the guitar.
2 She cans speak four languages. ________
3 How fast you can swim? ________
4 I could ran very fast when I was a child. ________
5 I didn't could understand what he said. ________
6 **A** Does he can cook? **B** Yes, he can. ________
7 **A** Could he walk before his accident? **B** Yes, he did. ________

d Now go to p. 81.

8B *have to / don't have to*

a Match questions 1–8 with answers a–h.

1 [d] Do we have to take our shoes off?
2 [ ] How much do you have to pay for a ticket?
3 [ ] Do you have to be a member to use the swimming pool?
4 [ ] Does she have to walk home?
5 [ ] Do you have to walk the dog every day?
6 [ ] Do you have to help in the kitchen?
7 [ ] I want to stay at home. Why do I have to go for a walk?
8 [ ] What time do you have to leave for work?

a Because you have to stay fit.
b No, I don't. My parents do everything.
c Yes, I do. Every day.
d No, you don't. You can keep them on.
e At eight o'clock.
f Nothing. It's free.
g No, you don't. It's open to everybody.
h No, she doesn't. She's got enough money for a taxi.

b Complete the sentences with the correct form of *have to* or a short answer.

1 In a kitchen, ___you have to work___ (you / work) very carefully.
2 **A** ________ (you / buy) any new clothes for your new job?
B Yes, ________.
3 ________ (I / not / pay) rent right now, because I'm living with my parents.
4 I usually wear jeans and a T-shirt, but at work ________ (I / wear) a suit.
5 **A** What ________ (we / do) before we start the game?
B I don't know. Read the instructions.
6 **A** Do ________ (I / give) them a present?
B No, ________. But it's a nice idea.
7 My son would like to see this film. How old ________ (he / be)?
8 To get fit, I think ________ (you / walk) for at least half an hour a day.

c Put a tick (✓) or a cross X (✗) next to each activity and write sentences that are true for you.

1 I / study for three hours every evening ✓
I have to study for three hours every evening.
2 I / cook dinner every night ✗
I don't have to cook dinner every night.
3 I / do a lot of homework
____
4 My teacher / help me with grammar
____
5 My best friend / sometimes / wait for me
____
6 My father / go to work at eight o'clock
____

d Now go back to p. 83.

9A Present continuous

We use the present continuous to describe an activity now or at the moment of speaking. The activity started in the past and will finish in the future.

09.08

	+		–	
I	*I'm*	***waiting**.*	*I'm **not***	***waiting**.*
you / we / they	*You'**re***	***waiting**.*	*We **aren't***	***waiting**.*
he / she / it	*He'**s***	***waiting**.*	*It **isn't***	***waiting**.*

Full forms: *am waiting, are waiting, is waiting; am not waiting, are not waiting, is not waiting*

	Yes/No **questions**		**Short answers**	
I	***Am** I*	***waiting**?*	*Yes,* *No,*	*you **are**.* *you **aren't**.*
you / we / they	***Are** you*	***waiting**?*	*Yes,* *No,*	*I **am**.* *I'**m not**.*
he / she / it	***Is** he*	***waiting**?*	*Yes,* *No,*	*he **is**.* *he **isn't**.*

	***Wh-* questions**		
I	*Why*	***am** I*	***waiting**?*
you / we / they	*Where*	***are** you*	***waiting**?*
he / she / it	*Who*	***is** he*	***waiting** for?*

9B Present simple or present continuous

The present simple is about things that are normally true. We use it to describe habits, routines, facts and feelings:
*I usually **wear** trousers.* *He **loves** cars.*

The present continuous is about now. We use it to describe what is happening now / today / this week etc.:
*Today I'**m wearing** a dress.* *I'**m studying** hard this week.*

There are some verbs which we don't usually use in the present continuous:

like love hate not mind want know
need understand remember forget

*I **want** to go home.* (NOT ~~*I'm wanting to go home.*~~)

Tip

We don't use *have* in continuous form for possession. We use *have / has got*:
*I'**ve got** a new car.* (NOT ~~*I'm having a new car.*~~)
*She'**s got** red hair.* (NOT ~~*She's having red hair.*~~)
We can use *have* for actions in continuous sentences:
*We'**re having** dinner right now.*
*I'**m not having** fun.*

9A Present continuous

a Write about the pictures using the present continuous.

he / drink / coffee

1 *He's drinking coffee.*

they / talk

2 ______

he / not / ride / a horse

3 ______

I / do / a grammar exercise

4 ______

she / not / wear / shoes

5 ______

they / play / tennis

6 ______

b Complete the conversations using the present continuous and the verbs in brackets. Use short answers where possible.

1 **A** Who *are* you *waiting* (wait) for?
  B I *'m* *waiting* (wait) for you.

2 **A** Why ______ she ______ (smile)?
  B I don't know. Maybe she ______ ______ (feel) happy.

3 **A** ______ you ______ (sleep)?
  B No, I ______ ______.

4 **A** Where ______ they ______ (stand)?
  B They ______ ______ (not stand). They're sitting at a table.

5 **A** ______ your brother ______ (play) football today?
  B No, he ______. He ______ ______ (play) basketball.

c Complete the telephone conversation using the present continuous forms of the words in brackets.

A What [1] *are you doing* (you / do)?
B [2] ______ (I / shop) in the city centre. Where are you?
A [3] ______ (We / look) for a parking space. [4] ______ (we / drive) past the museum.
B Really? [5] ______ (I / stand) outside the museum right now!
A I can't see you. What [6] ______ (you / wear)?
B [7] ______ (I / wear) a red T-shirt.
A OK, I can see you now, but [8] ______ (we / not stop). The traffic is too busy!

d Now go back to p. 91.

9B Present simple or present continuous

a Choose the correct words to complete the sentences.

1 She *usually* / *today* wears black clothes.
2 She's wearing bright colours *usually* / *today*.
3 They *never* / *are not* visit museums. They don't like them.
4 My parents aren't at home. They're visiting a museum *sometimes* / *this morning*.
5 Wow! Look! Tom *dances* / *'s dancing*! He doesn't usually dance.
6 I *enjoy* / *'m enjoying* the party. Thanks for inviting me!
7 I always watch football *at weekends* / *at the moment*.
8 We don't go out *now* / *often*.

b Complete the conversations with the correct form of the verbs in brackets. Use the present simple or the present continuous.

1 **A** What *are you doing* (you / do)?
  B ______ (we / get) ready to go out. Would you like to come with us?
  A Not really, no. ______ (I / watch) a film. It's really good.

2 **A** What's that noise?
  B Sorry, it's my friend Harry. ______ (he / sing).
  A Wow! He's quite good.
  B Yes, ______ (he / sing) in a band every weekend. ______ (They / often / play) concerts.

3 **A** ______ (you / play) that video game again?
  B No, ______. ______ (I / try) to sell my guitar on the Internet.
  A Really? Why ______ (you / do) that?

c Choose the options that are true for you and write sentences.

1 wear bright colours usually ✓ ✗ now ✓ ✗
I usually wear bright colours.
I'm not wearing bright colours now.

2 feel happy usually ✓ ✗ now ✓ ✗
______
______

3 listen to music when I study usually ✓ ✗ now ✓ ✗
______
______

4 wear a watch usually ✓ ✗ now ✓ ✗
______
______

5 use a computer when I study usually ✓ ✗ now ✓ ✗
______
______

6 study in my bedroom usually ✓ ✗ now ✓ ✗
______
______

d Now go back to p. 93.

10A Comparative adjectives

10.02

We use a comparative adjective + *than* to compare two or more things, people, etc.

*My new smartphone is **bigger than** my old one.*
*My tablet is **heavier than** my phone.*
*My phone is **more expensive than** my sister's.*
*Your laptop is **better than** mine.*

One syllable			End in -*y*			Two or more syllables		
adjective + -*er*			adjective – -*y* + -*ier*			*more* + adjective		
old	→	*old**er***	*heavy*	→	*heav**ier***	*useful*	→	***more** useful*
cheap	→	*cheap**er***	*easy*	→	*eas**ier***	*expensive*	→	***more** expensive*
light	→	*light**er***	*pretty*	→	*prett**ier***	*difficult*	→	***more** difficult*

Tip
good and *bad* are irregular:
good → *better* *bad* → *worse*

Life is **easier** with new technology.

SPELLING: adjective + -*er*

most adjectives → add -*er*	*short* → *short**er*** *clean* → *clean**er***
adjective ends in -*e* → add -*r*	*large* → *large**r*** *nice* → *nice**r***
adjective ends in consonant + -*y* → change -*y* to -*i* then add -*er*	*dry* → *dr**ier*** *easy* → *eas**ier***
adjective ends in one vowel (*a, e, i, o, u*) and one consonant (*g, n, t,* etc.) → double the consonant and add -*er*	*hot* → *hot**ter*** *thin* → *thin**ner***

10B Superlative adjectives

We use the superlative form of adjectives to talk about extremes.
We usually use *the* before superlatives.

10.06

***The most useful** language is English.*
***The easiest** language is Spanish.*
*What's **the hardest** language in the world?*
***The best** language practice is speaking.*

Tip
We don't use *the* with words like *my*, *your*, etc.
She's my best friend. (NOT ~~She's my the best friend~~.)

One syllable			End in -*y*			Two or more syllables		
the + adjective + -*est*			*the* + adjective – -*y* + -*iest*			*the most* + adjective		
old	→	***the** old**est***	*heavy*	→	***the** heav**iest***	*useful*	→	***the most** useful*
cheap	→	***the** cheap**est***	*easy*	→	***the** eas**iest***	*expensive*	→	***the most** expensive*
light	→	***the** light**est***	*pretty*	→	***the** prett**iest***	*difficult*	→	***the most** difficult*

Tip
good and *bad* are irregular:
good → *the best* *bad* → *the worst*

SPELLING: adjective + -*est*

most adjectives → add -*est*	*short* → *short**est*** *clean* → *clean**est***
adjective ends in -*e* → add -*st*	*large* → *large**st*** *nice* → *nice**st***
adjective ends in consonant + -*y* → change -*y* to -*i* then add -*est*	*dry* → *dr**iest*** *easy* → *eas**iest***
adjective ends in one vowel (*a, e, i, o, u*) and one consonant (*g, n, t,* etc.) → double the consonant and add -*est*	*hot* → *hot**test*** *thin* → *thin**nest***

10A Comparative adjectives

a Write the comparative form of the adjectives.

1 angry	*angrier*	11 modern	______
2 bad	______	12 noisy	______
3 clean	______	13 old	______
4 cold	______	14 popular	______
5 comfortable	______	15 sad	______
6 crowded	______	16 strange	______
7 fast	______	17 strong	______
8 fat	______	18 thin	______
9 good	______	19 wet	______
10 interesting	______	20 wide	______

b Write sentences using the present simple of *be* and comparative adjectives.

1 my new phone / cheap / my old phone
My new phone is cheaper than my old phone.
2 the film / interesting / the book
______
3 her children / noisy / my children
______
4 she / a good cook / my dad
______
5 Dubai / modern / Dublin
______
6 this hotel / comfortable / the last hotel
______
7 my friends / fit / me
______

c Correct one mistake in each sentence.

1 She quicker than me. She always finishes first. ______
2 The book is good than the film. ______
3 My marks are always worser than yours. ______
4 This dress is prettyer than that one. ______
5 The English weather is weter than the weather in Spain. ______
6 Their family is more big than mine. ______
7 My new teacher is most interesting than my old teacher. ______
8 Is your Internet faster mine? ______

d ≫ Now go back to p. 101.

10B Superlative adjectives

a Write the superlative form of the adjectives.

1 clean	*the cleanest*	8 good	______
2 fit	______	9 big	______
3 funny	______	10 nice	______
4 dry	______	11 safe	______
5 pretty	______	12 exciting	______
6 bad	______	13 tiring	______
7 friendly	______	14 hot	______

English is not **the most beautiful** language in the world. Some people say it's not **the easiest**. But when you're lost, it's probably **the most useful**.

b Complete the sentences using the superlative form of the adjectives in brackets.

1 One of *the longest* (long) words in English is *floccinaucinihilipilification*. But I don't know what it means!
2 ______ (short) words in English are *a* and *I*.
3 In spoken English, one of ______ (popular) words is *I* – because we think we're ______ (interesting) topic in the world!
4 ______ (useful) noun in English is *time*. We use it all the time!
5 ______ (fast) way to learn a language is to go and live in a different country.
6 Some people think ______ (important) thing for language learners is speaking.
7 I think ______ (good) way to improve your English is to learn a lot of words – I try to learn ten new words every day.
8 When you're reading in English, ______ (bad) thing you can do is check all the words in a dictionary. It takes too long and it's not much fun!

c ≫ Now go back to p. 102.

11A Present perfect

We use the present perfect to talk about past actions in a time period which starts in the past and continues now, for example: today, this week, this year, your lifetime.

*I'**ve seen** that film four times (**in my life**).*
*I **haven't had** any coffee **today**.*
***Have** you **been** to the gym **this week**?*

We make the present perfect from the verb *have* + the past participle of the main verb.

For regular verbs, the past participle is the same as the past form:
*I **walked** to work yesterday.*
*I'**ve walked** to work three times this week.*

For irregular verbs, the past participle is usually different. You have to learn the different forms. (See page 129 for a list of irregular verbs.)
*I **drove** to work yesterday.*
*I'**ve driven** to work three times this week.*

11.06

	+	
I / you / we / they	*I'**ve***	***seen** the film 400 times.*
he / she / it	*He'**s***	***seen** the film 400 times.*

	–	
I / you / we / they	*They **haven't***	***seen** the film.*
he / she / it	*She **hasn't***	***seen** the film.*

We often use the present perfect to talk about experiences:
*I'**ve seen** the film once.* (in my lifetime)
*She'**s met** him three times.* (in her lifetime)
When we ask a question about experiences, we often use the word *ever*.
***Have** you **ever read** this book?* = Have you read this book in your lifetime?
We use *never* with the present perfect to say there is no experience.
*I'**ve never read** her book.* = I haven't read her book in my lifetime.

	Yes/No questions		Short answers	
I / you / we / they	***Have** you*	***seen** the film?*	*Yes,* *No,*	*I **have**.* *I **haven't**.*
he / she / it	***Has** he*	***seen** the film?*	*Yes,* *No,*	*he **has**.* *he **hasn't**.*

Tip
The past participle of *go* is *gone*. But we often use the past participle of *be* (*been*) instead of *gone*.
*I'**ve been** to France.* (= I'm not there now.)
*Claire'**s gone** to Scotland.* (= she's still there now.)

11B Present perfect or past simple

We use the present perfect to talk about the past experiences in our life, but we <u>don't</u> say when exactly.
*I'**ve been** to Buenos Aires.* (We don't know when.)

We use the past simple to say when something happened (e.g. *last year, yesterday, in 2012*).
*I **went** to the theatre **last week**.* (NOT ~~I've been to the theatre last week.~~)

We often start a conversation by asking about or describing an event using the present perfect, and then change to the past simple to ask about or describe the details of the event.

11.13

A ***Have** you **ever been** to Argentina?*
B *Yes, I **have**. I'**ve been** there <u>three</u> **times**.*
} Focus: my/your life; Tense: present perfect

A *I've been there, too. I **went** there **last year**.*
B *Really? Which cities **did** you **visit**?*
} Focus: a visit last year; Tense: past simple

11A Present perfect

a Write the irregular past participles. Use the list on p. 129 to help you.

1 see *seen*
2 write ______
3 swim ______
4 have ______
5 bring ______
6 do ______
7 drive ______
8 ride ______
9 run ______
10 be ______

b Complete the sentences with the present perfect forms of the verbs in brackets.

1 I have *read* (read) this book twice.
2 We ______ (visit) this museum three times this year.
3 He ______ (not borrow) my car today.
4 We ______ (never eat) at that restaurant.
5 I ______ (walk) down this street many times.
6 She ______ (play) for England in three Olympic Games.
7 They ______ (not do) the housework this week.
8 This country ______ (have) five big storms this winter.

c Complete the conversations with present perfect verb forms of the words in brackets.

1
A *Have you ever seen* (you / ever / see) *Star Wars*?
B Yes, ______ (I / see) it many times. It's my favourite film.
A Really? ______ (I / never / see) it.

2
A ______ (you / ever / meet) a famous person?
B Yes, ______ (I / meet) Bill Gates.
A Wow! ______ (he / visit) Cambridge?
B Yes, ______ (he / be) here many times.

d Now go back to p. 111.

I've **watched** my favourite film 400 times.

11B Present perfect or past simple

a Underline the correct words.

1 *Have you been* / *Did you go* out last night?
2 *I've never seen* / *I never saw* an opera.
3 *We went* / *We've been* to a rock concert on Saturday.
4 *Have you ever danced* / *Did you ever dance* the tango?
5 She's a fantastic actor, but *she never won* / *she's never won* an Oscar.
6 *We've visited* / *We visited* the theatre when we were in Budapest last year.
7 I *didn't eat* / *'ve never eaten* sheep's milk cheese in my life.
8 *Did he win* / *Has he won* the 100m at the Olympic Games?

b Match questions 1–8 with short answers a–h.

1 [g] Did she go out?
2 [ ] Have you ever been to Chile?
3 [ ] Was it a good concert?
4 [ ] Has she been in any bad films?
5 [ ] Were you tired when you got home?
6 [ ] Did they help you?
7 [ ] Have they ever visited Tokyo?
8 [ ] Did you have a good time?

a Yes, we were.
b Yes, we did.
c No, I haven't.
d No, they didn't.
e Yes, it was.
f No, they haven't.
g No, she didn't.
h Yes, she has.

c Complete the conversation using the correct present perfect or past simple form of the verbs in brackets.

A [1] *Have you ever been* (you / ever / go) to a jazz club?
B Yes, I [2] ______. [3] ______ (I / go) to a few. My favourite is *Jazz Cellar*. [4] ______ (I / go) there hundreds of times.
A Yes, I think [5] ______ (I / go) there, too. [6] ______ (I / go) there last year.
B [7] ______ (you / like) it?
A Yes, I [8] ______. [9] ______ (it / be) great. There [10] ______ (be) a brilliant singer – her name [11] ______ (be) Erica something.
B Erica Sousa. [12] ______ (I / see) her a few times. She's amazing. In fact, [13] ______ (she / play) a concert there last week.
A [14] ______ (you / go) to that concert?
B No, I [15] ______. [16] ______ (I / want) to go, but I had a meeting at work, and [17] ______ (I / finish) late.

d Now go back to p. 113.

12A *be going to*

We use *be going to* when we have a plan for the future:

12.06

	+		–	
I	*I'**m***	***going to travel** the world next year.*	*I'**m not***	***going to work** in an office.*
you / we / they	*They'**re***	***going to travel** the world next year.*	*You **aren't***	***going to work** in an office.*
he / she / it	*She'**s***	***going to travel** the world next year.*	*He **isn't***	***going to work** in an office.*

	***Yes/No* questions**		**Short answers**	
I	***Am** I*	***going to travel** next year?*	*Yes,* *No,*	*you **are**.* *you **aren't**.*
you / we / they	***Are** you*	***going to travel** next year?*	*Yes,* *No,*	*I **am**.* *I'**m not**.*
he / she / it	***Is** he*	***going to travel** next year?*	*Yes,* *No,*	*he **is**.* *he **isn't**.*

	***Wh-* questions**		
I	*Who*	***am** I*	***going to travel** with?*
you / we / they	*Where*	***are** you*	***going to go**?*
he / she / it	*What*	***'s** he*	***going to see**?*

I'**m not going to stay** in this job much longer.
I'**m going to travel** the world.

12B *should / shouldn't*

We use *should* to give advice.
*You **should** learn the local language.* (= It's a good idea.)

12.10

	+		–	
I / he / she / it / you / we / they	*I **should***	***go**.*	*They **shouldn't***	***go**.*

	***Yes/No* questions**		**Short answers**	
I / he / she / it / you / we / they	***Should** she*	***go**?*	*Yes,* *No,*	*she **should**.* *she **shouldn't**.*

	***Wh-* questions**		
I / he / she / it / you / we / they	*When*	***should** we*	***go**?*

Tip

We use the infinitive without *to* after *should*.
*You **should take** sun cream with you.*
(NOT ~~*You **should to take***~~ *…*)

12A *be going to*

a Match questions 1–8 with answers a–h.

1 [e] Where are you going to stay?
2 [ ] Are they going to visit us?
3 [ ] When are you going to clean your room?
4 [ ] Is he going to get a job?
5 [ ] Who are they going to meet?
6 [ ] Are you going to leave your job?
7 [ ] What are you going to take with you?
8 [ ] How long is he going to be away?

a Not much. Just a few clothes.
b No, he isn't. He's going to travel around the world first.
c Some of their friends.
d No, I'm not. I'm just going to take a long holiday.
e In a hotel.
f About six months.
g Tomorrow – I promise.
h No, they aren't. They don't have time.

b Complete the sentences using the correct form of *be going to* and the verb in brackets.

1 I *'m going to travel* (travel) to South America.
2 My sister ________ (get) married next year.
3 We ________ (do) a lot of sightseeing on holiday this summer.
4 They ________ (not / stay) in hotels this year.
5 My parents ________ (buy) a new house in the country.
6 I ________ (go) to the cinema tonight. Do you want to come with me?
7 He ________ (not / go) to university after he leaves school.
8 We ________ (not / visit) big cities when we go to France.
9 We ________ (stay) in small towns.

c Now go back to p. 121.

12B *should / shouldn't*

a Complete the sentences with the verb in brackets and *should* or *shouldn't*.

1 **A** He feels tired all the time.
B He *should go* (go) to the doctor.
2 You ________ (drink) a lot of water when you run.
3 You ________ (bring) a lot of books. We're only going for three days.
4 You ________ (drive) all night. Stop and get some sleep.
5 It's going to be cold, so you ________ (take) some warm clothes.
6 The children ________ (come) into the house – it's getting dark.
7 We ________ (pay) for the meal. The food was terrible.
8 I ________ (say) sorry to him. I broke his cup.

b Put the words in the correct order to make questions.

1 money / much / take / should / I / how ?
How much money should I take?
2 museum / we / go / a / should / to ?
____
3 clothes / should / what / wear / I ?
____
4 I / later / come / should / back ?
____
5 we / local / the / should / eat / food ?
____
6 we / should / time / arrive / what ?
____
7 we / where / stay / should ?
____
8 for / should / ask / who / we / advice ?
____

c Read the conversation and find six mistakes with *should*.

A I'm going to Thailand next month. Have you ever been there?
B Yes, I have.
A Where should I staying?
B You should look for a hotel when you arrive. You don't should book before you go.
A Really? I should go to Bangkok?
B You should to go to Bangkok for a few days, but you shouldn't stay long. You should visit an island.
A What do I should do on an island?
B Do you want to relax?
A Yes.
B You should go swimming every day. You should eat at restaurants on the beach. And you should leave your mobile phone at home!
A Should I take anything with me?
B Just some money. You should not to worry about money on holiday!

d Correct the mistakes with *should* in **c**.

1 *Where should I stay?*
2 ________
3 ________
4 ________
5 ________
6 ________

e Now go back to p. 123.

1A Countries and nationalities

a 01.04 Look at the map below. Write the correct number next to each country in the table. Listen and check.

Country	Nationality	Country	Nationality
A *(-ian)*		**C *(-ish)***	
Argentina /ɑːdʒən'tiːnə/	Argentin**ian** /ɑːdʒən'tɪniən/	Ireland /'aɪələnd/	Ir**ish** /'aɪərɪʃ/
Australia /ɒs'treɪliə/	Austral**ian** /ɒs'treɪliən/	Poland /'pəʊlənd/	Pol**ish** /'pəʊlɪʃ/
Canada /'kænədə/	Canad**ian** /kə'neɪdiən/	Turkey /'tɜːki/	Turk**ish** /'tɜːkɪʃ/
Colombia /kə'lɒmbiə/	Colomb**ian** /kə'lɒmbiən/	(the) UK /juː'keɪ/	Brit**ish** /'brɪtɪʃ/
Iran /ɪ'rɑːn/	Iran**ian** /ɪ'reɪniən/	Britain /'brɪtən/	
Italy /'ɪtəli/	Ital**ian** /ɪ'tæliən/	**D *(-ese)***	
Nigeria /naɪ'dʒɪəriə/	Niger**ian** /naɪ'dʒɪəriən/	China /'tʃaɪnə/	Chin**ese** /tʃaɪ'niːz/
Russia /'rʌʃə/	Russ**ian** /'rʌʃən/	**E *(-i)***	
		Pakistan /pɑːkɪs'tɑːn/	Pakistan**i** /pɑːkɪs'tɑːni/
B *(-an)*		**F (other)**	
Mexico /'meksɪkəʊ/	Mexic**an** /'meksɪkən/	New Zealand /njuː 'ziːlənd/	(a) New Zealander /njuː 'ziːləndə/
South Africa /saʊθ 'æfrɪkə/	South Afric**an** /saʊθ 'æfrɪkən/	Saudi Arabia /ˌsaʊdi ə'reɪbiə/	Saudi /'saʊdi/
(the) USA /juːes'eɪ/	Americ**an** /ə'merɪkən/	Thailand /'taɪlænd/	Thai /taɪ/

b Talk about five countries you want to visit.

> I'd like to visit China because I want to see the Great Wall of China.

c Match the parts of the world 1–6 with a–f on the map.

1 North America
2 Middle East and Asia
3 Central and South America
4 Africa
5 Europe
6 Oceania

d Underline the different country in each group below. Say why.

1 France, Italy, Greece, Poland, China, Germany, Ireland
2 Thailand, Saudi Arabia, Brazil, Iran
3 the USA, Russia, the UK, Australia, Canada
4 Argentina, Mexico, Colombia, Spain

e Look at groups A–F in **a**. Match each nationality below to a group.

1 Brazilian
2 Spanish
3 German
4 Iraqi
5 Japanese
6 French

f 01.05 **Pronunciation** Listen to the nationalities in the table. Underline the stressed syllable in each word.

<table>
<tr><td>A 2 syllables</td><td>Brit|ish, Chi|nese, Tur|kish</td></tr>
<tr><td>B 3 syllables</td><td>Mex|i|can, Ja|pa|nese, Bra|zil|ian</td></tr>
<tr><td>C 4 syllables</td><td>Aus|tral|i|an, Pa|ki|sta|ni, I|tal|i|an</td></tr>
</table>

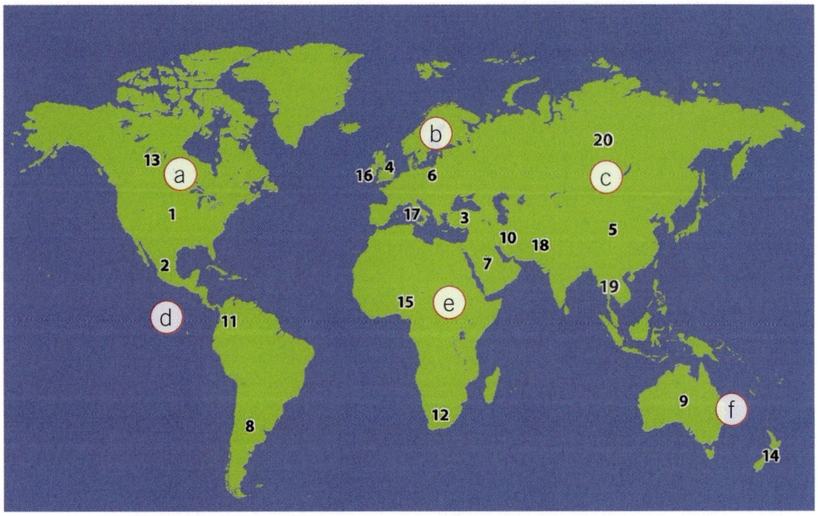

g 01.05 Look at the nationalities in **f** again and answer the questions. Listen again and check.

1 In A and in C, which word has a different stress pattern?
2 In B, do the words have the same or a different stress pattern?

h Student A: choose a new country and a nationality. Tell your partner the part of the world. Then answer his/her questions. Student B: ask questions to guess your partner's new country and nationality. Change roles and repeat.

> I'm from South America.
> Are you from Brazil?
> No, I'm not.
> Are you from Colombia?
> Yes, I'm Colombian.

i Now go back to p. 11.

1B Adjectives

a 01.08 Listen to these sentences. Do the adjectives in **bold** mean 'very good' or 'not very good'?

1 This wet and cold weather is **terrible**.
2 I like our new teacher – she's **wonderful**.
3 My new phone does so many new things – it's **amazing**.
4 This colour isn't very nice – it's **horrible**.

b 01.09 Listen to these sentences. Make pairs of opposites with the adjectives in **bold**.

1 My computer's quite **old** now. I need to buy a new one.
2 I don't think he's got a lot of money – he's quite **poor**.
3 Their new house is finished now and it's very **modern**.
4 He buys anything he wants, so I think he's **rich**.

c 01.10 **Pronunciation** Is the pronunciation of *o* in these words long (/ɔː/) or short (/ɒ/)? Listen and check.

1 m**o**dern 2 p**oo**r 3 h**o**rrible

d 01.11 Is the pronunciation of *o* in these words long or short? Listen and check. Listen again and repeat.

1 c**o**ffee
2 **o**ften
3 m**o**re
4 sh**o**rt
5 h**o**liday
6 d**oo**r

e Think of things you've got. Write notes. Do you have anything that's ... ?

- wonderful
- amazing
- terrible
- horrible
- old
- modern

f Tell a partner about your things using your notes in **e**.

g Now go back to p. 13.

2A Jobs

a 02.02 Match the jobs in the box with pictures 1–9. Listen and check. Listen again and repeat.

businessman /ˈbɪznɪsmən/ businesswoman /ˈbɪznɪswʊmən/ receptionist /rɪˈsepʃənɪst/
manager /ˈmænɪdʒə/ chef /ʃef/ actor /ˈæktə/ tour guide /ˈtʊə gaɪd/
farmer /ˈfɑːmə/ secretary /ˈsekrətəri/ mechanic /məˈkænɪk/

1

2

3

4

5

6

7

8

9

b Look at the jobs on p. 21 and in **a**. Read the sentences and write the correct job.

a I work in a hospital and look after people.
b I work outside and enjoy showing people my beautiful city.
c I sometimes work in a theatre and I sometimes make films.
d I drive people from one place to another.
e I work in a kitchen and cook amazing food.
f I help people if they have a problem with their teeth.
g I help people if they have a problem with their car.
h I fly people from one country to another.
i I am the first person people meet when they come to our hotel.
j I work outside, in the countryside.

c Talk about three jobs you would like to do and three jobs you wouldn't like to do. Say why.

d Now go back to p. 21.

NUMBERS

2B Time

a 02.08 Match the sentences (1–9) with the times (a–i). Listen and check.

1 It's (a) quarter past four. *or* It's four fifteen.
2 It's half past four. *or* It's four thirty.
3 It's (a) quarter to five. *or* It's four forty-five.
4 It's twenty past four. *or* It's four twenty.
5 It's ten to five. *or* It's four fifty.
6 It's five past four. *or* It's four oh five.
7 It's twenty-five to five. *or* It's four thirty-five.
8 It's four minutes to five. *or* It's four fifty-six.
9 It's seven minutes past four. *or* It's four oh seven.

b Write down five different times in numbers. Ask your partner to say your times.

c Now go back to p. 23.

PLACES

5A Places in a city

a 05.01 Match the places in the box with pictures 1–6. There are two extra words. Listen and check.

post office /ˈpəʊst ˌɒfɪs/ ☐ sports centre /ˈspɔːts ˌsentə/ ☐ theatre /ˈθɪətə/ ☐ police station /pəˈliːs ˌsteɪʃən/ ☐
concert hall /ˈkɒnsət ˌhɔːl/ ☐ stadium /ˈsteɪdiəm/ ☐ bridge /brɪdʒ/ ☐ park /pɑːk/ ☐

1

2

3

4

5

6

b Match the definitions with the places in **a** and on p. 51.

a You go there to watch a football match.
b This is a nice place to sit with trees and grass and flowers.
c When you want to send a postcard, you go to this place.
d You walk on this from one side of a river to the other side.
e You can see a play in this place.
f If someone steals from you, you go to this place.
g This is an open area in the centre of a town.
h You can listen to classical music in this place.
i When you want to do some exercise, you go to this place.

c 05.02 **Pronunciation** Listen to the words. Are the sounds in **bold** weak or strong? Listen again and repeat.

building **b**ridge **p**ark **p**ost office

d In pairs, ask and answer the questions.

1 Which of the places in **b** does / doesn't your city have?
2 Which does / doesn't your city need?

e Now go back to p. 51.

VERBS

3A Common verbs

a 03.06 Match 1–7 with a–g. Listen and check.

1 How much are the bananas?
2 Do you drink coffee in the morning?
3 Can I **help** you paint the kitchen?
4 Where's your passport?
5 Do you know where I can **buy** an English newspaper?
6 The film starts at 8:15 so let's **meet** outside at 8:00.
7 Do you want to go for a walk this evening?

a I think they **sell** them in the shop at the station.
b They're very cheap. They only **cost** €2 a kilo.
c No, I just want to **stay** at home and watch TV.
d OK. I'll **try** to be on time but I don't finish work till 7:30.
e Yes, please! But I can't **decide** what colour: blue or green.
f Sometimes, but I **prefer** tea.
g I don't know. I can't **find** it. It isn't in my bag.

b 03.07 **Pronunciation** Listen to the sounds in **bold** in these words and answer the questions. Listen again and repeat.

b**uy** f**i**nd dec**i**de tr**y** st**ay**

1 Which word has a different sound?
2 Are the two different sounds long or short?

c In pairs ask and answer the questions.

1 What do you prefer to drink in the morning?
2 Think of a small shop near your home. What do they sell? What do you buy there?
3 How much do these things cost in your country?
   a an ice cream
   b a cup of coffee
   c a loaf of bread
4 You decide to meet friends in town. Where do you meet?
5 Where do you usually stay on holiday?

d Now go back to p. 31.

6B Past simple: irregular verbs

a 06.15 Match the past simple forms in the box with 1–11. Listen and check.

brought won lost found did cut
read thought sold became gave

1 do	5 bring	9 become
2 read	6 win	10 cut
3 give	7 lose	11 sell
4 think	8 find	

b 06.16 **Pronunciation** Listen to these sentences. Do the letters in **bold** sound the same or different? Why?

- I r**ea**d a newspaper every day.
- I r**ea**d a wonderful book last month.

c 06.17 Read the story and underline the correct verbs. Listen and check.

How I [1]*won* / *lost* the lottery

One day, I went into town and [2]*did* / *made* some shopping. Then, on the way home, I [3]*brought* / *bought* a lottery ticket from a small shop by the bus stop. It had the number of my birthday: 24 11 1969. A beautiful woman [4]*spent* / *sold* it to me. When she [5]*gave* / *took* it to me, she smiled and said, 'Good luck. I hope you win.' I smiled back. A few days later, I opened the newspaper and [6]*gave* / *read* the winning number: 2-4-1 ... That was the moment I [7]*decided* / *found out*. My life completely changed and I [8]*became* / *came* rich. I immediately [9]*thought* / *told* of the woman in the shop. I [10]*cost* / *cut* some fresh flowers from my garden and went back to the shop to give them to her. 'Is the woman who was here on Saturday in today?' I asked. 'I've got some flowers for her.' But she wasn't there, and I never saw her again.

d Cover the text in **c** and practise telling the story from the pictures. Read it again to check.

e Now go back to p. 63.

6A Years and dates

a 06.09 Put the months in the correct order. Listen and check. Listen again and repeat.

June /dʒuːn/ September /sep'tembə/ April /'eɪprəl/
November /nəʊ'vembə/ January /'dʒænjuəri/
August /'ɔːgəst/ February /'februəri/
December /dɪ'sembə/ May /meɪ/ March /mɑːtʃ/
October /ɒk'təʊbə/ July /dʒʊ'laɪ/

b 06.10 Complete the sentences with *in* or *on*. Listen and check.

1 We were in Australia ____ 2012.
2 My birthday's ____ the nineteenth of June.
3 Our next holiday's ____ May.

c Correct the dates. Then write them in number form.

1 The next meeting's on twelfth of April.
2 Our party's on Saturday the twenty-one of February.
3 We were in Canada in twenty oh seven.
4 Next Saturday's the seventh July.
5 I was at university until one thousand nine hundred and ninety-eight.
6 I'd like to reserve a single room for December two.

d Think of two people in your family and two friends. Write down their names.

e Tell a partner the birthdays of the four people. Can they match the birthdays with the names?

f Now go back to p. 61.

FOOD AND CONTAINERS

4A Food

a 04.03 Match pictures 1–10 with definitions a–j. Listen and check.

1 garlic /ˈɡɑːlɪk/

2 salad /ˈsæləd/

3 burger /ˈbɜːɡə/

4 melon /ˈmelən/

5 cereal /ˈsɪəriəl/

6 yoghurt /ˈjɒɡət/

7 jam /dʒæm/

8 cola /ˈkəʊlə/

9 crisps /krɪsps/

10 curry /ˈkʌri/

a People often eat it in India, with rice or naan bread.
b It's a large fruit which grows in hot countries. It's yellow, orange or green.
c It's a quick, cheap meal: meat and salad inside bread, sometimes with cheese.
d It's uncooked vegetables mixed together that you can have with a meal. It's good for you!
e It's like onion and you can use it for cooking.
f It's made from milk. People often have it for breakfast.
g It's sweet and it's made from fruit. You can put it on bread.
h They're made from potatoes and usually come in small bags. They aren't very good for you!
i It's a drink, a bit like lemonade but it's brown.
j Many people eat it for breakfast with milk.

b 04.04 **Pronunciation** Listen to the sounds in **bold** in these words. Listen again and repeat.

/k/	**c**ola	**c**risps	**c**urry
/ɡ/	**g**arlic	bur**g**er	yo**gh**urt

c 04.05 Which words do you hear, *a* or *b*?

1 a could b good
2 a cold b gold
3 a class b glass
4 a back b bag

d Say a word from **c** for your partner to point to.

e Complete the sentences. Use words from **a** and p. 41.

1 What kind of meat do you want: c____n, s____k or l____b?
2 Let's have a s____d. We've got tomatoes, o____ns, c____ts, green b____ns and m____ms.
3 My wife has c____l and milk for breakfast, but I like y____t with fruit and then a piece of bread with butter and j____m.
4 We've got a lot of fruit: apples, p____rs, g____pes and a m____n.
5 Of course he's not fit. He always eats c____ps and drinks c____a between meals.

f Look at all the words in **a** and **e**. Talk about:

- things you eat or drink nearly every day
- things you eat or drink at least once a week
- things you don't often eat or drink
- things you never eat or drink

g Now go back to p. 41.

4B Containers

a Match phrases 1–6 with pictures a–f below.

1 a **jar** /dʒɑː/ of honey
2 a **bag** /bæɡ/ of potatoes
3 a **can** /kæn/ (or **tin** /tɪn/) of tomatoes
4 a **bottle** /ˈbɒtl/ of water
5 a **bar** /bɑː/ of chocolate
6 a **packet** /ˈpækɪt/ of biscuits

b 04.11 **Pronunciation** Listen to the phrases in **a**. Which words are stressed? Listen again and repeat.

1 the nouns
2 the article *a*
3 the preposition *of*

c Change the words in *italics* using phrases in **a**. Is more than one answer possible?

Yesterday I went shopping and bought [1] *some oil,* [2] *some jam,* [3] *some spaghetti,* [4] *some chocolate,* [5] *some tuna* and [6] *some apples.*

1 *a bottle of oil*
2 ____
3 ____
4 ____
5 ____
6 ____

d Write a shopping list. Use the words in **a** to help you. Tell a partner.

e Now go back to p. 43.

COLLOCATIONS

7A Transport collocations

a 07.01 Read and listen to the text. Match pictures 1–6 with phrases in **bold** a–f.

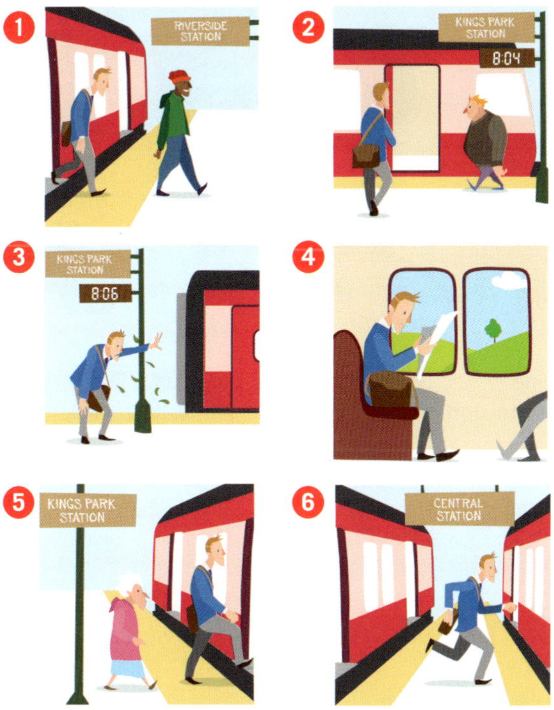

Erik works in the city centre and he [a]**takes the train** to work every morning. He [b]**gets on the train** at Kings Park Station, near his home. Then he [c]**changes trains** at Central Station in the city centre and he [d]**gets off** the train at Riverside Station, near his office. He usually gets to Kings Park Station at 8:00, so he can [e]**catch the train** at 8:05, but sometimes he's a few minutes late and he [f]**misses the train**. Then he has to wait for the next train.

b 07.02 <u>Underline</u> the correct verbs. Listen and check.

1 There were no buses, so I decided to *take / get on* a taxi.
2 It's nearly 10:30. Leave now or you'll *catch / miss* the bus.
3 Excuse me. I want to go to the City Museum. Where do I *take off / get off* the bus?
4 The concert finished at 9:30, so we just *caught / changed* the last tram.
5 The train was expensive, so we *take / took* a coach.
6 Quick! Let's get *on / off* the bus and find a seat! It leaves in a few minutes!

c 07.03 **Pronunciation** Look at these verbs and answer the question. Listen and check.

b**ough**t g**o**t s**aw** t**oo**k

1 Which verbs have the same sound as c**augh**t /ɔː/?
2 Is it a long or short sound?

d In pairs, ask and answer the questions.

1 When was the last time … ?
- you caught a bus or train at the last minute
- you missed a bus or train
- you changed trains

2 How do you get from here to your home? What kinds of transport can you take? Where do you get on and off?

e Now go back to p. 71.

8A Sport and exercise collocations

a Match the activities in the box with pictures 1–11.

running golf judo sailing
football snowboarding volleyball
exercises fishing rugby tennis

b Write the activities in **a** in the correct column in the table.

go	play	do
running	golf	judo

c Complete the rules with *go*, *play* or *do*. We use …

1 _____ when we talk about sports, games and music.
2 _____ when we talk about activities that end with *-ing*.
3 _____ when we talk about other activities.

d 08.04 **Pronunciation** Listen to the sounds in **bold** in these words. Are they long (*L*) or short (*S*)?

☐ f**oo**tball ☐ j**u**do

e 08.05 Are the sounds in **bold** in these words long (*L*) or short (*S*)? Listen and check.

1 f**u**ll 3 p**oo**l 5 f**oo**d
2 g**oo**d 4 p**u**t 6 bl**ue**

f Which activities in **a** do people do in your country? Choose a sentence which is true for each activity.

a It's very popular.
b Some people do it, but not many.
c It's very unusual.
d You can't do this in my country.

Some people go snowboarding, but not many.

g Now go back to p. 81.

APPEARANCE AND CLOTHES

8B Appearance

a Match sentences 1–4 with four of the pictures a–h.

1 He's got **short straight dark** hair.
2 She's got **long straight dark** hair.
3 He's got **short curly dark** hair.
4 She's got **long straight fair** hair.

b Notice the order of the adjectives in **a**. Which adjective always comes first?

c 08.09 Write sentences about the other four people's hair in **a**. Listen and check.

d Write a sentence about your hair and one about a partner's hair.

e Student A: choose a picture in **a**. Student B: ask questions to guess your partner's picture. Change roles and repeat.

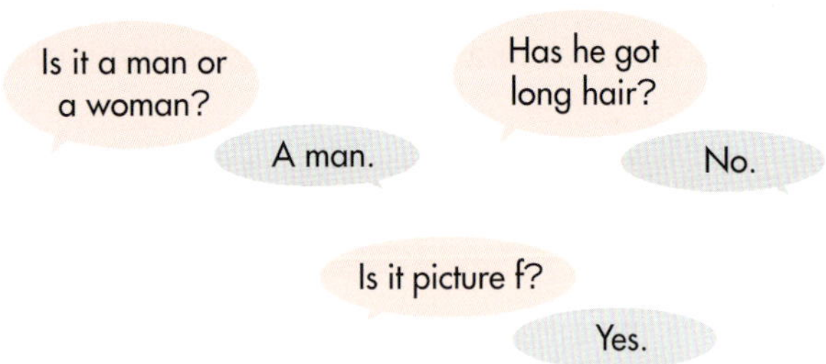

f Match sentences 1–6 with a–f.

1 People always look at her.
2 You can see he does a lot of sport.
3 Here's a photo of her at the age of five.
4 He always looks great in photos.
5 He should get more exercise.
6 I don't think she eats enough.

a He looks very **fit**.
b He's getting quite **fat**.
c She's looking much too **thin**.
d She was a very **pretty** girl.
e She's a very **attractive** woman.
f He's very **good-looking**.

g 08.10 **Pronunciation** Listen to these adjectives and underline the stressed syllable. Listen again and repeat.

prett|y a|ttrac|tive good-look|ing

h Talk about famous people who are:

- thin
- attractive
- good-looking
- fit

i Now go back to p. 83.

9B Clothes

a 09.12 Read and listen to the text. Match the words in **bold** 1–8 with pictures a–h. Listen and check.

- She looked lovely. She wore a red [1]**skirt** /skɜːt/ and a white shirt and she had a blue and yellow [2]**necklace** /ˈnekləs/.
- It was a hot day, so he decided to wear a [3]**T-shirt** /ˈtiːʃɜːt/, [4]**shorts** /ʃɔːts/ and [5]**trainers** /ˈtreɪnəz/ without socks.
- I never wear [6]**jewellery** /ˈdʒuːəlri/ – just a [7]**watch** /wɒtʃ/, of course, and my [8]**ring** /rɪŋ/.

b 09.13 **Pronunciation** Listen to this word. Which letter don't you hear?
jewellery

c 09.14 Cross out the letters you don't hear in these words. Listen and check.

1 vegetable
2 interesting
3 chocolate
4 camera
5 comfortable

d Student A: look at Picture 1 for one minute. Student B: look at Picture 2 for one minute. Try to remember everything the people are wearing. They are all words from **a** or p. 93. Cover the picture and say what you remember.

e Now go back to p. 93.

9A Money and prices

a 09.02 Tick (✓) the correct way of saying each price: a or b. Listen and check. Listen again and repeat.

1 £25 a twenty-five pounds b five pounds and twenty
2 £4.50 a four fifty pounds b four pounds fifty
3 60p a point six pounds b sixty p
4 €7.40 a forty cents and seven euros b seven euros forty
5 €0.25 a twenty-five cents b quarter euros
6 $28 a eight and twenty dollars b twenty-eight dollars
7 70¢ a seven oh cents b seventy cents
8 $15.50 a fifteen dollars fifty b fifteen and half dollars

b Take turns saying these prices.

1 £2.70
2 $120
3 €4.30
4 85p
5 $4.75
6 $0.60
7 £10.10
8 €49.95
9 €55.90
10 £9.99

c Now go to p. 91.

10B High numbers

a Match phrases 1–10 with numbers a–j.

1 a/one hundred thousand
2 one million three hundred thousand
3 one hundred and twenty
4 a/one million
5 one thousand one hundred
6 one hundred thousand two hundred
7 one hundred and thirty thousand
8 one thousand one hundred and thirty
9 five million six hundred thousand
10 a/one thousand and three

a 120
b 1,003
c 1,100
d 100,000
e 100,200
f 1,000,000
g 1,300,000
h 5,600,000
i 1,130
j 130,000

b 10.09 Look at these phrases. Add *and* to four more phrases (sometimes twice). Listen and check. Listen again and repeat.

1 340 = three hundred and forty
2 2,002 = two thousand two
3 45,800 = forty-five thousand eight hundred
4 381,245 = three hundred eighty-one thousand two hundred forty-five
5 2,000,670 = two million six hundred seventy
6 15,680,430 = fifteen million six hundred eighty thousand four hundred thirty

c Write down a number between:

- 600 and 699
- 3,001 and 3,010
- 20,000 and 20,999
- 1,000,000 and 1,499,999

d Ask a partner to say your numbers.

e Now go back to p. 103.

11A Irregular past participles

a 11.03 Look at these past participles. What are their infinitive forms? Listen and check.

broken /ˈbrəʊkən/ read /red/ been /biːn/ caught /kɔːt/
written /ˈrɪtən/ seen /siːn/ had /hæd/ eaten /ˈiːtən/
bought /bɔːt/ heard /hɜːd/ flown /fləʊn/
forgotten /fəˈɡɒtən/ fallen /ˈfɔːlən/ grown /ɡrəʊn/

b Complete the questions with past participles from **a**.

1 Have you ever ______ a fish?
2 Have you ever ______ an email in English?
3 Have you ever ______ octopus?
4 Have you ever ______ in a helicopter?
5 Have you ever ______ to Paris?
6 Have you ever ______ flowers for someone?
7 Have you ever ______ your own phone number?
8 Have you ever ______ an English newspaper?
9 Have you ever ______ an elephant?
10 Have you ever ______ South African music?
11 Have you ever ______ your leg?
12 Have you ever ______ breakfast in bed?
13 Have you ever ______ down the stairs?
14 Have you ever ______ vegetables?

c 11.04 **Pronunciation** Listen to the sound in **bold** in h**ear**d /ɜː/.

Which of these words have the same sound as h**ear**d? Listen and check.

girl hear learn nurse German work year

d In pairs, ask and answer the questions in **b**.

e Now go back to p. 111.

12A Geography

a Read the emails. Notice the words in **bold** and write them in the pictures.

a The ____________

We have a holiday house that we go to at the weekend. It's on the **coast** /kəʊst/, but behind us is a **jungle** /ˈdʒʌŋɡl/ with lots of very green trees. Next to the house is a small **hill** /hɪl/. You can walk to the top and the view is wonderful.

d The ____________

We live outside the city in the **countryside** /ˈkʌntrɪsaɪd/. There are **fields** /fiːldz/ all around the house and in the distance there is a small **wood** /wʊd/. I like walking there. It's so quiet – I love it.

b 12.02 **Pronunciation** Listen to the words in **a**. Which words have more than one syllable?

c Underline the different word in each group below. Say why.

1 lake, river, field, waterfall
2 forest, hill, wood, jungle, rainforest
3 island, mountain, coast, beach

d Think of the countryside in your country. Talk about what there is and there isn't.

> In my country, there are many hills, but there's no desert. We've only got two lakes, but there are about seven or eight rivers.

e Now go back to p. 120.